FREDERICK III

Recent Titles in
Contributions to the Study of World History

The Legend of the Mutilated Victory: Italy, the Great War, and the Paris
Peace Conference, 1915–1919
H. James Burgwyn

Spain in the Nineteenth-Century World: Essays on Spanish Diplomacy, 1789–1898
James W. Cortada, editor

The Entangling Alliance: The United States and European Security, 1950–1993
Ronald E. Powaski

Kings of Celtic Scotland
Benjamin T. Hudson

America's Feeble Weapon: Funding the Marshall Plan in France and Italy, 1948–1950
Chiarella Esposito

The Jews of Medieval France: The Community of Champagne
Emily Taitz

Royalist Political Thought During the French Revolution
James L. Osen

Theatre in the Third Reich, the Prewar Years: Essays on Theatre in Nazi Germany
Glen Gadberry

Between Ideology and *Realpolitik*: Woodrow Wilson and the Russian
Revolution, 1917–1921
Georg Schild

Stanley K. Hornbeck and the Open Door Policy, 1919–1937
Shizhang Hu

The French Revolution of 1789 and Its Impact
Gail M. Schwab and John R. Jeanneney

Gladstone's Imperialism in Egypt: Techniques of Domination
Robert T. Harrison

FREDERICK III

Germany's Liberal Emperor

Patricia Kollander

Contributions to the Study of World History, Number 50

GREENWOOD PRESS
Westport, Connecticut • London

Library of Congress Cataloging-in-Publication Data

Kollander, Patricia.
    Frederick III : Germany's liberal emperor / Patricia Kollander.
      p. cm.—(Contributions to the study of world history, ISSN
0885–9159 ; no. 50)
    Includes bibliographical references and index.
    ISBN 0–313–29483–6 (alk. paper)
    1. Frederick III, German Emperor, 1831–1888. 2. Germany—Kings
and rulers—Biography. 3. Liberalism—Germany—History—19th
century. 4. Conservatism—Germany—History—19th century.
5. Germany—Politics and government—1871–1918. I. Title.
II. Title: Frederick the Third. III. Series.
DD224.K65 1995
943'.07'092—dc20
  [B]   94–39268

British Library Cataloguing in Publication Data is available.

Library of Congress Catalog Card Number: 94–39268
ISBN: 0–313–29483–6
ISSN: 0885–9159

First published in 1995

Greenwood Press, 88 Post Road West, Westport, CT 06881
An imprint of Greenwood Publishing Group, Inc.

Printed in the United States of America

The paper used in this book complies with the
Permanent Paper Standard issued by the National
Information Standards Organization (Z39.48–1984).

10 9 8 7 6 5 4 3 2 1

Copyright Acknowledgments

The author and publisher gratefully acknowledge the following sources for granting permission to
use copyrighted materials:

Excerpts from *Letters of the Empress Frederick*, edited by Sir Frederick Ponsonby, London, 1929,
reprinted by permission of the archives of the Hessische Hausstiftung (formerly the Kurhessische
Hausstiftung).

Excerpts from *The War Diary of Frederick III*, edited by Otto Meisner and translated by A. R. Allinson,
London, 1957, reprinted by permission of the Geheimes Staatsarchiv Preussischer Kulturbesitz,
Merseburg.

To My Parents

Contents

	Acknowledgments	ix
	Introduction	xi
1	Frederick's Conversion to Liberalism, 1831–1861	1
2	Rebellion against Conservatism, 1862–1863	25
3	The Failure of "Moral Conquests," 1864–1866	55
4	Unification by Force, 1866–1871	79
5	From Optimism to Disillusionment, 1871–1879	109
6	The Succession Crisis, 1880–1887	137
7	The Illness, Reign, and Legend of Frederick III	167
	Conclusion	195
	Selected Bibliography	201
	Index	211

Acknowledgments

The completion of this book was facilitated by generous grants from the German Academic Exchange Commission (DAAD), the Institute for International Studies at Brown University, the Florida Atlantic University Foundation, and the Schmidt College of Arts and Humanities at Florida Atlantic University. I am deeply grateful to His Highness, Landgraf Moritz von Hesse, who graciously granted me permission to study the papers of his great-grandparents, Emperor Frederick III and Empress Victoria. I am also indebted to the following for their invaluable advice and their painstaking efforts to improve the manuscript: Norman Rich, Volker Berghahn, Tom Gleason, David Barclay, and Eric Tscheschlok. Finally, I would like to thank my parents, August and Maia Kollander, and my fiancé, Bruce Fuller, for their unwavering support and encouragement.

Introduction

In the first decades following World War II, historians generally agreed that the failure of Germany's nineteenth-century liberal movement to inculcate democratic values in German politics and society contributed to Hitler's triumphs. Historians have pointed to a variety of reasons for liberalism's failure. Some have stressed its ideological deficiencies,[1] others the lack of unity in the movement,[2] and still others its willingness to ally with conservative forces—to achieve German unification and economic betterment—at the expense of furthering the movement's original commitment to political liberty.[3] A common theme that pervades these works is that liberalism had much to offer, but in the end it contributed little, if at all, to Germany's political development.

In recent years, however, a new generation of scholars has challenged this traditional framework for analysis of the liberal movement. In their work *The Peculiarities of German History,* Geoff Eley and David Blackbourn charge that historians have been too preoccupied with liberalism's failure to transform state and society in accordance with Anglo-American standards of political liberty and equality. As a result, they have overlooked the positive contributions made by liberalism to the course of German history.[4] Blackbourn and Eley hold that German society, in fact, underwent a "silent bourgeois revolution" during the period of unification, which not only allowed the middle class to attain many of its goals but also set the stage for further liberal political development, which endured until the end of the Weimar republic.[5] This debate has reinvigorated the study of German liberalism and invites historians to reassess previously held assumptions about individuals and events that affected the course of Germany's liberal development.

This study provides a new interpretation of Emperor Frederick III's liberalism and its contribution to the course of Germany's liberal development. When asked to comment on the death of Frederick III in 1888, Liberal British prime minister Gladstone called him "the Barbarossa of German liberalism." Many German liberals felt the same way. As crown prince, Frederick had maintained ties with prominent liberals and rejected the conservative domestic and foreign policies of

Germany's chancellor, Otto von Bismarck. Frederick's marriage to Princess Victoria, the eldest daughter of Queen Victoria of England, had strengthened his liberal impulses. But when Frederick came to the throne in 1888, he was mortally ill with cancer and reigned only for three months.

Frederick's biographers, along with a majority of historians of nineteenth-century Germany, believe that liberalism would have triumphed had it not been for his untimely illness and death.[6] In 1944, Erich Eyck wrote:

No one will ever be able to say how Frederick would have ruled the German Empire if fate had given him good health and normal span of life. But one thing is for certain: he was a man of liberal and humane ideas, which he would not have forgotten on becoming King and Emperor – How different the course of German history would have been if in his [William II's] stead there had arisen a man who knew the true worth of liberty and who spoke words of humanity![7]

Eyck's views have been supported by other noted historians. Veit Valentin wrote that Frederick "clung obstinately to parliamentary principles," and that "the imminent possibility of a redirection of domestic and foreign policy toward western Europe perished with him."[8] Hajo Holborn concurred: "The crown prince–was a believer in liberal and constitutional methods of government. Unquestionably, he would have tried to put his ideas into practice, for he was an earnest and devoted man."[9] Koppel S. Pinson was perhaps the most ardent of Eyck's followers on this issue:

Frederick III was the great hope of German liberals. Married to the oldest daughter of Queen Victoria of England, he became familiar with British parliamentary institutions through his travels in England. He was greatly impressed with English constitutional government and became critical of Prussianism as practiced by Bismarck. His wife, Victoria, strengthened these tendencies in him, and exercised a great deal of influence over him up to his death.[10]

Others who regarded Frederick as a true liberal include Johannes Ziekursch and Julius Heyderhoff.[11]

Only a small number of historians have argued that Frederick had no intention of supporting the liberal movement when he came to the throne. In 1931, Arthur Rosenberg wrote: "The emperor Frederick's brief reign brought about no real change in the situation in Germany. Although as Crown Prince, Frederick had been more in sympathy with the Liberals than his father, he was still a convinced believer in the Bismarckian system, and even had he reigned longer, he would not have altered it in any way."[12] During the following decade, Andreas Dorpalen agreed, adding that Frederick was "dependent" on Bismarck and "maintained the attitudes of a Prussian officer throughout his life."[13] In the 1970s, James Sheehan wrote: "There was little in his character and conduct upon which to base optimistic expectations about a liberal reign."[14] Sheehan points out that the liberal left, which intended to support Frederick when he came to the throne, was politically impotent by the 1880s.[15] Some have also made the case that the crown prince was weak and tractable and hence would have been incapable of carrying through a program of liberal reforms.[16]

Whether Frederick could have changed German history is a question rendered moot by historians such as Hans-Ulrich Wehler, who maintains that the liberal movement was so fatally compromised by its own weaknesses and the hostility of Bismarck's conservative "system" that a liberal resurgence would have been impossible by the time Frederick came to the throne.[17] This view is founded on the premise that Bismarck's conservative legislation of the late 1870s ushered in a period of reaction that effectively destroyed democratic aspirations for another generation.[18]

While diverging opinions about Frederick's liberal views and his potential to change German history can be attributed to ideological differences, a lack of historical sources has caused confusion as well. Though Frederick's diaries from 1848 to 1866 and his diary from the Franco-Prussian war of 1870–1871 have appeared in print,[19] little primary source material is available for 1867–1869 or 1872–1888. Historians who believe that Frederick would have changed the course of German history have tended to rely on his wife's published correspondence with her mother, Queen Victoria, for information about Frederick's political beliefs.[20] But lack of access to Frederick's own words leaves open the question of whether we have an accurate picture of the man.

This study is based on documents recently made available from the Hessische Hausstiftung at the Schloss Fasanerie in Fulda, Germany. This archive contains the unpublished correspondence between Frederick and his wife, which provides fresh insight into their relationship and their politics. This book is not a traditional biography, but rather a study of the evolution of Frederick's liberal views and how they fit into the larger context of liberal development during the course of his lifetime. Frederick's contribution to the liberal movement will then be analyzed within the framework of questions posed by the historical debate on the impact of liberalism previously: Did Frederick's alleged weaknesses contribute to the failure of the liberal movement? Or was he buffeted by forces beyond his control? Or did his actions have a positive impact on the course of liberal development?

The following chapters attempt to prove that Frederick was, first and foremost, a constitutional liberal and an influential agitator on behalf of the preservation of constitutionalism on several occasions when conservatives threatened it with extinction. At the same time, however, Frederick's liberal constitutionalism favored adoption of liberal reforms only within the framework of the constitutional status quo, and he firmly resisted his wife's attempts to convince him to support increasing the powers of the representative branch of government at the expense of the monarchy. Therefore, while Frederick's liberal constitutionalism played a decisive role in ensuring the survival of constitutionalism in Germany, it is also true that some accounts on the extent of his liberal views have been exaggerated.

The chapters highlight the following: Chapter 1 describes Frederick's conversion from a conservative to a constitutional liberal and explains his opposition to the adoption of British-style political institutions in Prussia and Germany. Chapter 2 focuses on his struggle against the king and conservatives who wished to subvert the constitution to put an end to the constitutional conflict. Chapter 3 shows how the crown prince's hostile attitude toward Bismarck's foreign policy changed when the latter assured him that he would pursue German unification in a liberal-constitutional framework. Chapter 4 focuses on the fruits of Frederick's alliance with Bismarck during the late 1860s and his dreams for a liberal Germany as outlined in his war diary. Chapter 5 shows why the crown prince's hopes for a liberal Germany were dashed by Bismarck's alliance with anti-liberal forces in 1870. Chapter 6 discusses the hostility between the crown prince and Bismarck during the 1880s and highlights Frederick's determination to prevent the latter from subverting the constitution during his coming reign. Chapter 7 shows how Bismarck was able to exploit Frederick's illness during the latter's brief reign and discusses the genesis of the legend of Frederick III, which made the late emperor the progressive liberal he never was in life. The legend, in the end, ultimately obscured Frederick's contributions as a constitutional liberal.

NOTES

1. Leonard Krieger charges that the ideological underpinnings of the liberal movement were deficient since they failed to conform to Western notions of political liberty. Leonard Krieger, *The German Idea of Freedom: History of a Politcal Tradition* (Chicago, 1957). Fritz Stern's *The Politics of Cultural Despair* (Berkeley, 1961), and George Mosse's *The Crisis of German Ideology* (New York, 1964) both focus on the strength of antiliberal ideologies in German political culture.

2. Theodore Hamerow holds that the unwillingness of liberals to co-opt the lower classes into its ranks left the former open to manipulation by conservative forces in the government, which in turn neutralized the power of the liberal movement. Theodore Hamerow, *The Social Foundations of German Unification 1858–1891*. 2 Vols. (Princeton, NJ, 1969–1972). Toni Offerman holds that the liberals did try to lure the lower classes during the 1850's, but that their efforts in this direction were misguided and aroused only resentment of the working class. See Toni Offermann, *Arbeiterbewegung und liberals Bürgertum in Deutschland 1850–1863* (Bonn, 1979).

3. See E. N. Anderson, *The Social and Political Conflict in Prussia 1858–1864* (Lincoln, Nebraska, 1954), and Gordon Craig, *Germany 1866–1945* (New York, 1978).

4. *The Peculiarities of German History: Bourgeois Society and Politics in the Nineteenth Century* (New York, 1984). Thomas Nipperdey has also broken away

from the traditional emphasis on the weaknesses of the liberal movement; he praises liberal opposition to universal suffrage and their compromise with Bismarck in the 1860s. See Thomas Nipperdey, *Deutsche Geschichte 1800–1866. Bürgerwelt und starker Staat* (Munich, 1984).

5. Blackbourn and Eley's thesis is supported by Dieter Langewiesche, whose work has shown that left-wing liberalism experienced a revival in the early twentieth century. Dieter Langewiesche, *Liberalismus in Deutschland* (Frankfurt am Main, 1988). Many historians hold that liberal failure produced political passivity, but Stanley Suval's work on electoral politics in during the Wilhelmine era concludes that the voting public was far from passive. See Stanley Suval, *Electoral Politics in Wilhelmine Germany* (Chapel Hill, NC 1985). Larry Jones has also provided a poisitive reassessment of liberal politics during the Weimar republic. Larry Jones, *German Liberalism and the Dissolution of the Weimar Party System* (Chapel Hill, NC, 1988).

6. Eugen Wolbe's *Kaiser Friedrich: Die Tragödie des Übergangenen* (Hellerau bei Dresden, 1931) concludes with Victoria's prediction on the course that German history would take after Frederick's premature death: "I believe that the monarchy will have to endure harsh trials and tribulations, and I shudder when I consider the rough transition [of power] that lies before us." (p. 234). The introduction of Michael Freund's work on Frederick's fatal illness highlights the following: "The Emperor Frederick died of cancer. Had he lived longer, then two world wars would have been avoided." Michael Freund, *Das Drama der 99 Tage* (Berlin, 1966), p. 9. In his biography of Frederick, *Friedrich III: Leben und Tragik des Zweiten Hohenzollern Kaisers* 2nd ed. (Munich, 1981), Werner Richter wrote, "There was hardly a crown prince in the Hohenzollern line whose ascension to the throne was more eagerly anticipated than Frederick William. He embodied the hopes of the bourgeoisie that had strived for German unificiation and individual freedoms" (p. 15). See also Margarete von Poschinger, *Life of the Emperor Frederick* (New York, 1971) and Martin Philippson, *Das Leben Freidrichs III* (Wiesbaden, 1900).

7. Erich Eyck, *Bismarck and the German Empire* (London, 1968), pp. 298–299.

8. Veit Valentin, *The German People. Their History and Civilization from the Holy Roman Empire to the Third Reich* (New York, 1962), p. 502.

9. Hajo Holborn, *History of Modern Germany 1840–1945* (New York, 1969), p. 299.

10. Koppel S. Pinson, *Modern Germany: Its History and Civilization* 2nd ed. (New York, 1966), p. 274.

11. J. Heyderhoff and P. Wentzke, eds. *Deutscher Liberalismus im Zeitalter Bismarcks* 4 Vols. (Bonn, 1925–1926), Vol. 1, pp. 10–11. Johannes Ziekursch, *Politische Geschichte des Neuen Deutschen Kaiserreiches* (Frankfurt am Main, 1925–1930), p. 416. Thomas Kohut is far more tentative regarding the character of Frederick's liberalism: "By nature Friedrich was probably somewhat less liberal than Victoria; if left to his own devices, he might have developed political views more acceptable to traditional Prussian conservatives." See Thomas Kohut, *Will-*

iam II and the Germans. A Study in Leadership (New York, 1991), p. 21. The same is true of historian Ernst Huber: "The emperor Frederick and empress Victoria were not nearly as liberal as their friends and enemies made them out to be." See *Deutsche Verfassungsgeschichte seit 1789* 4 Vols. (Stuttgart, 1970), Vol. 4, p. 175.

12. Arthur Rosenberg, *The Birth of the German Republic* (New York, 1931), p. 34.

13. Andreas Dorpalen, "Frederick III and the Liberal Movement," *American Historical Review*, Vol. 54, No. 1 (October 1948), pp. 1–31.

14. James J. Sheehan, *German Liberalism in the Nineteenth Century* (Chicago, 1978), p. 216.

15. Ibid.

16. In 1884, Friedrich von Holstein, senior counsellor in the foreign office wrote, "Every one is agreed that the Crown Prince's character grows weaker year by year." See Norman Rich and M. H. Fisher, eds., *The Holstein Papers* 2 Vols. (Cambridge, 1957), Vol. 2, p. 164. Two years later, Albrecht von Stosch, an intimate of the crown prince commented, "The crown prince has not an atom of action–or reliability either." Frederick B. M. Hollyday, *Bismarck's Rival A Political Biography of General and Admiral Albrecht von Stosch* (Durham, NC, 1960), pp. 232–233. In his biography of William II, Thomas Kohut describes Frederick as "a tractable man whose initiative was stifled by his willful and stubborn spouse." Kohut, *William II* p. 25

17. Hans-Ulrich Wehler, *Das Deutsche Kaiserreich* (Göttingen, 1973) and *Bündnis der Eliten: Zur Kontinuität der Machstrukturen in Deutschland 1871–1945* (Düsseldorf, 1979). In the latter work, Wehler argues that landed aristocrats and wealthy industrialists together managed to thwart democratic and social reform in the late nineteenth and early twentieth centuries. See also Helmut Böhme, *Deutschlands Weg zur Grossmacht* (Cologne, 1973).

18. See Kenneth Barkin and Margaret L. Anderson, "The Myth of the Puttkamer Purge," *Journal of Modern History*, Vol. 54, (1982), p. 647.

19. Heinrich Otto Meisner, ed., *Kaiser Friederich III. Tagebücher von 1848 bis 1866* (Leipzig, 1929); *Kaiser Friederich III. Kriegstagebuch 1870–1871* (Berlin, 1926) and Georg Schuster, ed., *Briefe Reden und Erlasse des Kaisers und Königs Friedrich III* (Berlin, 1907) contain documents from the post-1871 period, but they shed no light on Frederick's liberal views.

20. Roger Fulford edited the following volumes of correspondence between Victoria and her mother: ed. *Dearest Child. The Private Correspondence of Queen Victoria and the Princess Royal: 1858–1861* (London, 1964), *Beloved Mama: The Correspondence of Queen Victoria and the German Crown Princess 1879–1885* (London, 1981), *Darling Child: The Private Correspondence of Queen Victoria and the German Crown Princess 1871–1878* (London, 1976), and *Dearest Mama: Private Correspondence between Queen Victoria and the German Crown Princess 1861–1864* (London, 1968). See also Frederick Ponsonby, ed., *Letters of the Empress Federick* (London, 1929). Major biographies of Victoria

include Egon Caesar Conte Corti, *The English Empress. A Study in the Relations between Queen Victoria and Her Eldest Daugher Empress Frederick of Germany* (London, 1957), Richard Barkeley, *The Empress Frederick* (London, 1956), Daphne Bennett, *Vicky: Princess Royal of England and German Empress* (London, 1971), and Evelyn Tisdall, *She Made the World Chaos: The Story of the Empress Frederick* (London, 1944).

FREDERICK III

Chapter 1

Frederick's Conversion to Liberalism, 1831–1861

Prince Frederick William of Prussia, the only son of Prince William and Princess Augusta of Prussia, was born on 18 October 1831. Prince William was the second son of King Frederick William III of Prussia. Upon the accession of William's brother Frederick William IV in 1840, William became the heir to the throne since his brother's marriage was childless.

The marriage between Frederick's parents was not happy, for they had nothing in common. Princess Augusta was raised in Weimar, a state distinguished by its intellectual atmosphere and cultural life. Though regarded as a high-strung, humorless woman, Augusta was also considered highly intelligent and corresponded with the greatest thinkers of her day, including Goethe.[1] William, on the other hand, received an entirely military education and was an enthusiastic soldier as well as a rigid disciplinarian. He was noted for his modesty and steady character but shared neither his wife's intelligence nor her interest in the artistic and intellectual life of the period.[2]

The clash between William's and Augusta's personalities and tastes was exacerbated by the fact that they espoused opposing political views. Princess Augusta's homeland was the first state in Germany to grant its subjects a constitution, and the princess regarded herself as a liberal. The liberal vision of the ideal social order was based on progress, faith in the future, and timely reform.[3] Liberals wished to transform the autocratic and oppressive order that was re-established throughout Europe after the defeat of the French Revolution and Napoleon.[4] They agreed that the restoration of governments based on the personal rule of the monarch and on the suppression of individual liberties was detrimental to the human condition. If men could be entrusted to govern themselves with a minimum of interference from outside authority, liberals argued, they would pursue their own best interests, and the sum of these individual efforts would benefit the welfare of all. Hence, the role of government in liberal society was to adopt constitutions, bills of rights, and laws that would preserve and protect individual liberties.

Liberals supported self-government through popular representation. Only a tiny minority of radical liberals, however, advocated complete democracy and universal suffrage. The majority of German liberals wished to see political power extended to educated members of the middle classes, who, they believed, could be trusted to use it wisely.[5] As liberal publicist Julius Fröbel put it:

Liberalism . . . is by no means to be understood as the system of popular freedom in general, but as a system in the special interest of quite specific elements of society which are assembled in the commercial and industrial class. The liberal state in this conventional sense is the state which represents the interest of this social group. But that does not in any sense mean that it must also represent interests of all other classes of the population or even only the interest of the true majority of the people.[6]

This attitude remained true for German liberals long after Fröbel made his statement; it was only in 1918 that liberals accepted democratic suffrage.

Having rejected authoritarianism and popular sovereignty as a basis for government, liberals turned to the idea of *Rechtsstaat*, which placed both the monarch and society under the rule of law.[7] However, the liberal movement was divided on the question concerning the amount of power to be exercised by the representative institutions of government within the framework of a *Rechtsstaat*. Right-wing liberals recognized the value of representative institutions but wanted to keep their influence over political affairs as limited as possible. Friedrich Dahlmann, a member of this group, held that representative institutions should "restrain the arbitrary power of the ruler, but not weaken the power of the government."[8] On the other hand, Dahlmann's critics argued that representative institutions should have more power to determine the business of the state. Members of this group desired the establishment of government on the English model, which deprived the monarch of the power to exercise arbitary authority and gave Parliament an influential voice in the affairs of the nation.[9]

Apart from their differences on these issues, German liberals were united in their desire to unify the German-speaking peoples into one nation. Liberals held that the nation-state should safeguard individual rights against interference by illiberal German princes and monarchs. This, in turn, would spur the achievement of other liberal goals such as popular education and progress in industrialization.[10] Once again, however, liberals disagreed on the question as to the form the unified Germany might take: some advocated union of all German states under Prussia, whereas others regarded Austria as the natural leader in German affairs.

Augusta shared the hopes and dreams of those liberals who supported the establishment of parliamentary government in Prussia on the English model and the unification of Germany under Prussian leadership.[11] When Augusta married Prince William of Prussia at eighteen, she tried to disseminate her liberal views at the ultraconservative Berlin court, but her efforts met with ridicule and scorn.[12] After Princess Augusta visited Queen Victoria in 1846, the queen wrote her uncle, King Leopold of Belgium: "Her position is a difficult one. She is too enlightened and too liberal for the Prussian Court. She seems to have some enemies, for there are whispers of her being *false*, but from all that I have seen of her . . . I *cannot* and will not believe it."[13]

Augusta's most noted critic was her own husband. At the time of his marriage, William was a reactionary conservative and a divine right monarchist.[14] He was a staunch defender of the established political order, and as such he perceived the philosophies of liberalism and nationalism to be nothing less than subversive. As he saw it, the enactment of the reforms that his wife supported would undermine the power of the Prussian monarchy and ultimately invite a repetition of the revolutionary events that had led to Napoleon's reign of destruction.[15] William defended Austria's traditional predominance in German affairs and had no interest in the idea of German unification under Prussia.

The lack of harmony between Augusta and William made Frederick's childhood miserable. As an adult, Frederick confessed to his future wife, Princess Victoria of Britain:

It is not easy for me to put my feelings concerning my family life into words. Unfortunately Mama has increasingly made it her habit to raise strong objections to many of my father's actions. This, along with her delicate state of health, has made my infrequent evenings alone with my parents very unpleasant. Since I no longer have the desire to play the role of mediator between the two of them, I often find myself in the most embarrassing of situations. Papa tries to do everything to please her, but Mama does not think so. If Mama would only recognize that Papa's efforts on her behalf were sincere![16]

The young prince was also frustrated in his efforts to win his parents' approval and support. Augusta saw to it that he was brought up in accordance with her enlightened views. The tutors she selected for her son included Frederic Godet, a youthful Swiss theologian, and Dr. Ernst Curtius, a professor of classics and a republican his political outlook.[17] Frederick's tutors praised his kindness and obedience but were unanimous in concluding that he was not particularly intelligent. Frederick's intellectual limitations, together with the fact that he showed little interest in her progressive views, came as a tremendous disappointment to Augusta, who never concealed from her son her low opinion of his abilities.[18] William, on the other hand, succeeded in instilling in his son a sense of devotion to the Prussian monarchy and army. But the young prince was unable to establish a close relationship with his father, whom he appears to have admired and feared at the same time. Augusta once confessed to a friend that her son was nervous and agitated in William's presence.[19]

As a young man, Frederick's political views were influenced by the conservatism of his father and the Berlin court.[20] His lack of sympathy with popular agitation for constitutional reform and the unification of Germany was evident in his response to the revolutionary events of March 1848. After King Louis Philippe of France was deposed in February 1848, Germans were encouraged to believe that they, too, could bring about changes, establish parliamentary government in Germany, and unify the German states. When King Frederick William IV of Prussia resisted popular pressure for change, he was confronted with angry demonstrations on the part of the people of Berlin.[21]

On 18 March 1848, the king gave in to this pressure and granted Prussia a constitution, but the demonstrations continued, and shots were exchanged between rioters and loyal palace guards. On the following day, the demonstrators forced the king to salute the bodies of the dead revolutionaries in the palace square, a scene witnessed by Prince Frederick. Thereafter, he and his sister (Princess Louise) fled to Potsdam for safety. Meanwhile, his father had fled to England incognito. Later, Frederick learned that his uncle, the king, had ridden through the streets of Berlin wearing a revolutionary tricolor armband, the symbol of revolutionaries agitating for German unification. He himself would never fall so low, he told his cousin, Prince Frederick Carl: "I intend to keep my Prussian cockade on my cap and will not wear the German one."[22] In his diary, Frederick called the months March through May of 1848 "the most tragic spring of my life."[23] He referred to democratic reformers as "the unruly mob" who had "trampled the majesty of the crown under their feet."[24]

The revolution was defeated several months later. Although the king kept his promise to give Prussia a constitution, it was revised to increase the powers of the king at the expense of the newly established parliament. The king exercised complete control over the executive branch of the government: he was supreme commander of the army and had the power to make war and conclude peace, appoint and dismiss ministers, and suspend civil rights in the event of an emergency. The king was granted decisive legislative powers as well. He had the right to call, prorogue, close, or dissolve parliament and the power to initiate emergency measures when parliament was not in session.[25]

The composition of the representative bodies of government reflected the conservative character of the constitution. The upper house of parliament (Herrenhaus) was composed of nobles, and members of the lower house (Abgeordnetenhaus) were elected on the basis of universal, but indirect and unequal, suffrage. The electoral law of 1849 divided voters into three classes according to taxes paid, so that the members of classes I and II, who paid two-thirds of taxes, chose two-thirds of the electors. The electoral law was designed to favor election of politically conservative landowners, who paid the most taxes.[26]

The constitution limited the powers of the lower house. While the lower house could propose changes in legislation, they could be approved only with the assent of the king and the upper house. However, the lower house did have important fiscal powers: if the lower house did not accept the budget, it could not be enacted. A literal interpretation of the constitution meant that in the event that the lower house rejected the budget, all payments by the state would have to cease and thus put an end to effective government.[27] Thus, the power of parliament in budgetary matters put it in a position to influence the policy of the government by holding the purse strings. In the years after 1849, however, the lower house was dominated by conservatives who approved the dictates of the government and hence were not inclined to use the power at their disposal to influence government policy.

The conservative revision of the constitution was accompanied by a period of reaction. Constitutional provisions for free speech and freedom of the press were ignored by the government. Liberal political clubs were closed, public demonstrations were forbidden, and censorship stifled the liberal press. The police subjected the government's critics to arbitrary arrest and persecution. The integrity of the constitution itself was threatened by the king's reactionary advisers, who were suspected of illegally manipulating elections in favor of candidates who shared their desire to do away with the constitution altogether.[28]

The reactionary era precipitated a profound shift in William's political views. As a conservative, he had regarded with dismay the implementation of a constitution forcing the king to share his power with parliament. Nonetheless, he opposed the illegal practices of his brother's government, which, he believed, undermined Prussia's prestige. He became attracted to the views of the parliamentary opposition, which used the journal *Wochenblatt* to condemn the corruption of the regime of Otto von Manteuffel and promote adherence to the constitution.[29] Thanks to the influence of the so-called *Wochenblattspartei* or Constitutional party, William came to regard the constitution as a hallowed contract between the crown and the people. By the same token, however, he opposed agitation on behalf of radical liberals to revise the constitution to increase the powers of parliament at the expense of the crown, as well as their demands for German unity.

William's views on this score were passed on to his son through his friend and political ally, Leopold von Auerswald, who advised Frederick on constitutional affairs.[30] Auerswald's influence on Frederick was evident when the young prince shocked a reactionary member of the king's cabinet by indicating his support for constitutionalism. When archconservative General Leopold von Gerlach told the prince that he envied his youth "because he would certainly live to see the end of absurd constitutionalism," Frederick replied, much to the general's astonishment, "[but] there must be a parliament!" By this he meant that the integrity of a parliament provided by the monarchy had to be respected.[31]

As much as Augusta approved her son's acceptance of constitutionalism, she was still committed to converting her son to her more liberal point of view.[32] With difficulty, Augusta persuaded her husband to depart from the conservative educational tradition of Hohenzollern princes by sending Frederick to the University of Bonn. There the young prince attended lectures of liberal-minded professors such as Ernst Moritz Arndt, the author of inspirational nationalistic writings during the wars of liberation, and Friedrich Christoph Dahlmann, who had jeopardized his academic career by protesting the reactionary policies of the Hanoverian government in the 1830s. Frederick enjoyed university life and wrote his former tutor Curtius in 1852: "I have the feeling that I will make rapid progress this winter—good ideas are cropping up in my head all the time."[33] Frederick's efforts, however, did not measure up to Augusta's high standards: "Fritz's knowledge of human nature has certainly improved," she wrote, "but his intellectual development does not equal that of his peers."[34]

Augusta's disappointment with her son's response to university education did not deter her from seeking alternative methods to convert him into a supporter of her political views. She cultivated her friendship with Queen Victoria of Britain, in the hope Frederick could be converted to liberalism and nationalism through his marriage to the queen's eldest daughter, Victoria.[35] The queen's consort, Prince Albert, enthusiastically backed the marriage project. He was raised at the court of Saxe-Coburg-Gotha and became an ardent supporter of British-style liberalism after his marriage to Queen Victoria. He believed that Britain's greatness was based on its progressive institutions, such as free elections, free expression, free trade, and a ministry responsible not to the monarch (as was the case in Prussia) but to parliament. Albert held that ministerial responsibility was the essence of constitutional government. Though he conceded that obstacles to such a reform were great in Prussia, he insisted that, "a new leaf *has to be* turned over and there *must* be government with the majority."[36]

Albert knew that Prussian ruling circles had rejected constitutional reforms on the grounds that they would compromise the traditional power and influence of the monarchy. He refuted this argument by insisting that attachment to the old order did not require a rigid adherence to every tradition. England, he argued, had been able to adapt itself to inevitable changes without any weakening in the loyalty to the crown and in the respect of the historical past represented by the monarchy.[37]

By Albert's lights, Prussia could spearhead the unification of Germany under Prussian leadership if the monarchy adopted a plan for reform. In September 1847, Albert wrote a lengthy memorandum on German affairs in which he concluded that the development of forms of popular government in Germany was making rapid strides and that "the yearning for German unity will not merely be increased, but the means will also be provided for its attainment." He added:

My own view is that the political reformation of Germany lies entirely in the hands of Prussia, and that Prussia has only to will, in order to accomplish these results. Prussia is next to Austria the most powerful State in Germany. Prussia. . . . has placed herself at the head of the development of German popular institutions. Prussia has for many years stood at the head of the Zollverein[38] and on Prussia the political expectations of all Germany are concentrated. If Prussia were really to adopt the plan of reform . . . she would become the leading and directing power in Germany, which other Governments and people would have to follow, and in this way would come to be regarded as one of the most important European powers.[39]

The united Germany that Albert envisaged would be closely allied to Britain and support its desire to block Russian or French expansion. In response to

Albert's commentary on German affairs, Prime Minister Palmerston wrote a memorandum stressing the advantages of a close alliance between England and Germany: "Both England and Germany are threatened by the same danger and from the same quarters ... that danger is an attack from Russia or from France separately, or from Russia and from France united." Palmerston believed that a Franco-Russian alliance would pose a greater threat to Germany than England, since the latter was protected by its navy, but that England would nonetheless be far better off allied with Germany. "England and Germany," he concluded, "have mutually a direct interest in assisting each other to become rich, united and strong."[40]

These ideas played a major role in Albert's desire for a marriage between his daughter Victoria and Prince Frederick William. The introduction of popular forms of government in Prussia and German unification under Prussia leadership could all be accomplished if Frederick, the future ruler of Prussia, could be won over to Albert's ideas through Victoria.

Albert's pronouncements on Prussia and Germany, however, were not always in tune with actual conditions in Germany. He overestimated the strength and scope of the liberal movement, which was confined to a still relatively small middle class and a group of intellectuals. More important, he underestimated the hostility of Germany's conservatives—including the king of Prussia—toward liberal reform and the unification of Germany.[41] They jealously guarded their power and were loath to sacrifice it to satisfy the demands of the middle classes for German unity.

Princess Victoria, Albert's favorite child, worshipped her father, and it never occurred to her that some of his views on Prussia and Germany were inaccurate. The attention and support the young princess received from her parents in childhood made her more confident and self-assured than her prospective husband. At the age of two, she already exhibited "great intelligence and a particular aptitude for foreign languages, as well as a definite personality of her own."[42] But the precocious young princess was not without faults. According to one of her ladies-in-waiting, Countess Hohenthal, Victoria was rather stubborn and not a very good judge of character:

The Princess, often for no particular reason, took violent fancies to people. She used at first to think of them quite perfect and then come to bitter disillusion. She also took first-sight dislikes to persons, based often on a trick of manners or an idle word dropped about them in her presence, and thus she often lost useful friends and supporters. She was no judge of character, and never became one, because her own point of view was the only one she could see.[43]

The princess's faults were not apparent to Frederick, who was charmed by the intelligence and wit of the ten-year-old Princess Royal when he met her for the first time while visiting the Great Exhibition with his family in 1851. He began to correspond with her and intensified his studies of the English language. In 1855, Frederick visited the British royal family at Balmoral Castle in Scotland. Frederick basked in the happy domestic atmosphere of the English court, for the British royal family gave him the affection and approval that he had never received from his own. He was attracted to the Princess Victoria and told his parents, "She speaks intelligently, her eyes are expressive; her presence and movements are very gracious."[44]

One week after his arrival at Balmoral, the prince asked the queen and her husband for permission to marry their eldest daughter. Victoria's parents were enthusiastic about the match but asked that the marriage be postponed for two years until the prospective bride was seventeen years of age. That evening, Frederick confided to his diary, "Since my declaration of today I feel as if a sudden change has taken place inside of me. I will look to the future with different eyes if I can go through life's hardships and joys with the Princess Royal. I believe that we are well-suited to each other."[45] As he told his parents: "I am hardly capable of putting into words how happy I am at the thought that she [Victoria] will be mine [and] that I will be a part of this precious family!! . . . I am so serene, and I look to the future with a sense of calm . . . and the love and trust that the parents shower upon me makes me happier with each passing day!"[46]

Frederick's biographers suggest that the young prince was converted to English-style liberalism during his courtship with the princess.[47] However, his letters and diary entries during his courtship belie any interest in, or preference for, the British political system. As Frederick told his English tutor, Mr. Perry: "Neither politics or ambition has brought it [the marriage] about, but my heart."[48] His letters to Victoria after their betrothal show that he was anxious to have her bring happiness to his home life; his mother's nervous behavior in particular made him miss "my dear Vicky and her sweet disposition all the more!"[49]

Prince Albert, however, wished to see his daughter do more than alleviate Frederick's domestic woes. He spent hours preparing his daughter to play an active role in making his dream of German unification under a liberalized Prussia a reality. "Vicky has learned many and divers [sic] things," Albert wrote, "Now she comes to me every evening from six to seven . . . then, if I find that she has misunderstood something, I make her work it out in writing without any help, then she brings it to me for correction."[50] The young princess enjoyed these sessions with her father. As she wrote her fiancé, "From dear Papa I can learn more than anyone else in the world; he explains everything so well and discusses things like no one else. In fact, the hours I spend with my parents are the happiest in the day."[51]

Albert, however, underestimated the hostility of powerful conservatives toward the introduction of "British influence" to the Prussian court in the form of the British marriage. General Leopold von Gerlach was shocked when the king told him of his approval of the union. Gerlach relayed his concern to his protégé, Otto von Bismarck, Prussia's representative at the Diet of the Germanic Confederation in Frankfurt. Bismarck replied:

You ask me . . . what I think of the English marriage. I must separate the two words to give you my opinion. The English in it does not please me, the marriage may be quite good, for the Princess has the reputation of a lady of brain and heart. If the Princess can leave the Englishwoman at home and become a Prussian, then she may be a blessing to the country. If our future Queen on the Prussian throne remains the least bit English, then I see our Court surrounded by English influence . . . What will it be like when the first lady in the land is an English-woman?[52]

The marriage of Princess Victoria and Prince Frederick William took place on 25 January 1858 at the Chapel Royal in St. James' Palace. The bride did not appear to exhibit any "bridal nervousness and flutter," whereas the groom, according to Queen Victoria, was "pale and agitated."[53] An English observer called Frederick "a handsome lieutenant, but not in the least clever."[54] The couple honeymooned in England and departed for Prussia one week after their marriage. Victoria's departure was a wrenching experience for the queen and her family: "The separation," the queen wrote, "was awful and the poor child was *quite* brokenhearted at parting from her dearest beloved papa, whom she *idolises*."[55]

The new princess made a favorable impression upon her arrival in Berlin, which pleased her father, who wrote: "Your exertions, and the demands which have been made upon you, have been quite immense; you have done your best, and have won the hearts . . . of all."[56] He warned her to be wary of criticism that would come her way:

In the nature of things we may now expect a little reaction. The public, just because it was rapturous and enthusiastic, will now become minutely critical; and take you to pieces anatomically. This is to be kept in view, although it need cause you no uneasiness, for you have only followed your natural bent . . . It is only the man who presents an artificial demeanour to the world who has to dread being unmasked.[57]

It was precisely Albert's advice, however, that made Victoria a target of criticism. When Albert insisted that she retain the title of princess royal of Britain, he failed to acknowledge the extent to which her English background was disliked by conservatives at court: " the delicacy of your position," he wrote his daughter, "may be eased by the fact that the Prussian people regard your British background as an asset. There is great enthusiasm among the Prussian people of Fritz's choice of the Princess Royal for a bride; the people would therefore consider it to be a great error if you let your British title drop or if you allowed that it may be used along with your Prussian title as the Queen [Elizabeth of Prussia] and the Court seem to desire."[58] The princess was too young, naive, and anxious to please her father to raise any objections to this request. As she dutifully replied, "When the people hear my English title, they will always be reminded of a useful alliance, and that was the real reason behind this marriage."[59] Albert also expected his daughter to send him detailed reports: "I trust that you will waste no time in replying to this letter, and I expect you to address the issues I have raised point by point."[60] Victoria was also instructed to report to her father any changes in the "moods of the Royal Family and others," while remaining "silent and neutral" in her observations about international politics.[61]

Victoria's filial duties kept her busy, but she was far from happy. Her residence in Berlin was dark and gloomy and lacked modern conveniences. The birth of her first child, Prince William, was difficult. Mother and child nearly died, and William's left arm was deformed.[62] Although Victoria appeared to adore her new husband, he was frequently away on military tours, leaving her alone to face the hostility of Queen Elizabeth and other reactionary members of the Berlin court, who resented her because of her British background. Victoria would have been better able to withstand such hostility had she been able to form a close friendship with Augusta, who sympathized with her daughter-in-law's political views. But Victoria found herself hard-pressed to tolerate Augusta's bouts of nerves and her domineering personality. As she told her husband, "Why must she [Augusta] come here and make such scenes just to work her temper off on me? . . . I won't put up with it, particularly when it concerns my private affairs, in which I will have no interference, except from you, my darling husband!"[63]

Victoria also discovered that it would be more difficult to convert Frederick into a supporter of English-style liberalism than she and her father had anticipated. Though Frederick professed great affection for his wife and British relatives[64] and came to accept their views on nationalism and the unification of Germany under Prussian leadership, he rejected their belief that reforms to strengthen parliament would have to be enacted before Prussia could assume leadership in the German question. The prince saw unification as a means to strengthen Prussian prestige, but he did not want the powers of the crown undermined by the unification process.[65]

Frederick's devotion to the military also overrode his willingness to accept English-style liberal views. His enthusiasm for life in the army is evident in the following letter to his wife:

Today we viewed a parade of the Königsberg garrison. As I rode behind Papa . . . he stopped suddenly, called me to his side, and said, "I appoint you Colonel in Chief of this regiment." He took me so by surprise that I thought I had misunderstood what he meant. It was only after I had him repeat what he had said, and after my startled reply, "Me?" that I began to comprehend what he meant. So with drawn sword, I led it [the regiment] in the march, and was in such a dither of joy that I was really a little crazy![66]

Frederick added that he was proud of his wife's performance at a ceremony for her honorary regiment and added, "Papa was especially pleased about this . . . as he said, 'This is behavior worthy of Prussian princess.' Papa is really on my side after all!"[67] Frederick's preoccupation with military affairs disturbed Albert, who wrote, "that Vicky's husband has lapsed into his family's and his country's playing at soldiers is to be regretted, though it is not to be wondered at."[68]

Feeling alienated in her new homeland, Victoria became more than ever dependent upon her father's advice. As she told her mother: "There are such thousands of things I would like to hear Papa's opinion about. Whatever I hear or see I always think what would Papa say, what would he think. Dear Papa has always been my oracle."[69]

Prince Albert was also anxious to become Prince William's "oracle" and corresponded with him frequently on political matters. However, Albert's advice shows that he was poorly informed about conditions in Prussia. In 1857, Prince William became his brother's deputy after the latter suffered a stroke. Although the title of deputy did not empower William to change the reactionary practices of his brother's regime, Albert advised William to do just that: "The way the Manteuffel ministry abused their influence at the last election roused in the minds of all patriotic and thinking men a feeling of disgust so deep and well-founded, that you are not only justified, but bound, as a sacred duty, to forbid, and to prevent any repetition of these shameful proceedings under the sanction of your name."[70] He added, "How far it is possible for you, standing alone as you unhappily do, to exercise control over the Government which they will require, I am unable at this distance to form an opinion. But the firm exercise of the will on your part will probably be sufficient."[71]

Albert repeated the same advice to his son-in-law:

When I consider what I should do in the present state of things, I would record a solemn protest against such proceedings, not by way of opposition to the Government, but in defence of the rights of those, whose rights I should regard as inseparable from my own—those of my country and my people—and in order that I might absolve my conscience from any suspicion in the unholy work. At the same time, however, that my conduct might be divested of every semblance of being dictated by a spirit of opposition or desire for popularity—and in order, it may be, to make those who are contemplating the wrong aware that, if it were persisted in, I should feel myself compelled to adopt this course. This done, I should entertain no animosity towards my friends, but, on the contrary, should live on terms of peace with the reigning powers.[72]

He added, "I am satisfied that an attitude of this kind would inspire the delinquents with a certain measure of alarm, and help to keep the nation from losing all hope."[73] Albert, however, was apparently oblivious to the fact that as deputy to his brother, William lacked the power to follow Albert's advice.

Albert applauded William's efforts to initiate reform when the latter became regent of Prussia after his brother, King Frederick William IV, was declared insane in October 1858. William's first act as regent was to dismiss the reactionary Manteuffel cabinet. Anxious to establish a regime that had support of the people, William selected a new cabinet drawn from the ranks of the liberal opposition (or the Constitutional party) in the Prussian parliament of the early 1850s. These men were not liberal reformers in the British sense, since they had absolutely no intention of increasing the power of parliament at the expense of the monarchy.[74] But despite the rather conservative emphasis on royal power, the new era cabinet was committed to respect the rights of parliament. From these ministers William expected "a new moral tone, obedience to the constitution, reforms of a moderate nature, but no fundamental changes."[75]

William's pronouncements were hailed by Prussian liberals, who dubbed the new regime the "new era." Satisfaction with William's program was reflected at the polls: the elections of 1858 produced 263 backers of the new era in the Prussian parliament; only 57 backed the policies of the deposed Manteuffel.[76]

The election results indicated not only the dissatisfaction of voters with the reactionary policies of William's predecessor but the transformation of Prussian society as a result of the Industrial Revolution. Thanks to the increased tempo of industrialization, the wealth of the liberal-minded industrial middle class began to exceed that of the landed gentry. Since liberal industrialists paid enough taxes to enter classes I and II of the electoral system, it was they who selected two-thirds of the electors to parliament. Only nine years after its enactment, the electoral law of 1849, designed to guarantee the predominance of politically conservative landowners in parliament, now worked to favor liberal representation in that body.[77]

The inauguration of the "new era" pleased Albert, who wrote William:

If some extravagant demands or even absurdities should crop up in the new Diet [parliament], this, I hope, will neither alienate nor alarm you, nor lead you to adopt a hostile attitude in defence. In any case it is a free assembly of several hundred men, who will represent . . . those interests and feelings of the most diverse kinds. . . . The Regent's position is that of moderator, and your readiness to use it everywhere with firmness will be of essential service to the general weal.[78]

It gradually became clear, however, that the regent and the liberal majority in the parliament were working at cross-purposes. Liberals expected that the regent shared their goals to reform Prussia in the liberal sense and unify Germany. However, while the regent was anxious to do away with the constitutional abuses of his brother's regime, he was determined to keep his power and had no enthusiasm for German unity. In theory, William approved of German unity at some time in the future but did not expect to live long enough to see this liberal ideal realized. Hence his policy toward German unity was vague, at best.[79] In 1861, liberals frustrated with the regent's policies formed the German Progressive party, which aimed to unite men of all liberal groups, from right-wing Constitutionalists to left-wing democrats, who wished to work vigorously for the execution of liberal ideals and national unification.[80]

That Albert shared expectations of left-wing liberals on the question of reform was evident in his request that his daughter write a memorandum on the advantages of ministerial responsibility. According to Albert's biographer Theodore

Martin, the memorandum was composed "with the view of removing the appre-
hensions entertained in the high quarters of the Prussian courts as to the expedi-
ency of a contemplated measure of this kind."[81] Her efforts earned high praise from
her father, who reiterated what he considered to be the highlights of the memorandum. Like his daughter, he could not understand why monarchs on the Continent
were wary of ministers responsible to parliament:

They [the ministers] can say "We will not do this or that which the Sovereign wishes,
because we cannot be responsible for it." But why should a sovereign see anything here to
be afraid of? To him it is in truth the best of safeguards. A really loyal servant should do
nothing for which he is not prepared to answer, even though his master desires it! This
practical responsibility is of the utmost advantage to the Sovereign. Make independence,
not subservience, the essential of service, and you compel the Minister to keep his soul
free toward the Sovereign, you ennoble his advice, you make him staunch and patriotic,
while time-servers, the submissive instruments of a monarch's extreme wishes and com-
mands, may lead, and often have led him, to destruction.[82]

William, however, was not interested in such ideas, and the same could be said for
his son. Frederick believed that Prussia was not ready for a government responsible to the legislature.[83] This view was shared by prominent liberals such as
Theodor von Bernhardi who wrote: "Parliamentary life among us is still a weak,
delicate plant that needs to be cared for and nursed. It does not good to pretend
that our situation is already like that in England, for instance, and to talk and act
accordingly. That leads only to a reaction, first in a conservative, then in a democratic sense."[84]

Unlike his father, however, Frederick was sympathetic to liberals' demands for
German unification under Prussian leadership. The movement to unify Germany
became increasingly popular when the Italians, with French support, unified their
country after defeating the Austrians in the war of 1859. Politically minded Germans on both sides of the political spectrum believed that the wartime successes
of Napoleon III had revived the threat of French expansionism, and German unification was recommended as a means to put a stop to it.

Since the war resulted in the decline of Austrian power and prestige, the movement for unification under Prussia gained ground. In September 1859, liberal advo-
cates of unification under Prussia formed the Nationalverein, an organization designed to cooperate with the Prussian government for national ends. According
to liberal leader Rochau, the general aim of the Nationalverein was "the concentra-
tion of all military and democratic power in one single hand, the restoration of
general representative assembly for the nation, alert protection of all true German
interests against foreign nations . . . the supplanting of an illegal bureaucratic and
police regime by a rationally constituted system of self-government in province,
community and association."[85] Frederick supported this movement, because it
was led by moderate liberals willing to accept the unification of Germany under a

constitution preserving the autocratic authority of the Hohenzollern monarchy.[86]

After the death of King Frederick William IV in January 1861 and William's accession to the throne, Albert tried to convince the new king that his leadership of the nationalist movement would protect Germany from the pretensions of Napoleon III: "If the nationalist movement can be guided by one prince who possesses the trust of his people," he wrote, "the German people will be satisfied and the German nation will have nothing to fear . . . from France, and Germany can become a power which will command respect from its neighbours."[87] He also urged the king to abide by the constitution and to protect himself from "corrupting influences":

My hope, as well as the hope of most German patriots [for a better future] lies with you, and with Prussia. All that is required of Prussia is that it merely act upon the principles found in its constitution—in this way Prussia can live up to the challenges of our time and provide an example to the rest of the German states and win their support, so they too will wish to become Prussia's ally . . . Your person . . . represents the nucleus of European security . . . and you must protect it from harm or corrupting influence . . . Avoid any act that could be seen as representing a lack of trust between you and the German people and the German nation.[88]

William ignored this advice, for he was preoccupied with the issue of army reform. Prussia's mobilization during the Austro-Italian war revealed the army was deficient in size and organization. As a military man, William firmly believed that the source of Prussia's strength was its army, not the nationalist movement. The king's preoccupation with military reform led Albert to believe that William had reverted back to the reactionary ideas he had held prior to 1848 and that the future of constitutionalism in Prussia was in jeopardy. In a letter to his uncle, King Leopold of the Belgians, Albert made clear his disappointment in William:

There exists in Prussia a great Junker and bureaucrats' party which comes together in the Army and particularly in the Guards, which is determined not to allow the constitution and constitutional government to develop, and which for this purpose does not shrink from cunning, fraud and violence for the provocation of a revolution of of a coup d'etat, and . . . the King *himself* belongs to this party by sympathy and tradition.[89]

William's unwillingness to take a leading role in German affairs did not dampen long-term enthusiasm for united Germany. Members of the middle classes continued to agitate on behalf of German unity, and one impatient fanatic named Becker attempted to assassinate the king because he had not done enough for this cause.[90] The king, however, refused to give in to this pressure, and the new era cabinet began to lose popularity because of its inertia in the German question.

Some liberals believed that the cabinet could be rescued only by a strong initiative in German affairs. Frederick himself expressed enthusiasm for this course, which, he believed, would restore the confidence of German patriots in the regime. Albert disagreed and wrote his son-in-law:

An *external* war for the elimination of *internal* dissension and evils is always a morally unjustified undertaking. . . . [Also] the very evils, personal weaknesses, internal contradictions etc. which form the obstacles to the solution of internal difficulties are . . . just the ones which would most impede success in war . . . Prussia, with its broken territory, which is only a part of Germany and whose other members are hostile to it, with a policy which has not yet found its own principle, entangled with alliances and treaties of all kinds, and vulnerable at all corners, is not in a position to risk a daring undertaking without perishing. The altogether exceptional case of Frederick the Great misleads and blinds many a Prussian.[91]

Albert also reminded Frederick that Austria had adopted such a policy in 1859 with disastrous results and that Napoleon III's foreign policy had made him the scourge of Europe because his wars did not have the mandate of his people, but were engineered by the emperor to satisfy his own selfish needs.[92] Frederick rejected this advice. By his lights, Albert overlooked the fact that it was precisely the nationalists, not the government, who supported a decisive stand by Prussia in German affairs.

Once again, Albert tried to convince Frederick that Prussia would have to be liberalized before it could assume leadership in the German question:

Prussia must first become the *moral* leader of Germany before it can raise itself as a power in Europe and this will not happen by adoption of hasty policies or by making outrageous claims; but by adoption of a bold, confident, truly German and completely liberal policy that corresponds to the needs of our time and the needs of the German nation, which will in turn make it impossible for any of the other German states to adopt any alternative course.[93]

Since the Prussian nobility and reactionary members of the government were hostile to liberal policy, Prussia, said Albert, was not ready to assume leadership in the German question. It appears that what Albert really meant was that German unity under Prussian leadership would be impossible unless William would see fit to take Albert's advice. Albert urged Frederick to be patient with regard to German unity and maintain hope that his government would one day see its way clear to adopting a more sensible policy.[94]

He gave the same advice to his daughter:

I am for Prussia's hegemony; still Germany for me is first in importance, Prussia as Prussia second. Prussia will become the chief if she stands at the head of Germany: if she merely seeks to drag Germany down to herself she will not herself ascend. She must, therefore, be magnanimous, act as one with the German nation *(Deutsch handeln)* in a sacrificing spirit, prove that she is not bent on aggrandisement, and then she will gain pre-eminence, and keep it.[95]

Victoria agreed with her father's views, but her husband did not. As far as Frederick was concerned, Prussia was in a good position to lead Germany as long as the government upheld the constitution and as long as parliament did not pressure the government for amendments to increase its powers at the expense of the crown.[96]

Albert did not live to see the rejection of his prescription for Prussian leadership in the German question. His sudden death on 14 December 1861 from typhoid deprived Victoria of the only person whom she deemed capable of guiding her in her role as an English princess in a hostile, foreign country. After his death, Victoria made it her mission to make sure that Albert's ideas and ideals would never be forgotten. However, she observed Germany with Albert's eyes, meaning that she emulated his habit of making ill-informed judgments on conditions in Germany.

Victoria spared no effort in trying to convince her husband to follow the example of her father and put his ideas into practice. Like her father, she believed that Prussia would have to be liberalized before it could assume leadership in the German question. Victoria also wished to see Prussia and Germany adopt the British political system, an ideal shared by left-wing members of the Prussian parliament. In the years that followed, she supported any German political party that advocated ministerial responsibility and greater parliamentary control of government activities.

Victoria's mission was not a complete success. Although she was able to sway Frederick on certain issues, the core of his political philosophy was, and remained, essentially different.[97] The two clashed on the timing and the character of the liberalization process in Prussia. Like many moderate German liberals, Frederick held that the process of liberalization could be achieved only after unification. In order for Prussia to emerge as a leader of the German states, it had to have the strength necessary to overcome the hostility of other German rulers to unification. As the liberal deputy Max von Forckenbeck said, Prussia could not be liberalized without German unity. Only unified Germany could relieve Prussia from its dependence on military power and make absolutism no longer justifiable on military grounds.[98]

However, Frederick opposed liberals whose idea of liberalization involved increasing powers of parliament at the expense of the crown. By Frederick's lights, liberal reforms such as free expression, free trade, and popular education could be achieved without revision of the constitutional status quo. At bottom, Frederick's political views were in line with those liberal new era ministers who favored maintaining existing constitutional guarantees but did not want the powers of the monarchy subordinated to parliament. They believed that the job of parliamentarians was to defend existing laws and to institute progressive reforms only if they could be achieved through mutual cooperation between the crown and parliament; their slogan was "Do not press."[99]

Frederick's unwillingness to accept his wife's views created tension in their marriage, which their biographers have overlooked. This tension was exacerbated by the fact that their personalities clashed. According to her eldest son, Victoria was "a woman of unwearied energy, she was passionate, impulsive, argumentative, and had an undeniable love of power."[100] Frederick, on the other hand, was far more introspective; he shied away from conflict and controversy as much as possible. His son wrote that Frederick was "subject to fits of depression, and what he used, laughing at himself, to call 'Weltschmertz [weariness of life].'"[101] Given Victoria's passion for politics, it is not surprising that she chafed at her husband's apparent unwillingness to use his position to change Prussian policy along liberal lines. She never appreciated the fact that his position as heir to the throne did not automatically enable him to influence government policy. In fact, Frederick was permitted to do no more than attend meetings of the crown council and council of ministers and serve as his father's representative abroad. Frederick's political power and influence were also exaggerated by his liberal supporters, who on many occasions expected far more from him than he was able to deliver.

This is not to say that Frederick lacked the ability to influence his wife. During the first years of her marriage, the princess abided by Albert's view that Prussia should become a champion of morality and legality and thereby peacefully attract other German states to the idea of unification under Prussian leadership: unification need not be achieved by force but by moral conquests. Later, however, her views on this score became far more similar to those of her husband and many liberals, who, in effect, radically revised the idea of moral conquests. While Frederick and liberals in theory approved of the idea of nonviolent unification, in practice they advocated decisive action on behalf of the nationalist cause when Prussia faced a foreign policy crisis. Force was an acceptable alternative as long as it was used on behalf of liberal-national goals such as unification, self-determination of German people under foreign rule, and the preservation of constitutionalism.

Though Frederick rejected his wife's more radical liberalism, the constitutional liberalism that he exhibited during the late 1850s shows that he had clearly renounced the ultraconservatism of his youth. In 1860, Victoria wrote her husband: "You were not . . . sure of, not versed in, the old liberal and constitutional conceptions and this was still the case when we married. What enormous strides you have made during these years!"[102] And as he told his wife in 1861, "You . . . know how my position has become more comfortable since Papa has begun to rule, and the more my self-confidence increases, the more I view my actions in the past as questionable in retrospect."[103] By the end of the decade he hoped that the new era cabinet would cooperate with the Nationalverein in realizing the goal of a unified Germany.

At the end of 1861, however, the influence of the new era cabinet and its supporters in parliament waned when the king came to loggerheads with parliament over the question of military reform. The conflict between crown and parliament faced Frederick with a dilemma. Like the king, he felt that liberals' opposition to military reforms was unwarranted. At the same time, however, he opposed the king's methods for dealing with the conflict with parliament, which included dismissal of the new era cabinet in favor of more conservative ministers and rejection of parliamentary rights guaranteed by the constitution. Frederick fought to preserve and uphold the Prussian constitution, but his efforts put him in a precarious position vis-à-vis the parliamentary opposition, which mistakenly regarded him as one of their own, and the king, who became alienated from his son for the same reason. Frederick's position in the constitutional conflict and the ways in which it was misinterpreted by both the king and parliament are the subjects of the following chapter.

NOTES

1. Werner Richter, *Friedrich III: Leben und Tragik des Zweiten Hohenzollern Kaisers* 2nd ed., (Munich, 1981), p. 32. See also Marie von Bunsen, *Kaiserin Augusta* (Berlin, 1940), Hermann von Petersdorff, *Kaiserin Augusta* (Leipzig, 1900) and Königin Augusta von Preussen, *Bekentnisse an eine Freundin* (Dresden, 1935).

2. Major biographies of William include Erich Marks, *Kaiser Wilhelm I* (Leipzig, 1897) and Karl Heinz Börner, *Kaiser Wilhelm I* (Cologne, 1984).

3. Dieter Langewiesche, "The Nature of German Liberalism" in Gordon Martel, ed., *Modern Germany Reconsidered, 1870–1945* (London, 1992) p. 96

4. The liberal movement is traditionally seen as having been dominated by intellectuals and owners of small businesses. Recent research on the social composition of the movement, however, shows that the liberals came from a variety of backgrounds and religious convictions. Historian Wolfgang Schieder has concluded that "the unity of the liberal movement in Germany came only from its diversity." See Wolfgang Schieder, ed., *Liberalismus in der Gesellschaft des deutschen Vormärz* (Göttingen, 1983), p. 83.

5. According to his biographer, Fröbel continued to oppose universal suffrage and supported social Darwinism. See Rainer Koch, *Demokratie und Staat bei Julius Fröbel, 1805–1893: Liberales Denken zwischen Naturrecht und Sozialdarwinismus* (Wiesbaden, 1978). Generally speaking, liberals held that the introduction of universal suffrage to an unprepared constituency would upset the balance in state and society. This principle held true not only for German liberals but for all European liberals at the time of the revolutions of 1848. See Dieter Langewiesche, "Gesellschaft-und verfassungspolitische Handlungsbedienungen und Zielvorstellungen europaeischer Liberaler in der Revolution von 1848" in W. Schieder, ed., *Liberalismus in der Gesellschaft des deutschen Vormärz* (Göttingen, 1983)

6. Quoted in Theodore Hamerow, *The Social Foundations of German Unification. Ideas and Institutions* (Princeton, NJ, 1969), p. 138.

7. Otto Pflanze, *Bismarck and the Development of Germany. Volume 1: The Period of Unification, 1815–1871* (Princeton, NJ, 1990), p. 13.

8. James J. Sheehan, *German Liberalism in the Nineteenth Century* (Chicago, 1978), p. 44.

9. See Paul Kennedy, *The Rise of the Anglo-German Antagonism, 1860–1914* (London, 1987), pp. 7–8.

10. Theodore Hamerow, *Social Foundations of German Unification*, p. 139.

11. Egon Caesar Conte Corti, *The English Empress. A Study in Relations Between Queen Victoria and Her Eldest Daughter, Empress Frederick of Germany* (London, 1957), p. 10.

12. King Ernest of Hanover half-jokingly referred to Augusta as the "little Jacobin." Martin Philippson, *Das Leben Friedrichs III* (Wiesbaden, 1908), p. 5.

13. Corti, *English Empress,* p. 10.

14. Erich Marcks, *Kaiser Wilhelm I*, 9th ed.,(Berlin, 1943), p. 65.

15. H. W. Koch, *A Constitutional History of Germany in the Nineteenth and Twentieth Centuries* (London, 1984), p. 36. See also Friedrich Wilhelm Prinz von Preussen, ed., *Preussens Könige* (Gütersloh, 1971), p. 176.

16. Hessische Hausstiftung, Schloss Fasanerie, Fulda (hereafter HH), Prince Frederick William to Princess Victoria, 22 December 1857.

17. Richard Barkeley, *The Empress Frederick* (London, 1956) p. 20. Curtius authored *Greek History*, which became famous through excavations in Olympia.

18. Richter, *Friedrich III*, p. 17.

19. Königin Augusta von Preussen, *Bekentnisse an eine Freundin* (Dresden, 1935), p. 165.

20. Georg Schuster, ed. *Briefe, Reden und Erlasse des Kaisers und Königs Friedrich III* (Berlin, 1907), pp. 10–21.

21. Standard works on the revolutions of 1848 in Germany include Veit Valentin's *1848: Chapters of German History* (London, 1940) and Rudolf Stadelmann's *Social and Political History of the German 1848 Revolution* (Columbus, OH, 1975). Historian Karl Faber sees the revolution of 1848 as reflective of pre-industrial circumstances in Prussia and Germany. See Karl G. Faber, *Deutsche Geschichte im 19. Jahrhundert: Restauration und Revolution von 1815 bis 1851* (Wiesbaden, 1979). Herbert Obenhaus' *Anfänge des Parlmentarismus in Preussen bis 1848* (Düsseldorf, 1984) makes a case for the existence of protoparliamentary institutions prior to the revolutions of 1848 and explains the liberals' wish for a political alliance not with the people but with the monarch.

22. Heinrich Otto Meisner, ed., *Kaisers Friedrich III. Tagebücher von 1848 bis 1866* (Leipzig, 1929), p. 28.

23. Ibid., p. 32.

24. Ibid., p. 27. See also Ernst Rudolf Huber, *Deutsche Verfassungsgeschichte seit 1789.* 4 Vols. (Stuttgart, 1957–1969), Vol 3, pp. 11–24.

25. Koch, *Constitutional History*, p. 79.

26. This electoral system was initially supported by liberals, who had viewed the general male franchise—an experiment during the revolutions of 1848–1849—with considerable skepticism. Ibid., p. 80.

27. Ibid., p. 82.

28. Huber, *Deutsche Verfassungsgeschichte*, pp. 162–164.

29. Hajo Holborn, *History of Modern Germany, 1840–1945*, (New York, 1969), p. 124. The *Wochenblattspartei* also opposed provincialism, and supported a pro-British foreign policy and the separation of church and state. See Huber, *Deutsche Verfassungsgeschichte*, pp. 179–182.

30. Schuster, *Briefe, Reden und Erlasse*, p. 69.

31. Richter, *Friedrich III*, p. 29.

32. After the revolution of 1848, Augusta wrote her son: "The day may come when the people won't wish to settle accounts with the representatives of the princes, but with the princes themselves. If this happens to you, then accept your loss with dignity and be prepared to devote your energy to another occupation. If this does not happen, then you [must] protect the crown, and if God keeps you on your father's throne—then you must preserve it with honor, carry Prussia with Germany in [your] heart and rule as a good, constitutional monarch." Eugen Wolbe, *Kaiser Friedrich III: Die Tragödie des Übergangenen* (Berlin, 1931), p. 27.

33. Ibid., p. 39. During the third semester of his studies at the University of Bonn, Frederick wrote an essay entitled, "On the Uses of a University Education," which emphasized the need for heirs to the throne to study at university as a means by which to become acquainted with the different classes of society. Schuster, ed. *Briefe, Reden und Erlasse*, p. 28.

34. Wolbe, *Kaiser Friedrich*, p. 27. In 1851, Queen Victoria of England advised her friend Augusta to tone down her criticism of her son: "I beg of you to show confidence in your dear son, so that he may likewise show confidence in himself. I am always afraid in his case of the consequences of a moral clash, should his father recommend something and his mother warn him against it. He will wish to please both, and the feat of not succeeding will make him uncertain and hesitating, and his attempts to do so will train him in falsehood—two of the greatest evils which can befall a Prince." Barkeley, *Empress Frederick*, p. 19.

35. According to Egon Caesar Corti, Queen Victoria's uncle, King Leopold of the Belgians originated the idea of a marriage between Princess Victoria and the Prussian prince. He encouraged Queen Victoria to cultivate her friendship with Princess Augusta, and in 1846, the queen wrote her uncle: "I believe that she [Augusta] is a friend to us and our family, and I do believe that *I* have a friend in her, who may be most useful to us." Corti, *English Empress*, p. 11.

36. Frank Eyck, *The Prince Consort. A Political Biography* (London, 1959), p. 77.

37. Ibid., p. 80.

38. The Zollverein was the German customs union, established in 1834, had

profitably eliminated customs barriers between German states.

39. Theodore Martin, *The Life of HRH the Prince Consort*, 5 Vols. (London, 1880) Vol. 1, pp. 439–446.

40. Ibid., Vol. 1, p. 447. See also Günter Hollenberg, *Englisches Interesse am Kaiserreich. Die Attraktivität Preussen-Deutschlands für Konservative und Liberale Kreise in Grossbritannien, 1860–1914* (Wiesbaden, 1974), pp. 15–17.

41. Barkeley, *Empress Frederick*, p. 18.

42. Ibid., p. 10.

43. Barkeley, *Empress Frederick*, pp. 54–55. Victoria's governess was concerned that "Vicky's" emotional sensitivity could make her "very unfit for roughing it through a hard life." For an interesting profile of Victoria's personality, see Thomas Kohut, *William II and the Germans, A Study in Leadership* (New York, 1991, pp. 19 ff.

44. Prince Frederick William to Prince William and Princess Augusta of Prussia, 14 September 1855, Meisner, ed., *Tagebücher,* p. 41.

45. Ibid., p. 49.

46. Prince Frederick William to Prince William and Princess Augusta, 25 September 1855, Ibid., p. 53.

47. According to Richter: "He gained from those weeks in England a happiness previously unknown to him . . . was there a way to bring the fresh clear sea air of England to Prussia? Was there a way to bring together the best of both countries: the industriousness of Prussia and the open and liberating form of English political life?" Richter, *Friedrich III,* p. 46. See also Wolbe, *Kaiser Friedrich,* pp. 40–41.

48. Philippson, *Friedrich III,* p. 48.

49. HH: Prince Frederick William to Princess Victoria, 22 December 1857.

50. Corti, *English Empress,* pp. 24–25.

51. Ibid., p. 25.

52. Bismarck to Gerlach, 8 April 1856, Barkeley, *Empress Frederick*, pp. 43–44.

53. Sir Frederick Ponsonby, *The Letters of the Empress Frederick* (London, 1929), p. 9.

54. Ibid.

55. Ibid.

56. Prince Albert to Princess Victoria of Prussia, 8 February 1858. Martin, *Life of the Prince Consort*, Vol. 4, p. 175.

57. Ibid., pp. 175–176.

58. HH: Prince Albert to Princess Victoria of Prussia, Osborne, 24 March 1858.

59. Corti, *English Empress,* pp. 43–44.

60. Ibid.

61. Ibid., 3 March 1858.

62. Prince William (born in January 1859) was the first of eight children born to Frederick and Victoria. He was followed by Charlotte (born 1860), Henry, (born 1862), Sigismund (1864–1866), Victoria (born 1866), Waldemar (1868–1879), Sophie (born 1870), and Margaret (born 1872). For an interesting explanation of Victoria's

inability to conform to her Prussian surroundings, see Kohut, *William II*, pp. 19 ff.

63. Corti, *English Empress,* p. 122.

64. In August 1861, he told his wife how happy her parents made him: "I've just received letters from your precious parents, and your mother writes me in such affectionate terms, just as a mother would write her own son. Your Papa wrote me many interesting things. . . . You can imagine how happy I am to possess such proof of your parents' approval and trust . . . Until recently I always wished to do well by my parents, but their difficulties were always a burden to me." HH: Crown Prince Frederick William to Crown Princess Victoria, Neues Palais, 25 August 1861.

65. Andreas Dorpalen, "Frederick III and the Liberal Movement," *American Historical Review* Vol. 54, No. 1 (October 1948), p. 15.

66. HH: Crown Prince Frederick William to Crown Princess Victoria, Hembinnen, 4 June 1860.

67. Ibid.

68. Eyck, *Prince Consort,* p. 244.

69. Princess Victoria to Queen Victoria, 16 February 1858. Roger Fulford, ed., *Dearest Child. The Private Correspondence of Queen Victoria and the Princess Royal: 1858–1861* (London, 1964), p. 46.

70. Prince Albert to Prince William of Prussia, 18 May 1858, Martin, *Prince Consort*, Vol. 4, p. 326.

71. Ibid., p. 326.

72. Martin, *Prince Consort*, Vol. 3, pp. 386–387.

73. Ibid., p. 387. In subsequent years, however, Frederick was to use Albert's tactics to express his opposition to the policies of his father's government.

74. Huber, *Verfassungsgeschichte*, p. 273.

75. Eugene Anderson, *The Social and Political Conflict in Prussia, 1858–1864* (Lincoln, NE, 1954), p.121.

76. Ibid., p. 122.

77. Koch, *Constitutional History*, pp. 90–91.

78. Prince Albert to Prince William of Prussia, 22 December 1858. Martin, *Prince Consort*, p. 328.

79. Anderson, *Social and Political Conflict in Prussia*, pp. 119–120.

80. Ibid., p. 280.

81. Martin, *Prince Consort*, Vol. 5, p. 260.

82. Ibid., pp. 261–262.

83. HH: Crown Prince Frederick William to Crown Princess Victoria, 23 March 1862.

84. Hamerow, *Social Foundations*, p. 146.

85. Hans Rosenberg, *Die nationalpolitische Publizistik Deutschlands,* 2 Vols. (Munich, 1935) Vol. 1, p. 219.

86. Pflanze, *Bismarck,* Vol. 1, p. 129.

87. HH: Prince Albert to King William I of Prussia, Buckingham Palace, 12 March 1861.

88. Ibid.

89. Eyck, *Prince Consort,* p. 249.

90. Pflanze, *Bismarck,* Vol. 1, p. 144.

91. Eyck, *Prince Consort,* p. 248.

92. HH: Prince Albert to Prince Frederick William, 1 May 1861.

93. Ibid., 1 May 1861.

94. Ibid.

95. Prince Albert to Princess Victoria of Prussia, 13 September 1859. Martin, *Prince Consort*, Vol. 4, p. 490.

96. Frederick made his views on this score quite clear in a letter to his father discussing the latter's coronation: "The despotic act of assuming the crown of our ancestors is, just in our time, a solemn proof that it is not conferred by any earthly power, in spite of the many prerogatives which were abandoned in 1848." He added, "Just as Frederick I by his coronation at Königsberg laid the foundation of a new state life, so you, dear father, as the founder of a new form of government which opens up the way for our future, the defenders of the affairs of united German territories, allow this important ceremony to take place in the centre of Prussia." Crown Prince Frederick William to William Osborne, 15 July 1861, quoted in Margarethe von Poschinger, *Life of the Emperor Frederick* (New York, 1971) pp. 125–126.

97. In his letters to his father, Frederick intimated that the English simply did not understand the way things worked in Prussia. From England, Frederick wrote William, "Our projected army reforms are a topic of discussion here; the English find it difficult to grasp the idea that we have universal conscription; Mr. Sidney Herbert asked me yesterday, for example, whether we would introduce the proxy (Stellvertreter) system [of conscription]!" Geheimes Staatsarchiv Merseburg, HA Rep 52 (Nachlass Friedrich III) J. 313, Prince Frederick William of Prussia to Regent William, 18 November 1869.

98. Anderson, *The Social and Political Conflict in Prussia,* pp. 123–124.

99. Huber, *Verfassungsgeschichte,* p. 274.

100. Kohut, *William II,* p. 20.

101. Ibid., p. 21

102. Quoted in Robert K. Massie, *Drednought. Britain, Germany and the Coming of the Great War* (New York, 1991), p. 26.

103. HH: Crown Prince Frederick William to Crown Princess Victoria, Neues Palais, 25 August 1861.

Chapter 2

Rebellion against
Conservatism, 1862–1863

Frederick's constitutional-liberal views were put to a severe test when his father proposed to break with his new era ministers because of their inability to induce parliament to accept the king's military reforms. Although conservatives and liberals agreed that military reforms were necessary,[1] a clash threatened when the crown revealed details of the reform plan. The reforms were expensive, and the proposed tax increases alarmed liberal deputies from the commercial classes, whose constituents were just recovering from the depression of 1857.[2] The liberals also opposed the government's proposal to incorporate a large part of the citizen's militia into the regular army, since this would put the militia under the command of the conservative professional military. Since the militia, unlike the latter, was sympathetic to the political hopes and demands of the liberals, parliament saw this particular reform as a poorly disguised attempt by the Junker military caste to strengthen the authority of the monarchy at the cost of the bourgeoisie.[3] The same criticism was levelled at the crown when the government announced its intention to extend the term of required military service for new recruits from two to three years. The liberals in the parliament rejected the army reforms for fear that the new army would bolster monarchical power and be used to suppress liberal agitation for genuine constitutional government.[4]

Despite the strong air of suspicion between crown and parliament, the disagreement brewed for two years before an impasse was reached. In 1860 and 1861, parliament approved the funds for the expansion of the army but rejected the king's plans for the militia and the three-year term of service. Surprisingly, the government opted not to do battle with parliament on the issue and asked for only a "provisional appropriation" so that it could proceed with army expansion and technological improvements for one year.[5]

Parliament agreed, but the aura of compromise was illusory. In early 1861, the government reorganized the militia without parliamentary approval of the necessary funds. The liberals were outraged at what they regarded as a breach of parliament's budgetary rights granted by the constitution and blamed the new era ministry for giving in to the king and the conservatives. Feelings against the ministry and the government were reflected in the results of the elections of December 1861: despite the three-class voting system, the elections returned a liberal majority hostile to the military reforms. Conservative strength shrank from 236 to 57 seats, while the liberals increased their representation from 116 to 281 seats.[6]

More important, there was a shift within liberal representation toward the Left: the Constitutionalists, with 91 seats, were now outnumbered by the Progressive Party, which won 109 parliamentary seats. The shift to the Left reflected liberals' disillusionment with the new era, which was based not only on the military reforms but also on the ministry's lack of initiative in the areas of liberal reform and German unity. Conservatives in general and the crown in particular had every reason to be wary of the Progressives' gains, for the party was determined not only to block the military reforms but to use the conflict to initiate a national German policy in Prussian foreign affairs. Many Progressives were also intent on undermining the powers of the crown by achieving parliamentary government.[7] Hence, the conflict between crown and parliament involved much more than the issue of military reform. At the heart of the conflict was the question as to whether the parliament or the crown were the power center in the state.[8]

Even before the elections, the deepening conflict between crown and parliament caused the king to lose faith in the new era ministry. In November 1861, he told his son that he was tempted to dismiss the ministry in favor of a more conservative cabinet, and his incentive to do so was only increased by the election results of the following month. Frederick, however, evaluated the situation differently. While he supported the military reforms and had no sympathy whatsoever with the Progressives' aims,[9] he did not believe the ministry was the source of the conflict between crown and parliament. In November 1861, he wrote his father that the dismissal of the ministry would only exacerbate the conflict between crown and parliament. He maintained that the presence of the ministry and its adherents in the Constitutional party was necessary to maintain the delicate balance between reactionary conservatives and radical liberals. He added that the appointment of a conservative ministry would reduce the attractiveness of Prussia as a potential leader in the German question among reform-minded members of the middle states.[10]

Frederick bemoaned the election results of December and was sympathetic to the dilemma that the ministers faced after the elections. If they sided with William, they would betray their political convictions and lose popular support.[11] But if they supported parliament, they would be dismissed and replaced by more conservative ministers. Perhaps remembering Frederick's warnings with regard to dismissal of the new era ministry, the king did not give his cabinet an ultimatum and gave them one more chance to end the conflict.

Despite the efforts of the new era ministry, the gulf between crown and parliament continued to widen. Parliament not only continued to refuse the extension of military service but also came up with proposals to limit the ability of the government to procure funds. In February 1862, the parliament proposed the Hagen motion, which required itemization of the military budget, thereby making it impossible for the government to continue shifting funds for purposes not authorized by parliament. If passed, the motion would make the passage of even "provisional appropriations" difficult, if not impossible.[12]

Frederick was not confident in the ministry's ability to block the Hagen motion. In an effort to forestall what appeared to be the inevitable dismissal of the new era cabinet, Frederick conceived of a plan to use a "moral" conquest in foreign affairs to make the liberals tone down their agitation for liberal reforms. In a memorial, the crown prince reasoned that parliament would drop the Hagen motion and cooperate with the government if the army marched on Hesse-Kassel, where the elector had subverted the liberal constitution of the principality.[13] Liberals wanted the constitution in Hesse-Kassel to be restored.[14] As the crown prince saw it, a Prussian directive on behalf of constitutionalism in Hesse-Kassel would prove to the parliament that the Prussian government defended constitutionalism. This, in turn, would neutralize the agitation of those radicals in parliament who believed that the army reforms constituted a step toward the elimination of constitutionalism. Normally, the task of disciplining errant German rulers was the joint responsibility of Prussia and Austria as co-leaders in the German Confederation. But if Austria refused to participate in delivering a joint ultimatum to the elector, the crown prince wrote, Prussian troops could march into Hesse-Kassel to force the issue.[15]

Frederick's plan to exploit the Hesse-Kassel issue was rendered moot when the Austrians agreed to put pressure on the elector to reinstate the constitution of his principality. The crown prince, however, continued to support a foreign policy venture as a means to diffuse the conflict, and this feeling was shared by many liberals. On 3 March, members of the Nationalverein appealed to the Prussian government to pursue an active policy in the Schleswig-Holstein question.[16] German patriots ardently supported the cause of the German-speaking residents of the duchies of Schleswig and Holstein, who were protesting their treatment at the hands of their Danish overlords. The Nationalverein called for a Prussian foreign policy that would wrest Holstein and the German parts of Schleswig from Denmark. Frederick wholeheartedly agreed with the views expressed at the Nationalverein meeting. As he told his wife: "Our . . . views were supported at the meeting. . . . I did not expect them [members of the Nationalverein] to speak in such a moderate way. I hope Papa is relieved since he expected rebellious views to be expressed."[17]

The new era cabinet, however, turned a deaf ear to the Nationalverein's demands. Although Prussian foreign minister Count Bernstorff wished to follow an active policy in the Schleswig-Holstein question, he held that the Nationalverein's demands lay outside the limits of Prussian foreign policy, which, he believed, was paralyzed by the constitutional conflict.[18]

The ministry's efforts to block the passage of the Hagen motion were in vain. After it passed on 6 March, the king threatened to dismiss the ineffective ministers and dissolve parliament. Although Frederick supported his father's decision to dissolve parliament, he wanted to keep the new era ministers. Unlike the king, he did not blame the ministers for the passage of the Hagen motion. He blamed "the untalented and unenlightened members of the Chamber—it was impossible to bring them to reason."[19] In a meeting of the council of ministers on 9 March, Frederick supported those ministers who favored an active policy in the Schleswig-Holstein question and the introduction of a liberal program as a means to stave off liberal opposition to the government.[20]

The king, however, was not interested in doing any favors for the liberal opposition. By his lights, the liberal experiment of the new era was a failure, since it had incited liberals against the crown. The time had come to reassert the crown's authority over parliament, and the appointment of a conservative ministry was, in the king's opinion, the only means to this end. The king was disappointed that his son did not agree with him on this score and told him his views were far too liberal and that it would be in his best interests not to express them again in future meetings of the crown council.[21]

The crown prince kept his wife informed of his efforts to support the new era cabinet. From London, the crown princess praised her husband and encouraged him to use the crisis as a forum for his liberal views:

You are acting so well, my darling, and I am proud of you. Be sure to remain firm and liberal. . . . You are making good strides for your future in Germany and you will command great respect outside Germany's borders. The hope of all people rises when it is evident that there is one practical and clearheaded man present among so many confused and short-sighted individuals. I am so glad that it is well known over here that you hold these opinions. . . . I would like to encourage you to acknowledge your faith in them fearlessly and publicly—our position in the future and our power depend on that alone![22]

Victoria added that although Frederick's views were not appreciated by his father, the opposite was true where the English court was concerned:

Everyone is singing your praises over here—all are so glad that you think differently than your Papa, because many are aware how outdated and vague principles can endanger the reign of even the best and most popular of kings. Everyone is talking about "the last gasp of the New Era." I hope that you will one day be able to resurrect the notion of the new era in the fullest sense of the word and let it prosper and become great. Papa could have done this whilst accruing the greatest advantages for himself—without sacrificing anything—but his principles are outdated and have disappointed the great hopes for a better future.[23]

Frederick, however, was unwilling to declare his support for the liberal ministers in public, since he was sensitive to warnings from conservatives that any overt move on his part would indicate to the opposition that he had joined their ranks.[24] He added that the opposition in Prussia was not comparable to its British counterpart. The German people, he told her, were "politically immature," adding that, "they must learn to share power and not pursue it blindly."[25] In response to his wife's request that he fearlessly acknowledge his liberal views, he replied that his first priority was to be of service to his troubled father.

The king, however, saw his son's continued support for the new era cabinet as evidence that Frederick had joined the ranks of his father's enemies. When the crown prince took the side of the new era ministers in opposing the appointment of August von der Heydt as minister of finance on the grounds that he was not qualified for the post, the king replied that von der Heydt, unlike the liberal ministers, could be trusted. Frederick's support for the liberal ministers on this point gave William additional grounds to accuse his son of sympathizing with the opposition in parliament.

The charge disturbed Frederick, since it was completely false, but he chose not to defend himself, for it was clear to him that William's resentment of liberalism had grown to the point where he regarded even moderate liberals as his enemies. As he explained to his wife, rebuttal of his father's charges against him would be pointless: "From that moment on I naturally remained silent, for what more could I say since Papa had identified me completely with his enemies?"[26]

In March 1862, William told his son that he intended to dismiss the new era cabinet on the grounds that he was duty-bound to defend the military policies of his ancestors and could not afford to give in to liberals' demands for a reduction in the military reforms without appearing like a fool in the face of the army. He added that he would rather abdicate than face such a humiliation, and then his son, whose views indicated that he bore no allegiance to the great Prussian military tradition, could do as he wished. William added that his son's liberal views had been publicized in the democratic press. As the crown prince reported to his wife:

[Papa said]: "The democrats consider you to be far more reasonable than the king," and I replied, "Why should the democrats wish to count a Prince among their ranks and pin their hopes on me?" Papa then told me that I should be more careful about my choice of acquaintances. The next morning Papa told me [that] he could no longer work with the liberal ministers, and I told him to act according to his convictions and select ministers whom he trusted.[27]

Frederick was quite shaken by this altercation with his father. As he told his wife, "You can imagine how I felt! I never dreamed that Papa would want to accuse me of such things." He added, "Papa has always been so good to me, so you can imagine how I cried . . . after our argument."[28] Despite his distress, the crown prince was determined not to join the conservative camp for his father's sake: "The influence of our enemies has spread far and wide," he told his wife, "[but] I will never give up [my liberal views]."[29]

Backed by his trusted advisers Edwin von Manteuffel and Albrecht von Roon (chief of the military cabinet and minister of war, respectively), the king replaced the remaining members of the new era cabinet with conservatives on 19 March. Although the crown prince labelled the new ministers as "solid men," he was upset that his father did not consult him during the selection process and believed that the appointment of the new ministry would only widen the gulf between crown and parliament. As he confided to his diary, "May God help us; I cannot expect anything good to come from this change."[30]

Victoria's reaction to the appointment of new ministry was far more drastic: "The only more 'moderate' ministers than those who were dismissed could only be reactionaries!" she exclaimed. She added: "We must prepare ourselves for a lengthy period of reaction and unpopularity abroad." Victoria's immediate concern was that her husband not be swept away by what she referred to as the "reactionary tide." As she told Frederick: "Please stay away from all of this, for God's sake. As you can see, no one has use for your ideas. Reserve them for a more appropriate time, and forget nothing." The crown princess advised her husband to abstain from crown council meetings, lest it be presumed by the liberals that he had abandoned his liberal views, and added that he could exploit the crisis in order to enhance his liberal reputation: "Your behavior must be above suspicion—in this way poor Germany will never lose faith in you and will find in you all that it has ever hoped for! All hopes are now pinned on you—the hopes which could not have been realized during the new era! You should take pride and comfort in this hope—it is only unfortunate that you have to learn from the mistakes of your predecessors."[31]

Victoria also told Frederick that he had to make a choice as to whether his future course of action would be dictated by the king—who, in her opinion, was "deluded and confused"—or by the sterling example of her father: "All his life he [Albert] fought for justice with diligence and clarity of purpose and [he] overcame the obstacles that surrounded him. Now he is called 'the Good' and 'the Great' and England looks upon him as one of its greatest benefactors. He did not shy away from unpleasantries and annoyances in his quest for what he believed was right, and his efforts were rewarded!"[32]

Frederick was put off by Victoria's implication that he was found wanting in comparison to her father: "If you only knew just how much I grieve over his departure from our midst, you would begin to understand that I am not unworthy to be his son-in-law." He insisted that he, like Albert, had already endured "unpleasantries" for the sake of his liberal beliefs: did his tense meetings with his father not constitute proof of his willingness to suffer for the liberal cause? As the only person close to the king who espoused liberal views after the departure of the new era cabinet, he was already in a difficult position. As he saw it, to do his wife's bidding would have lent credibility to the rumor that he belonged to the opposition, and this, in turn, would have made any effort to dispel this impression in his father's eyes far more difficult. As Frederick told his wife:

I know that you would prefer that I stay away from [crown] council meetings, but what choice do I have after Papa commanded me to attend and told me that he needed my protection? But you can rest assured that I will conduct myself properly in the [cabinet] meetings and that I will not allow my professed views to be judged any differently. C'est le ton qui fait la musique—and I too can afford to abstain frequently from meetings. I find your sentiments to be quite correct and I have nothing against them—but you must consider the difficulty of my position at the present moment—many believe that I have insulted my father, who believes that I belong to the opposition.[33]

Victoria, however, refused to accept this line of reasoning. She charged that her husband was confusing the issues of passive opposition and duty to the king: "Passive opposition to a ruinous system of government does not preclude your duty to your father; passive opposition is determined by your conscience and your convictions, not by the king's command. I understand that your father needs to be protected, but I also believe that you owe it to yourself to avoid the negative influence of the king's advisers."[34] Victoria added that Frederick's reputation as a liberal could suffer if he stood by his father: "You must avoid anything that could hurt your position! How else can the world understand you unless you remain steadfast in your beliefs? You always complain that you are considered by many to be weak, but now you can show everyone that you intend to remain true to your beliefs and that you will not change them on command."[35]

Victoria also understood that Frederick's relationship with his father would suffer if he refused to attend crown council meetings, "but," she added, "your love for each other will prevent a serious break between the two of you." She believed that Frederick's viability as a future liberal monarch would be undermined if he chose to protect his father: "I fear that your childlike love for your father could work to your disadvantage. I believe that you will be able to put these feelings temporarily aside and remain true to your duty, conscience and convictions." She advised him to associate himself "with those [people] who truly wish the best for the king and who would do anything for him but consider their own convictions and conscience to be more important than the king's command."[36]

Despite these arguments from his wife, Frederick refused to stay away from crown council meetings. At bottom, he did not feel compelled to adopt a hostile posture toward the king and the conservative ministry as long as they did not revert to the unconstitutional practices of the Manteuffel era; this was a far more favorable alternative to being associated with the opposition, since he rejected its policy and its goals. He also told Victoria that she had misjudged recent political developments and that the new ministry was not as reactionary as the English newspapers had led her to believe:

It is easy to see how the cabinet changes could be seen as a victory for the Kreuzzeitung Party,[37] but it is questionable that those who were appointed would go so far as to wish to warrant themselves such a negative reputation. However, the danger does exist that they could drift more to the right and/or will be incapable of influencing the elections or that they will be incapable of dealing with the complications that could arise if the elections do not go their way.[38]

Frederick was enthusiastic when another opportunity for Prussian intervention presented itself in Hesse-Kassel, where the elector stubbornly refused to abide by Austro-Prussian demands to observe legal electoral procedures. The cabinet recommended that a Prussian delegate be sent to Kassel with instructions to advise the elector to accept an Austro-Prussian solution to the problem; if the elector refused to cooperate, he would face Prussian military intervention. When the cabinet voted to present this ultimatum to the elector, Frederick confided to his diary, "Thank God—the power of Prussia will finally make itself evident!" Once again, he expressed the hope that a Prussian victory in Kassel would solve the constitutional conflict. As he confided to his diary: "Our delegates will certainly become more cooperative and will realize that the king has not altered his views on the protection of constitutional rights."[39]

Frederick and his wife disagreed on the uses of foreign intervention. Following Albert's dictum, Victoria held that only a liberalized Prussia—not a Prussia led by a conservative ministry—could pursue an active policy in the German question. Hence she considered her husband's wish for a foreign policy victory under the auspices of a conservative ministry a case of putting the cart before the horse. She explained her feelings on the subject when she voiced her opposition to the appointment of the archconservative Otto von Bismarck as minister to Paris:

Bismarck espouses a doctrine to which Papa [Prince Albert] was vehemently opposed, namely that any action in foreign affairs will ease domestic turmoil. This is an immoral principle. One cannot use an affliction to promote healing. It is difficult enough to deal with domestic problems; how is it even possible to believe that they can be solved via foreign policy? This is a completely erroneous idea that a man like Bismarck can be of use to our country—he has no principles![40]

This belief was shared by many members of the opposition, who maintained that the liberalization of Prussia was the prerequisite for its leadership in the German question.

Frederick's hopes for a foreign policy victory were dashed when the elector accepted the Austro-Prussian ultimatum. In the end, the Kassel affair proved to be but a minor distraction from the serious difficulties at home. The elections in May resulted in a devastating defeat for the government: conservative strength in parliament shrank to 15, and 85 percent of parliamentary seats were filled with members of the opposition: the left liberals gained 96 seats while the winners of the elections were the Progressives, with 133 seats. The Catholic faction that had supported the military reforms was reduced from 54 to 28 seats. The Constitutionalists also suffered heavy losses: they dropped from 91 to 65 seats, and this loss was regarded as the death knell of the party.[41]

With parliament under domination of radical liberals, the prospect of compromise between government and parliament appeared to be impossible.[42] The king was determined to prevent any attempt by parliament to undermine the royal prerogative, while the parliamentary majority, on the other hand, was determined to throw out the military budget and impose parliamentary government upon the crown. What was at stake was nothing less than the subjugation of the crown to parliament.[43]

Not all liberals, however, were determined to impose parliamentary government on the crown. Some liberals offered to abandon their opposition if the government gave in to their demand to reduce the term of army service from three to two years. Some of the ministers were willing to accept this compromise but William would not hear of it, and told them that he would prefer to rule without a budget. The ministers, however, rejected this suggestion on the grounds that it would place the crown in violation of the constitution.[44] On the other hand, conservative war minister von Roon recommended that the king give a cabinet post to arch conservative Otto von Bismarck in order to strengthen the case of the crown against parliament. None of these alternatives appealed to the king, who summoned his son to Babelsberg and told him that he wished to abdicate.

Without hesitation, the crown prince begged his father to reconsider his decision. Although Frederick was nominally opposed to the two-year service term,[45] he tried to convince the king that giving in to the two-year term could not be compared with the ruinous consequences of his abdication, which would exacerbate domestic unrest and threaten the stability of the monarchy and the dynasty. He added that abdication in the face of demands by the intractable parliament would only set a dangerous precedent for future monarchs.[46] The king, however, was not moved by his son's arguments. Frederick then tried to convince the cabinet to support the king so that abdication could be avoided, but the ministers remained divided on the question of the two-year service term.[47]

The crown princess, however, did not view the abdication threat in negative terms at all. She told her husband that he had little choice but to take the throne:

I am actually glad that things have come to a head at this moment. For once we may be able to do more than remain silent in the face of this awful situation, which is so full of indecision and ignorance. What is expected of you as a dutiful son and subject is so very difficult and severe, but this cannot be compared to what you would have to contend with if you stood idly by watching your father forfeit his popularity (a process that is already underway) and watching errors being committed that could threaten crown and country![48]

The crown princess had no doubts whatsoever that her husband, as king, would be able to put an end to the constitutional conflict: "If you came to the throne and had a liberal government, the reorganization of the army would be safe and I believe that this is what your father feels." On the other hand, if the king retained power and refused to initiate liberal reforms, and if he took up Roon's suggestion to appoint Bismarck, the crown princess predicted a dim future for Prussia: "Should a truly reasonable 'new era' emerge as a result of this crisis, our future happiness will be assured and all will be well. If not, we will have to endure absurdities, unreasonableness and intolerance. The parliament will remain in opposition, the military question will not be resolved, and Bismarck will have to tackle it, and he will do this like a man who cannot swim but jumps into the water where it is deepest!"[49]

Victoria hinted that she wished to see Frederick's accession lead to establishment of British-style government in Prussia. She told her husband that the political crisis at hand served as proof that the traditional Prussian system of government had outlived its usefulness: "The policy-makers have been much too hesitant," she wrote, "They have acted either too late or not at all or have pursued harmful policies; they have ultimately destroyed the legitimate status of Germany in Europe—all of this has happened because they do not have the courage and strength to rule according to the spirit of our time." Given Victoria's liberal views, it is reasonable to assume that a Prussian government that would "rule according to the spirit of the time" would adopt British-style political institutions. In short, she wished Frederick to succeed where new era liberalism had failed.

As a constitutional liberal, Frederick was no advocate of such radical changes, and this helps explain why he opposed his father's abdication.[50] When he told his father that the abdication would put him in an "embarrassing position,"[51] he meant that he found himself uncomfortably wedged between liberal and conservative forces in the country. If he were to come to the throne, he knew that he would be confronted by die-hard conservative opposition to his liberal views. Three months before the abdication crisis, the crown prince became privy to rumors that the army would never allow him to ascend the throne if he became too closely affiliated with liberal aspirations. Frederick also heard rumors of an army plot to remove the crown prince from the line of succession in favor of his conservative cousin, Prince Frederick Charles, who was supported by the military clique.[52] Even if the rumors were untrue, Frederick knew that the hostility that ultraconservatives bore him because of his liberal views was quite genuine and would make his reign as king difficult indeed.[53]

Given Frederick's constitutionalist views, there is also good reason to believe that he would have had trouble cooperating with the radical liberal majority in parliament. The king's abdication in favor of his more liberal-minded son would have signalled the liberals' victory in the constitutional conflict. It is a foregone conclusion that the liberals' first order of business under King Frederick would have been demands for genuine parliamentary government. Since the crown prince opposed the idea of sacrificing the powers of the crown to parliament, it is likely that another conflict between crown and parliament would have erupted during his reign.[54]

Frederick met with the king again on 20 September to report on his meeting with the ministers of the previous day and told him that some of them favored agreeing to the two-year term, whereas others suggested that the government simply go about its business without a budget approved by parliament. The crown prince raised objections when he learned that William was far more inclined to rule without a budget, since such a step would place the king in violation of the constitution. Frederick's disappointment was mitigated somewhat by his father's promise not to appoint Bismarck as minister-president. Still, the possibility that William would rule without a budget compelled Frederick to leave Babelsberg, lest it be assumed by his presence that he approved such a policy.

Only two days after Frederick's departure, it was clear that he had underestimated Roon's determination to have Bismarck appointed minister-president. As the crown prince was en route to Reinhartsbrunn, Roon prevailed upon William to reconsider his misgivings about Bismarck, and the king finally met with the latter on 22 September. Bismarck told the king precisely what he wished to hear. If made a member of the cabinet, Bismarck would not give into parliament's demands in the military question and would rule without parliament if necessary. The king was impressed and appointed Bismarck minister-president and foreign minister.[55]

The crown prince and his wife were stunned by Bismarck's appointment after having received assurances from the king to the contrary only a few days before. By their lights, Bismarck was bound to make a bad situation only worse, for Frederick and Victoria knew that he had no qualms about violating the constitution in order to secure the army reforms.[56]

On the advice of Victoria and her liberal-minded private secretary, Ernst von Stockmar, the crown prince wrote the new minister-president five days after his appointment and warned him that any attempt to violate the constitution would create an atmosphere of mistrust between the people and the crown, which would, in turn, cripple the government in its domestic and foreign relations. The crown prince recommended that any solution to the conflict would have to be achieved in accordance with the constitution and the will of the people.[57]

It would have surprised Frederick to find out that Bismarck was not averse to Frederick's way of thinking. Upon assuming office, the new minister-president made an honest effort to effect a compromise with parliament. Bismarck hoped that the conflict could be resolved if minor concessions could be made to the liberal opposition. Like the crown prince, Bismarck was not opposed to the two-year service term. He devised a plan whereby conscripts could purchase their release from military service after two years. Those unable or unwilling to pay would serve a third year, and the money raised could be used to attract volunteers.[58] This plan, however, was dismissed out of hand by the king, who insisted that anything less than the three-year term would mean death to the army. Bismarck then tried to appease the opposition by offering cabinet posts to liberal deputies Vincke, Simson, and Sybel. But this plan failed when the candidates insisted on the two-year term as the condition for their acceptance. Although Bismarck told the liberals in private that he would persuade the king to accept the two-year term, the liberals, who were aware of the king's stubbornness on the issue, refused to enter the government.[59]

Having failed to bring either the king or the opposition closer to a compromise, Bismarck had to look for new ways to resolve the conflict. Following royal orders, he withdrew the budget for 1863, which had been submitted to parliament along with the budget for 1862, thus making it impossible for the opposition to eliminate funds for the army reorganization for 1862. In a speech before the budget committee on 30 September, he declared that if parliament refused funds for 1863, he would rule without a budget. He justified this procedure by pointing out that parliament had no exclusive power over military appropriations. Instead, it was necessary for parliament, together with the crown, to come to an agreement. Rejection of the budget by either of these powers constituted an emergency, which, in turn, gave the government the right to govern without a budget, since the crown retained all those rights not expressly allocated to parliament by the constitution.[60]

When Progressive party member Rudolf Virchow declared that it was unconstitutional for the government to rule without a budget, Bismarck replied that the constitution made no provision for what was to happen in the event that a budget was rejected by parliament. Since the constitution was deficient in this regard, it was the government's duty to prevent a standstill of all business. Government, said Bismarck, had to continue even if that implied expenditure without lawful parliamentary enactment. This was the gist of Bismarck's famous *Lückentheorie*, or gap theory.[61]

Bismarck angered the liberals even more with his speech to the parliamentary finance committee, in which he stated that the German people looked to Prussia not for its liberalism but for its power. Since Prussia's frontiers, as fixed by the Congress of Vienna, were not suitable for healthy development, Prussia's primary goal was the development of its power: "Not through speeches and majority decisions will the great questions of the period be decided, but through iron and blood."[62]

Bismarck's strong words failed to intimidate the liberals into accepting his demands. Although they assented to the budget for 1863, they rejected the military expenditures. Bismarck responded by dissolving parliament on 13 October 1862. He proclaimed a state of emergency and announced that the government would rule without a budget approved by parliament and would submit a bill of indemnity only when "normal" conditions had returned.[63]

If Bismarck was willing to declare war on the liberal majority in parliament, the same was not true in the case of the crown prince. After parliament was dissolved, he wrote Frederick that his ministry would continue to do everything possible in order to bring about an amicable solution to the conflict. He added, however, that the uncooperative stance of parliament could bring about the necessity of measures that were "incompatible with the letter of the constitution."[64] Bismarck confided that he was frustrated by the prolongation of the conflict and hinted that the situation had become desperate: "The friction in our government system is so strong that it will be almost impossible to alleviate it by human means." Nonetheless, he insisted that he was committed to removing the obstacles to compromise between crown and parliament.[65]

The tone of Bismarck's first letters as minister-president to the crown prince show that the former was anxious to convince the latter to accept his policies. Bismarck insisted that he was not a reactionary and did not claim allegiance to any political party. He had nothing against the liberals, he told Frederick, but insisted that he was forced to refrain from adopting a liberal policy lest parliament interpret this as submission of the government to the will of parliament.[66] Bismarck also insisted that he, like the crown prince, was interested in using a foreign policy victory to solve the constitutional conflict. He was as good as his word. He tried to pursue a policy in the ever-festering Hesse-Kassel affair precisely along the lines previously suggested by the crown prince, but his efforts were in vain.[67]

Frederick, however, rejected Bismarck's proffered friendship. As far as Bismarck's domestic policy was concerned, Frederick had no interest in supporting measures that were "incompatible with the letter of the constitution." Though Frederick also supported a foreign policy victory as a means to solve the conflict, he, like many other liberals, balked at the prospect of a reactionary Junker like Bismarck leading the nationalist cause.

The first months of 1863 marked a period of increased hostility between crown and parliament. Issues of military reform and the budget crisis were virtually ignored since the deputies were preoccupied with the task of bringing pressure to bear on the ministry because of its questionable policies. Bismarck, however, defeated liberals' attempts to discredit his ministry: he refused to give the king a petition signed by deputies protesting the conduct of the minsters, and he denied parliament its right to inquire into the reasons that the government made the unpopular decision to support Russian suppression of the Polish rebellion of 1863.[68]

Popular opinion now began to turn against the king, who supported the unscrupulous minister-president. In order to offset the growing unpopularity of the monarch, Bismarck and the king staged an elaborate celebration of the fiftieth anniversary of the founding of the Prussian militia, to rekindle the spirit of a time when the people had rallied enthusiastically to their king. The attempt miscarried; the celebration was poorly attended, and those who did come cheered the crown prince but did not give the same homage to the king. This demonstration reinforced the hope of many liberals that the days of Bismarck's ministry were numbered. Theodor von Bernhardi wrote, "Everyone thinks Bismarck's government is finished and is convinced that he cannot hold on any longer."[69]

Bismarck, however, stayed in power, and liberals now looked to Frederick to make public his disapproval of the minister-president and his policies. Those close to Frederick knew that his silence stemmed from a desire to avoid a break with his father but felt such a break was justified at a time when the viability of parliament's existence was being challenged by Bismarck. In February 1863, popular novelist Gustav Freytag summed up the frustration of many liberals when he wrote: "The country is being alienated from the dynasty as a result of the passive attitude of the crown prince. The opposition demands that he state his position and take sides."[70] Some liberals even went so far as to suggest that Frederick be supplanted in line of succession for the throne by the liberal Grand Duke Frederick I of Baden. Liberal leader Hermann Baumgarten believed that Frederick's silence confirmed rumors of his personal weakness: "I have reason to assume that nothing has been left undone to inform the crown prince about the situation and the duties it imposes upon him. But from what I hear I must consider him unable to achieve anything in important matters. Evidently he is as insignificant in intellect as he is in character. I have long ceased to expect anything from him."[71]

Gustav Freytag took it upon himself personally to persuade the crown prince to speak out against Bismarck. His remarks appeared to have some effect; the crown prince wrote, "Freytag is right. It is good to be forced by circumstances to give up half-way measures."[72] Frederick received further encouragement from his brother-in-law, the grand duke of Baden, who urged him to say something against the existing system, "so the people could have hope."[73]

Frederick was put under even more pressure to break his silence when Bismarck proposed to issue an edict against the liberal press in a meeting of the ministerial council in May 1863. The crown prince knew that it would be difficult to justify a decree against the press on constitutional grounds. Although he did not voice his opposition to the decree in the meeting, he made no secret of his feelings on the subject to his father. Prior to his departure on a military inspection tour, Frederick wrote the king that he would break his silence and speak out against a decree that would compromise the integrity of the constitution and seriously endanger the prestige of the crown.[74] Frederick reminded his father that his silence had thus far been dictated by his respect for the king along with his wish that he not be identified with the opposition, which wrongly considered him to be an honorary member of its ranks. But he felt justified in abandoning passive resistance on the grounds that he could not remain silent if the king's prestige and the welfare of Prussia were being threatened.

The crown princess heartily approved of this letter. Her comments on the subject show how difficult it was for Frederick to write such a stern letter to his father:

When one does something because it is right, this can often be a heart-rending task. This is what you have done by writing that letter to Papa. [But] your dear Papa will thank you for this some day and not think less of his son because he has dared to tell him the truth and had the courage not only to have his own opinions, but to act in accordance with them. On such difficult occasions . . . when feelings of duty and conscientiousness collide with your obligation to be obedient, you must satisfy the demands of your conscience *before* those of your father and king.[75]

Frederick's efforts did not, however, make any impression on the king, who, shortly after dissolving parliament, signed an edict that silenced the opposition press. Justification for the decree was constitutionally ambiguous: it was issued under Article 63 of the constitution, which gave the king the right to issue decrees while parliament was not in session, but only when "urgently" required to do so, "for the protection of public safety or settlement of an unusual emergency."[76]

Liberals were justified in labelling the decree unconstitutional: it was created while parliament was still in session and there was no "unusual emergency." The liberal newspapers published a common protest, and on 4 June the Berlin city council voted to send a delegation to the king protesting the arbitrary actions of the government. All protests were quickly suppressed by the government.[77]

No member of the government took the trouble to telegraph the crown prince and princess about the promulgation of the press decree. Like their liberal friends, the royal couple read about it in the newspapers. Frederick immediately wrote his father expressing his disapproval. Unlike the liberals, the crown prince did not call the edict unconstitutional, but he pointed out that it went against the "true spirit of the constitution." While he admitted that the opposition press posed a threat to the government, he suggested that the threat could have been alleviated without resorting to extraordinary measures. He recommended that the decree be rescinded, since it would give the opposition further grounds for protest against the government.[78] Significantly, Frederick begged his father not to consider his opposition to the decree as evidence that he had joined the ranks of the opposition in parliament.[79]

This letter was not enough to convince Victoria that her husband had done everything in his power to protest the press decree. When Frederick arrived in Danzig on 4 June, she and Leopold von Winter, mayor of Danzig, told him that his sense of duty to the king had clouded his judgment. They argued that he stood to lose as much as his father in the way of popular support unless he spoke out publicly against the decree, and they added that his silence on the subject had given all the impression that he had supported it.

It is quite possible that Frederick's decision to break his silence was encouraged by the somber mood of the public upon his arrival in Danzig. He wrote in his diary: "people are truly enraged about the press decree."[80] Accustomed to cheering crowds wherever he went, he probably sensed that the people had assumed that he had approved of the press edict, and it may have been for this reason that he was anxious to dispel this notion.

After Mayor von Winter welcomed the crown prince to the Danzig town hall on 5 June and added his regret that they could not meet under happier circumstances, Frederick replied:

I too regret that I have come here at a time when a conflict has developed between the government and the people of which I learned with great surprise. I did not know anything about the decrees that have brought it about. I was away. I had nothing to do with the consultations which led to their promulgation. But we all, and I most of all, since I know best the noble and fatherly intentions and generous sentiments of the king, we are all confident that Prussia, under the scepter of His Majesty, will achieve the greatness for which Providence has marked her out.[81]

With these words, Frederick entered the political arena, albeit reluctantly. Unfortunately, many of the people whom the crown prince wished to reassure could read about the speech only in non-Prussian newspapers, since the Prussian liberal newspapers were silenced by the very decree that Frederick protested.[82]

Frederick's feelings about his political debut were decidedly mixed. On one hand, he observed proudly in his diary that his remarks would prove his sincerity to the liberals, who had heretofore been critical of his behavior: "I have made it known that I am an enemy of Bismarck and his unsavory policies, and I have proven to the world that I have no part in his schemes. It was my intention to make the ministry cringe [*sich getroffen fühlen*]." On the other hand, he feared that the speech would result in a break with his father.[83]

William's reaction was quite what his son feared; he was deeply hurt by the speech, which he considered to be an act of near treason. On 6 June, the king brusquely ordered his son to publicly retract the speech or resign his military posts. But the courage that enabled Frederick to make the speech proved sufficient to endure its immediate consequences: Frederick refused his father's request and added "The consequences of my behavior are completely clear to me, and I ask you to understand that I intend to stand by my convictions and endure any suffering and persecution."[84] The king was tempted to indulge his son on this score: since Frederick was an officer in the army, the speech made him guilty of insubordination, and he was hence liable to imprisonment. Such treatment was not without precedent; as crown prince, Frederick the Great was imprisoned by his own father for insubordination.[85]

Ironically, though Frederick's remarks at Danzig were directed against Bismarck, it was he who urged the king not to subject his son to imprisonment. Bismarck told the king that persecution of the crown prince would make him a martyr in the eyes of the liberals and strengthen their resistance against the government. Bismarck therefore urged William to limit his son's punishment to a sharp warning that a repetition of the Danzig speech would not be tolerated. Bismarck also persuaded the king to allow his son to continue his military inspection tour, since any deviation from his schedule could lead liberals to believe that the prince was planning further acts of insubordination. He finally recommended that the crown prince be kept preoccupied with ministry meetings and affairs of state so that he would have less time to fall under the influence of his liberal advisers.[86]

The king accepted the logic behind Bismarck's arguments and criticized Frederick's behavior in writing. Frederick was free to share the opinions of the opposition, the king wrote his son, but was forbidden to make them public. William reminded his son of his duty to accept the king's decisions on all matters. The letter ended on a conciliatory note: the king was willing to forgive the Danzig episode as long as his son promised to never again broadcast his antigovernment views.[87]

The crown prince was happy to accept his father's terms for reconciliation. He had no intention of making further criticisms of the government even before his father decided to forgive him. As the crown princess explained to her mother:

A year of silence and self-denial has brought Fritz no other fruits than that of being considered weak and helpless....The Liberals think that he is not sincerely one of them, and those few who think it, fancy he has not the courage to avow it. He has now given them an opportunity of judging his way of thinking and consequently will now again be passive and silent until better days come.[88]

The London *Times* echoed the satisfaction of the royal couple with the Danzig episode:

It is . . . felt that Prince Frederick William, in that short speech, cleared away the mist of doubt which hung around him and dimmed his popularity, that he greatly improved his position before the country, and gave, for the future, an implied pledge precious to the people and most important to his dynasty . . . this is the general feeling of the reflecting and impartially-judging men of all shades of the constitutional party . . . and of the great bulk of the bourgeoisie.[89]

This article, however, exaggerated German liberals' enthusiasm for the speech. Frederick immediately came under fire for this comment: "I knew nothing about the decrees that brought it [the press decree] about." The liberals knew that the crown prince attended crown council meetings and that he therefore must have known that the edict was under consideration; hence, the comment made Frederick appear either inept or insincere. As liberal deputy Vincke-Oldendorff wrote to Duncker: "This comment made me uneasy as well, because I know that the prince is well-informed about political issues. It is possible that he was misquoted or wished to say something else."[90] The comment was also puzzling to Queen Victoria, but it was defended by her daughter, who wrote, "his [Frederick's] speech in Danzig was intended to convey in a clear and unambiguous way to his audience, that he had *nothing* to do with the unconstitutional acts of the Government—that he was not even aware of their being contemplated!"[91] Liberals also criticized Frederick's tribute to his father in the speech, which was seen as inappropriate since the king sanctioned the unpopular practices of the Bismarckian regime.

The crown prince defended himself against these criticisms in a letter to the grand duke of Baden. He said that he had used the word "surprise" to connote the fact that he had been left in the dark about the *promulgation* of the press edict and that his remarks about his father "were the least I could do and the most appropriate a son could make."[92]

Despite their objections to the Danzig speech, prominent liberals tried to persuade the crown prince to make a stronger gesture or statement to demonstrate his opposition to Bismarck's government. The grand duke of Baden and his foreign minister, Roggenbach, urged Frederick to resign his military posts or refuse to perform any official functions until the ministry ceased its unconstitutional activities,[93] and liberal deputy Karl Mathy expressed the hope that the Danzig speech would be but the first in a series of statements against Bismarck.[94] Queen Victoria also encouraged her son-in-law to demonstrate his opposition to Bismarck's policies by breaking off his military inspection tour and coming to England. As she told her daughter: "The crown prince should respectfully refuse to travel about . . . and come here. . . . I speak in beloved Papa's name. . . . Fritz may be fatally compromised if you do not do this."[95] Perhaps remembering the fate of his predecessor Frederick the Great the crown prince refused the queen's invitation, knowing that premature termination of his tour would constitute another act of insubordination. This disturbed the queen, who told Victoria, "This news grieves me and disappoints all of your friends."[96]

Frederick's rationale for rejecting the advice of his mother-in-law and his liberal friends was that any further statements made against the government would push him into the arms of the Progressive Party. As he explained to Duncker:

If the progressives wish to make me one of their own . . . I cannot restrain their efforts any more than I could prevent Bismarck's attempts to bring me over to his point of view. My views are embodied in my words at Danzig; I refuse to say or do anything more because I do not want to be a leader of the opposition. If Waldeck[97] and company are progressives, I wish to have nothing to do with them. On the other hand, I do not consider all progressives as enemies simply because they have unfortunately split ranks with the old liberals.[98]

Before Frederick made the Danzig speech, he predicted that any protest on his part would be bound to generate confusion. In a letter to the grand duke of Baden, he wrote, "once the different explanations and interpretations start a nice controversy, who is going to find out the quintessence?"[99] This prediction was correct, for few, if any, understood the true meaning of the Danzig speech. Frederick's heavily criticized tribute to his father in the speech was meant to convince the people that the king had not turned against them and to hold out the hope that he would come to his senses and reverse his support for Bismarck's unconstitutional policies. Indeed, the speech was intended as a gesture of faith in the king, and its author had no intention of giving any support to a radical liberal majority, whose goals he opposed.

Victoria, however, was far more sensitive to criticism of the Danzig speech than was her husband. Sensing that her husband's unwillingness to take a stronger anti-government position could compromise his image as a liberal, which she was carefully cultivating, Victoria arranged the publication of Frederick's letters in the foreign press indicating his opposition to Bismarck's policies. On 11 June, Victoria asked her mother to publicize the Danzig speech in England, and she sent portions of Frederick's correspondence to her mother, adding that other letters had been given to Stockmar and the grand duke of Baden.[100] According to Frederick's biographer, Wolbe, the crown princess directed Stockmar to hand over Frederick's letters to liberal associates for publication in the *Grenzboten* and the *Süddeutsche Zeitung*.[101]

Victoria's efforts, however, had no effect in Prussia, where the press edict forbade publication of Frederick's letters. News about the indiscretion could be obtained only through leaflets and rumor. This, in turn, made Prussian liberals doubt the validity of the correspondence, and enthusiasm over the matter died quickly.[102] In the end, the incident did little to reassure the liberals of Frederick's devotion to their cause.

The press indiscretion enraged the king, who launched an investigation into the matter. Although the results of the investigation were inconclusive, Bismarck had little doubt that the crown princess had engineered the entire episode in order to "generate publicity for her husband's deeds and to acquaint public opinion with the crown prince's way of thinking."[103] The crown prince was deeply embarrassed by the affair and begged the recipients of his letters to show them to no one.[104] Victoria, however, felt that the furor over the matter had been exaggerated.[105]

Frederick's embarrassment over the press indiscretion did not deter him from attempting to convince his father that Bismarck and his unconstitutional policies were a liability to the monarchy. When the king met with his son in Gastein for the first time after the Danzig episode, Frederick insisted that the constitutional conflict could be ended if Bismarck stepped down and the king accepted the two-year service term. Angered at his son's adherence to his liberal constitutionalist opinions after he had been forgiven for the Danzig episode, the king told him that he would obtain the military reforms through a series of dissolutions of parliament until "obedience" had been reestablished.[106] The crown prince also spoke to Bismarck, who shocked Frederick with his comment that a constitutional regime was "untenable" in Prussia. When Frederick asked the minister-president why he continued to bother with the constitution at all, Bismarck replied that he would observe existing laws "as long as he could."[107]

After the cabinet voted to dissolve parliament on 2 September, Frederick asked his father whether he supported Bismarck's views on the future of constitutionalism in Prussia. The crown prince reported the substance of his conversation with the king to his wife:

I mentioned that I had heard Bismarck's ideas in Gastein. . . . Papa replied that these ideas would be acted upon and that he believed . . . that there would be no more constitutions in twenty years' time. When I asked him what would replace constitutions, he said that he did not know since he would probably not live long enough to find out. He added . . . that the King of Prussia was never intended to be a weak figurehead in the face of a more powerful parliament. When I asked him how often he intended to dissolve parliament, he replied that dissolutions would continue until it became obedient, or until barricades were raised in the streets, or until he ascended the scaffold.[108]

The king's words confirmed Frederick's worst fears; he was now convinced that the course planned by his father would ultimately result in revolution, civil war, and the downfall of the monarchy. As he told his wife: "This is the beginning of the end!"[109]

The king's threat to suspend the constitution forced the crown prince to assume a hostile stance toward the government. After the aforementioned exchange with the king, Frederick asked him for permission to abstain from crown council meetings, which indicated his intent to embark on a policy of passive resistance to the government. William would hear none of it. He declared that he needed his son's support more than ever and that Frederick's refusal to attend crown council meetings indicated that he was under the influence of the king's enemies. Frederick did not allow this to serve as the final word on the matter. His resolve was fortified by his wife, the British diplomat Robert Morier, and the privy counsellor in the ministry of justice, Friedberg, who encouraged him to write the king that he would raise a furor in crown council meetings if forced to attend against his will.[110]

The king passed his son's letter to Bismarck, who advised the king on how to deal with his troublesome son. Bismarck agreed that Frederick's oppositional behavior was the result of the influence of his liberal associates, but it was also the result of his inadequate knowledge of government affairs. The minister-president supported the latter point by citing several errors in Frederick's letter. The crown prince had written that he could no longer consider himself a part of the ministry or an adviser to the king in view of the unconstitutional practices of the government. Bismarck told the king that the crown prince had no voting privileges in the ministry and that the position "adviser to the king" did not exist.[111] Bismarck advised the king to allow his son to stay away from crown council meetings, since he believed that the crown prince could be disruptive. The minister-president added that Frederick would cause his father less trouble if he could spend more time learning about government affairs and less time in the company of liberal friends, particularly those in England, whose advice to the crown prince was not always compatible with Prussia's interests.[112]

Victoria's biographer Egon Caesar Corti pointed out that Bismarck's unflattering comments about the crown prince were indicative of his desire "to chalk up the score heavily against his enemies, the crown prince and his wife." Yet Frederick himself expressed doubts concerning his knowledge of government affairs. Shortly before he asked his father for permission to stay away from crown council meetings, he wrote his wife:

The more seriously I consider the present situation, the more troubled I am about my ability of dealing at some future date with similar difficulties as I should. My courage and persistence will no doubt prevail, but on the other hand I am increasingly aware of my startling lack of knowledge about domestic problems, foreign policy, and government personnel. Sometimes I imagine I hear the call to retreat getting louder and louder![113]

Frederick's crisis of confidence was somewhat relieved when his father finally agreed to his request to stay away from crown council meetings.

Frederick now shared the hope of liberal deputies that Bismarck's policies would lead to his downfall and that a liberal ministry would succeed him.[114] In the meantime, Frederick remained committed to his policy of passive resistance and chose not to speak out against Bismarck's threat to suspend the constitution. He told his wife that his absence from crown council meetings and his unwillingness to support Bismarck's policies could be just as effective as a public speech and not nearly as risky: "my behavior will eventually make clear attitudes that could be otherwise expressed by not remaining silent and sharply opposing [the government]. If I limit myself to the latter course of action, it is clear to me that I will be put in a most embarrassing position, and the long-term consequences of such action are too uncertain."[115] Indeed, since both sides of the political spectrum had failed to grasp the true meaning behind his words at Danzig, he could not see what good could possibly be done by additional speeches. Passive resistance, by Frederick's lights, was the logical alternative to delivering speeches that would be misinterpreted and misunderstood and put him in a difficult position as a royal prince.

Shortly after the crown prince embarked on his policy of passive resistance, Frederick had reason to believe that his dire predictions about the future of constitutionalism in Prussia were inaccurate. In October, the king wrote his son that Bismarck was not necessarily determined to suspend the constitution: "You always come back to Minister von Bismarck's utterance that we would reach the point of dispensing with the constitution. In his conversation with you at Gastein, he presented this as one of the eventualities which lies within the range of possibility, whereas you make it out to be the goal of his efforts."[116] By Frederick's lights, there was still hope for some sort of compromise in the conflict between crown and parliament as long as the constitution remained intact.

By late 1863, there were also signs that the radical liberal opposition was losing steam. Shortly after the press edict was promulgated, liberal deputy Vincke-Oldendorff reported that he could detect no enthusiasm for opposing the regime. The general attitude was : "Nothing comes of it; it is better to let the king rule by himself once more."[117] The liberals failed to pose a serious threat to the government when parliament was called into session in late 1863. They duly exercised their constitutional right to vote down the press edict, which became inoperative. Questionable government practices were investigated and duly recorded, and the army bill was rejected, but there was no widespread movement to call for the resignation of the cabinet.[118] The lack of fighting spirit among the opposition was confirmed by Rudolf Haym, editor of the *Preussische Jahrbücher*, who complained:

Whoever can, seeks a pretext to withdraw, saying "After all, we can't push our way through, we must let the storm blow over" and the like. He who is involved, fancies himself uninvolved, spares his strength, relaxes from the strain and leaves the struggle to others. Later he will appear and be all the louder when the friends of the constitution have been victorious, or when some favorable event in foreign affairs has turned the page.[119]

A favorable event in foreign affairs was precisely what Frederick had advocated all along to solve the constitutional conflict. An opportunity for Prussia to assert itself on behalf of the nationalist cause arose when liberal nationalists appealed to the Prussian government to support the liberation of German speaking denizens of Schleswig and Holstein from their Danish overlords. Frederick once again tried to persuade his father to back the nationalists' demands, since he held that a linkage of the interests of the government and the nationalists with regard to the Schleswig-Holstein problem would effect a moral conquest, which, in turn, would tone down liberal agitation for radical reforms. But his efforts were blocked by Bismarck, who, in turn, pursued a policy that appeared to be motivated by the latter's desire to increase Prussia's frontiers. By 1866, however, Frederick realized that Bismarck's ultimate goals in foreign policy were not so different from his own desire to preserve constitutionalism and unify Germany. The clash between Frederick and Bismarck's ideas on foreign policy and its resolution by 1866 are subjects of the next chapter.

NOTES

1. Prussian mobilization during the Austro-Italian War of 1859 had revealed that

the army was inadequate in size and organization. Even the liberals, who were wary of the army as a reactionary force, believed that a strong reformed army would be a crucial factor in realizing the goal of a unified Germany. Otto Pflanze, *Bismarck and the Development of Germany. Volume 1: The Period of Unification 1815–1870* (Princeton, NJ, 1990), pp. 165–168.

2. Ibid., p. 168.

3. Erich Eyck, *Bismarck and the German Empire*, 3rd ed. (London, 1968), p. 46.

4. The fears of the liberals were not unfounded. The king wished to create an expanded and loyal army that would inject military attitudes into civil life so that the events of 1848–1849 could not be repeated. When parliament rejected the military reforms, William suspected that it wished to bring the armed forces under its control. The liberals, on the other hand, became equally suspicious when the government continued to insist that all facets of the reform program be unconditionally approved—they accused the government of attempting to interfere with their constitutional right to approve budgetary legislation. See Pflanze, *Bismarck*, p. 169 and Gerhard Ritter, *The Sword and the Scepter: The Problem of Militarism in Germany* (Coral Gables, FL, 1969), pp. 121 ff.

5. Pflanze, *Bismarck* Vol. 1, p. 170.

6. Adalbert Hess, *Das Parlament, das Bismarck widerstrebte* (Cologne, 1964), p. 24.

7. George O. Kent, *Bismarck and His Times* (Carbondale, IL, 1978), p. 39.

8. Ernst Rudolf Huber, *Deutsche Verfassungsgeschichte seit 1789* 4 Vols. (Stuttgart, 1957–1969), Vol. 2, pp. 281ff.

9. He called the liberals' demand to reduce the term of military service "impossible and unacceptable." H. O. Meisner, ed., *Kaiser Friedrich III. Tagebücher von 1848 bis 1866.* (Leipzig, 1929), p. 131. Shortly before the December elections, Frederick wrote in his diary, "The elections are expected to return more Democrats [progressives] than before. Many appear to be laboring under the misconception that one can do the government a favor by voting for progressive, that is, democratic, candidates." Ibid., p. 131.

10. Crown Prince Frederick William to King William I, 4 November 1861. Meisner, *Tagebücher*, pp. 498–501.

11. Pflanze, *Bismarck* Vol. 1, p. 177.

12. Ibid., p. 165.

13. In his memorial, "Zur Situation, 22 February 1862," Frederick wrote: "An energetic policy . . . that would raise the possibility of using the army would persuade the majority of the representatives to immediately approve the budget without amendments. . . . I believe that the affair in Kurhessen should be ended since . . . the situation there is bordering on anarchy." Meisner, *Tagebücher*, p. 492

14. For commentaries from both sides of the political spectrum on the Hesse-Kassel situation, see Hans Rosenberg, ed., *Die Nationalpolitische Publizistik Deutschlands vom Entritt der Neuen Ära in Preussen bis zum Ausbruch des Deutschen Krieges* 2 Vols. (Munich, 1935) Vol. 1, p. 330ff.

15. While Frederick was aware that such a venture ran the risk of driving a wedge between pro-Austrian and pro-Prussian factions in the Confederation, he maintained that this was a small price to pay since bold Prussian action would ultimately end the conflict between crown and parliament, since it would prove the government's commitment to upholding constitutionalism: "Jedenfalls hätte Pruessen in einem solche Falle nicht bloss die Vertretung des Landes, sondern das gesamte Land und bedeutende Sympathien Deutschlands hinter sich." Meisner, *Tagebücher,* p. 494.

16. Liberal leaders Rudolf von Bennigsen and Theodor von Bernhardi both believed that the liberals' unwillingness to compromise with the government on the military question was conditioned by the indecisive foreign policy of the Prussian government. They also agreed that the government had to act in the Danish question or the credibility of the new era ministers would be lost. Theodor von Bernhardi, *Aus dem Leben Theodor von Bernhardi* 5 Vols. (Leipzig, 1893–1895), Vol. 4, p. 237.

17. Hessische Hausstiftung, Schloss Fasanerie, Fulda (hereafter HH) Crown Prince Frederick William to Crown Princess Victoria, 5 March 1862.

18. L. D. Steefel, *The Schleswig-Holstein Question* (Cambridge, 1941), pp. 47–48.

19. Meisner, *Tagebücher*, p. 129.

20. "Ein festes liberales Programm muss verkündet werden, womöglich eine thatkräftige action [sic] wozu sich die Herzogthümer Frage darbiete, lebhaft erfasst werden." HH: Memorial of Crown Prince Frederick William, 7 March 1862.

21. Ibid. Surprisingly, Max Duncker, an adviser to the crown prince sympathetic to the liberal cause, also believed that the liberal ministry was expendable. Duncker felt that a conservative ministry could be a favorable alternative to a weak liberal ministry that had failed to produce a foreign policy to enhance Prussia's position as a great power and satisfy the demands of the German nationalists. He tried to convince the crown prince that the appointment of a conservative ministry did not necessarily imply the onset of a period of reaction. As he put it, "If a conservative ministry does not produce a foreign policy victory, it will only be a brief experiment." Duncker to Stockmar, 6 March 1862. Johannes Schulze, ed., *Max Duncker, Politischer Briefwechsel aus seinem Nachlass* (Osnabrück, 1967), p. 323.

22. HH: Crown Princess Victoria to Crown Prince Frederick William, Windsor, 12 March 1862.

23. Ibid., 18 March 1862.

24. In a meeting with the temporary cabinet head, Prince von Hohenlohe, Frederick was warned to curb his enthusiasm for the new era ministers. Frederick agreed with Hohenlohe that it was necessary to dispel the impression that he supported the opposition. Meisner, *Tagebücher*, p. 131.

25. HH: Crown Prince Frederick William to Crown Princess Victoria, 10 March 1862.

26. Ibid., 13 March 1862.

27. Ibid., 18 March 1862.

28. Ibid.

29. Ibid.

30. Meisner, *Tagebücher*, p. 133.

31. HH: Crown Princess Victoria to Crown Prince Frederick William, 20 March 1862.

32. Ibid.

33. HH: Crown Prince Frederick William to Crown Princess Victoria, 20 March 1862.

34. HH: Crown Princess Victoria to Crown Prince Frederick William, 21 March 1862.

35. Ibid.

36. Ibid. Although the crown princess encouraged her husband to adopt a confrontational stance toward his father, she herself avoided arguing with the king. After the appointment of the conservative ministry, she wrote her husband: "I have sent birthday greetings to your father devoid of commentary on the situation because I do not wish to say anything that he does not want to hear." HH: Crown Princess Victoria to Crown Prince Frederick William, 19 March 1862.

37. The right-wing conservatives dominating the court and cabinet in Berlin were named after their press organ, the *Kreuzzeitung.*

38. HH: Crown Prince Frederick William to Crown Princess Victoria, 23 March 1862.

39. Meisner, *Tagebücher*, pp. 138–139. See also Huber, *Verfassungsgeschichte*, pp. 440–449.

40. HH: Crown Princess Victoria to Crown Prince Frederick William, 14 May 1862.

41. H. W. Koch, *A Constitutional History of Germany in the Nineteenth and Twentieth Centuries* (London, 1984), p. 94.

42. Frederick's liberal adviser Max von Duncker pointed out that the failure of the ministry to score a decisive victory in the Hesse-Kassel affair had damaged its already sorry reputation. Schulze, *Duncker*, p. 170.

43. Ibid., p. 94.

44. In a memorandum presented to the king, the ministers argued that a rejection of the budget by parliament would deprive the government of a constitutional basis of administration. Hence, the government would act unconstitutionally if it tried to spend revenue against the wishes of parliament. Eyck, *Bismarck*, p. 55.

45. Meisner, *Tagebücher*, p. 131.

46. Ibid., p. 160.

47. HH: Crown Prince Frederick William to Crown Princess Victoria, 19 September 1862.

48. HH: Crown Princess Victoria to Crown Prince Frederick William, 20 September 1862.

49. Ibid., 20 September 1862.

50. Frederick's detractors charge that he was simply afraid to assume power at a time when Prussia was wracked by political crisis, whereas his apologists make little

reference to Frederick's misgivings on the subject or assume that the king never truly meant to give up the throne in the first place. According to Andreas Dorpalen, "he could have been expected to welcome the chance of ascending the throne himself . . . [but] he was fearful at the thought of having to assume the reins of government in his father's place. Everything in him revolted against such a possibility." Andreas Dorpalen, "Frederick III and the German Liberal Movement," *American Historical Review*, Vol. 54, No. 1 (1948), p. 8. Frederick's biographer Werner Richter argues that the crown prince felt that he was too young [he was thirty-one years old (!)] to assume the throne and that he did not have the heart to see his father retire, bitter and humiliated over the struggle between parliament and the crown. Werner Richter, *Friedrich III: Leben und Tragik des Zweiten Hohenzollern Kaisers,* 2nd ed., (Munich, 1981) p. 75. Sir Frederick Ponsonby alludes to the abdication crisis only briefly: "The Crown Prince and Princess . . . were disarmed by the King's threat of abdication and by the opinion urged by the younger Stockmar, who was secretary to the Crown Princess, that they should not intervene in party strife." Sir Frederick Ponsonby, *Letters of the Empress Frederick* (London, 1929), p. 37. Eugen Wolbe believes that while the crown prince took the abdication threat seriously at first, he realized during his second meeting with his father that his threat to abdicate was a bluff designed to deter the ministers from acceptance of the two-year term. This being the case, Frederick's summons to Babelsberg and his attempt to persuade his father to agree to the demands of parliament were superfluous. See Eugen Wolbe, *Kaiser Friedrich, Die Tragödie des Übergangenen* (Hellerau, 1931), pp. 82–83.

51. Meisner, *Tagebücher*, p. 160.

52. Ibid., pp. 134–135.

53. During the abdication crisis, conservative General Gustav von Alvensleben warned Frederick that government's acceptance of the two-year term would give the liberals the impression that parliament controlled the army. He added that the king's acquiescence to the two-year term would place him in violation of the constitution, since it stipulated that the king was the undisputed head of the armed forces. Ibid., p.161. Frederick, however, did not take Alvensleben's views seriously, for several months later, he tried to persuade his father to give in to the two-year term in order to end the constitutional conflict.

54. This conclusion is hinted at in Franz Herre's biography *Kaiser Friedrich III. Deutschlands liberale Hoffnung* (Munich, 1987), p. 103.

55. Kent, *Bismarck*, p. 35.

56. The reaction of many liberals to Bismarck's appointment was, however, cautious; some even hoped that he would appoint a cabinet composed of political moderates. Conservatives, however, hoped that he would appoint a ministry of ultraconservatives. As Duncker aptly pointed out, "Bismarck is a chameleon to which every party has a claim." Schulze, *Max Duncker*, p. 178.

57. Crown Prince Frederick William to Count Otto von Bismarck, 28 September 1862, Meisner, *Tagebücher*, p. 504. After sending this warning to Bismarck, Frederick took advantage of a long-standing invitation to join the Prince of Wales on a lengthy

Mediterranean cruise. Frederick hoped that his absence would prove to the liberals that he neither condoned nor took part in plans by the new government to violate the constitution. Wolbe, *Kaiser Friedrich*, p. 86.

58. Huber, *Verfassungsgeschichte*, p. 305.

59. Kent, *Bismarck*, p. 41.

60. Pflanze, *Bismarck*, Vol. 1, p. 180. See also Huber, *Verfassungsgeschichte*, pp. 333–341.

61. Koch, *Constitutional History*, p. 95.

62. This phrase was often used by Bismarck's contemporaries and German historians to prove Bismarck's militarism, yet a look at the context of the speech itself leads to a different conclusion. It is often overlooked that the speech was an appeal to the parliamentary finance committee to fund military reforms; hence its emphasis naturally fell on the importance of military power. The speech, therefore, did not necessarily imply that Bismarck was committed to achieving unification through violent means. He was aware of the risks of war and was willing to go to war only under the most favorable circumstances. Prussia's ability to assume leadership in the German question depended not only on military power but also on alliances and on a foreign policy that would weaken the alliances of Prussia's enemies.

63. Kent, *Bismarck*, p. 42.

64. Bismarck to Crown Prince Frederick William, 13 October 1862, Meisner, *Tagebücher*, p. 505.

65. 29 October 1862, ibid., p. 510.

66. Meisner, *Tagebücher*, p. 510.

67. Pflanze, *Bismarck*, Vol. 1, pp. 182–183 and Huber, *Verfasssungsgeschichte*, pp. 447–449.

68. When liberals protested, Bismarck accused them of supporting the forces of revolution. Pflanze, *Bismarck*, Vol. 1, p. 196.

69. Theodor von Bernhardi, *Aus dem Leben Theodor von Bernhardi*, Vol. 5 (Leipzig, 1893–1895), p. 37.

70. Fritz Kämpf, *Gustav Freytag und das Kronprinzpaar Friedrich Wilhelm* (Leipzig, 1923), p. 23.

71. Hermann Baumgarten to Heinrich von Sybel, 22 May 1863. J. Heyderhoff and P. Wentzke, eds,. *Deutscher Liberalismus im Zeitalter Bismarcks*, 4 Vols. (Bonn, 1925–1926), Vol. 1, p. 151.

72. Samwer to Freytag, 28 February 1863. Heyderhoff, *Deutscher Liberalismus*, Vol. 1, p. 133.

73. Hermann Oncken, ed., *Grossherzog Friedrich von Baden und die deutsche Politik von 1854–1871* 5 Vols. (Stuttgart, 1927), Vol. 1, p. 346. Otto Meisner, *Der preussische Kronprinz im Verfassungskampf* (Berlin, 1931) p. 66.

74. Meisner, *Verfassungskampf*, pp. 65–66.

75 HH: Crown Princess Victoria to Crown Prince Frederick William, 1 June 1863.

76. Pflanze, *Bismarck*, Vol. 1, p. 204.

77. Ibid., p. 204.

78. Meisner, *Verfassungskampf*, p. 70.

79. He concluded the letter with the statement: "nichts liegt mir ferner als die Absicht, in eine oppositionelle Stellung gegen Dich zu treten." Ibid., p. 71.

80. Meisner, *Tagebücher*, p. 198.

81. Meisner, *Verfassungskampf*, p. 75.

82. This excerpt appeared in the *Leipziger Allgemeine Zeitung* on 8 July—a full month after the speech was originally delivered. According to Andreas Dorpalen, the excerpt represents a "toned down" version of the speech, yet it duplicates Frederick's own diary entry of 5 June for the Danzig speech. Compare Dorpalen, "Frederick III," *AHR*, p. 12, to Meisner, *Tagebücher*, p. 187.

83. Meisner, *Tagebücher*, p. 188.

84. Crown Prince Frederick William to King William I, Schlobitten, 7 June 1863. Meisner, *Verfassungskampf*, pp. 74–75.

85. Dorpalen, "Frederick III," *AHR*, p. 9.

86. Meisner, *Verfassungskampf*, pp. 75–79.

87. King William I to Crown Prince Frederick William, 10 June 1863. Meisner, *Verfassungskampf*, p. 78.

88. Ponsonby, *Empress Frederick*, p. 42.

89. London *Times*, 16 June 1863.

90. Schulze, *Duncker*, p. 347.

91. Crown Princess Victoria to Queen Victoria, 11 June 1863, Ponsonby, *Empress Frederick*, p. 43. Victoria's statement differs from her husband's diary, which shows that Frederick knew about Bismarck's plans to discipline the bureaucracy, which went against the letter of Article 88 of the constitution. Meisner, *Tagebücher*, p. 140.

92. Crown Prince Frederick William to Grand Duke Frederick of Baden, Oncken, *Friedrich von Baden,* Vol. 1, p. 349.

93. Roggenbach to Frederick of Baden, 12 June 1863, ibid., pp. 348–349.

94. Mathy to Gustav Freytag, 17 June 1863, Heyderhoff, *Deutscher Liberalismus*, p. 157. However, the left liberals had no need for additional statements from the crown prince. As left-liberal deputy Schultze-Delitzsch told Freytag: "As far as the relationship between the crown prince and the opposition is concerned, the creation of a crown prince party inspired by him would not do any good; at best it would attract a few weak-minded old liberals. Something of this nature—a gesture by him or his leadership in the struggle—is not expected of him. A party dedicated to his cause would find little appeal in the country." Hermann Schultze-Delitzsch to Gustav Freytag, Potsdam, 12 July 1863. ibid., Vol. 1, p. 161. In 1860, liberal historian Droysen complained about the ineffectiveness of the party that the crown prince supported. He lamented to a colleague, "Our party [the Constitutional Party] is a pitiful party." A year later, Progressive Party member Kosch diagnosed the ills of the Constitutional Party: "They, the Constitutionalists, are blood of our blood, but very much less flesh of our flesh. They are so gentle, they are so soft that every raw breeze affects them unpleasantly. The Progressives are of a less sensitive nature; their energy distinguishes them from others." Eugene Anderson, *The Social and Political Conflict in Prussia*

1858–1864 (Lincoln, NE, 1954) p. 280.

95. Queen Victoria to Crown Princess Victoria, 8 June 1863. Roger Fulford, ed., *Dearest Mama: Private Correspondence Between Queen Victoria and the German Crown Princess, 1861–1864* (London, 1968), p. 225.

96. Ibid., 17 June 1863, p. 232.

97. A leader of the extreme democratic faction of the Progressive Party.

98. Wolbe, *Kaiser Friedrich*, pp. 101–102.

99. Quoted in Dorpalen, "Frederick IIII," *AHR*, p. 14.

100. Victoria's complicity in the affair is hinted at in a letter to her mother of 8 June: "I hope you will make his [Frederick's] conduct known to your ministers and to all our friends in England." The queen duly passed this information to members of the British cabinet via her private secretary, General Grey. British foreign secretary Russell put his stamp of approval on the Danzig speech: "Nothing can be more judicious than the course which the crown prince has adopted—the hope of any good depends on his firm perseverance in it. With the crown princess by his side there seems to be no fear of his not being firm." Ponsonby, *Letters*, p. 45. Three days later, Victoria sent portions of her husband's correspondence to her mother and General Grey and added: "I cannot send you all of the papers I intended, as they are either with Stockmar, Fritz of Baden, or Prince Hohenzollern." Ibid., p. 44.

101. Wolbe, *Kaiser Friedrich*, p. 101.

102. Pflanze, *Bismarck*, Vol. 1, pp. 218–219.

103. Ponsonby, *Empress Frederick*, pp. 44–45. On 3 July, Victoria wrote her mother: "The articles in *The Times* have caused a tremendous sensation; people suppose I have got them put in and both our friends . . . and our foes consider me as 'la genie du mal.' " Fulford, *Dearest Mama*, p. 241.

104. As Frederick told the grand duke and duchess of Baden: "I hasten to request that you show the copy of my letter to Bismarck to absolutely *no one* . . . since my correspondence with Papa has inexplicably found its way into the newspapers." Oncken, *Friedrich von Baden*, p. 353.

105. Victoria tried to play down her husband's concern with the press indiscretion. As she told her mother: "Fritz is very frightened every time an article in the *Times* appears about him and fancies they do him an injury." Fulford, *Dearest Mama*, p. 241.

106. Meisner, *Tagebücher*, p. 209.

107. Ibid., p. 209.

108. HH: Crown Prince Frederick William to Crown Princess Victoria, 3 September 1863.

109. Ibid.

110. Frederick's memorandum, 17 September 1863, Meisner, *Tagebücher*, pp. 513–522.

111. Bismarck's comments appear in the marginalia of Frederick's memorandum. Bismarck also pointed out that the heir to the throne had had the right to countersign cabinet decisions, but that this right was eliminated after 1848. Since the crown prince

had no official vote in the ministry, he was free from accountability where ministerial decisions were concerned. Therefore, said Bismarck, the Danzig speech, inspired by Frederick's wish not to be associated with the policies of the government, was superfluous. Ibid., p. 520.

112. Bismarck hinted to the king that Victoria's influence was disruptive: "It is difficult when boundary lines are drawn between mother and daughter, brother and sister, but to deny that such boundaries exist poses a danger to the state." Meisner, *Tagebücher,* p. 521.

113. HH: Crown Prince Frederick William to Crown Princess Victoria, 16 September 1863. When he cited this letter, Corti failed to include Frederick's admission about his ignorance of government affairs. Egon Caesar Conte Corti, *The English Empress. A Study in the Relations Between Queen Victoria and her Eldest Daughter, Empress Frederick of Germany* (London, 1957), p. 114.

114. HH: Crown Prince Frederick William to Crown Princess Victoria, Letzlingen, 10 November 1863.

115. Ibid., Thlow bei Wrietzler, 20 September 1863.

116. William I to Crown Prince Frederick William, Babelsberg, October 1863, Meisner, *Verfassungskampf,* p. 73.

117. Schulze, *Duncker,* p. 347.

118. Pflanze, *Bismarck,* Vol. 1, p. 219.

119. Ibid., p. 215. According to historian Koppel S. Pinson, *The Preussische Jahrbücher,* founded in 1858, "came to be the most famous organ of the 'classical liberalism' of Prussian tendencies. . . . It aspired to represent the liberal national point of view with the weapons of science, to be more German than Prussian, to place the greatest emphasis on the historical approach, and hence to follow the English more than the French liberal tradition." Koppel S. Pinson, *Modern Germany* 2nd ed. (New York, 1966), p. 115.

Chapter 3

The Failure of "Moral Conquests," 1864–1866

Frederick's interpretation of moral conquests stipulated that Prussian sponsorship of the nationalist cause in foreign affairs would solve the constitutional conflict and increase Prussian influence in German affairs. An opportunity to test this theory arose in late 1863 when the German-speaking inhabitants of Schleswig-Holstein rebelled against the Danish king's attempt to incorporate Schleswig into his realm. This act violated the London treaties of 1852 and aroused the anger of German nationalists, who regarded both duchies as German states.[1] The nationalists demanded that the duchies be separated from Denmark and admitted to the German Confederation under the prince of Augustenburg, who claimed that the Danish king was not the rightful heir to the duchies.[2]

The issue of the duchies was important to German nationalists. If the German national movement failed to separate Schleswig-Holsteiners from Denmark, a minor power, it was hardly likely that the movement would be strong enough to create a German nation-state. German nationalists in Austria, Prussia, and the German Confederation therefore wished to exploit the popular indignation over Denmark's treatment of the duchies in order to spur their respective governments into action.[3] In December 1863, the Nationalverein and its rival, the Reformverein (which supported unification under Austrian leadership) staged a large rally in Frankfurt in support of the claims of Augustenburg and the liberation of the duchies from Danish rule. As historian Otto Pflanze put it, "The purpose of the rally was to demonstrate the existence of a national movement of great power which no German statesman could ignore."[4]

Frederick and his wife agreed that the Prussian government could effect an important "moral conquest" by supporting the nationalists' demands. The prince of Augustenburg, a close friend, assured the royal couple that the duchies, once placed under his leadership, would be ruled according to liberal principles.[5] From this the royal couple concluded that Prussia would appear to be a country sympathetic to liberal ideas if it played a decisive role in the creation of a new liberal state and that the movement for unification under Prussia would gain ground as a result.

Frederick also tried to convince his father that Prussia's support of the nationalists' demands would resolve Prussia's domestic problems with respect to the constitutional conflict. In a series of memoranda, the crown prince repeatedly reminded the king that Prussia's assumption of leadership in the Schleswig-Holstein issue would induce most members of the opposition in parliament to "accept the military budget for the sake of initiating a nationalist policy."[6] Yet Frederick expressed doubts about his ability to convince his father to take his advice. As he wrote in his diary after he sent his letter to William: "My letter will not be of much use and will not accomplish anything, but at least I did my best to speak my mind for the sake of the Fatherland."[7]

Frederick's prediction was correct, since the king was far more receptive to Bismarck's views on the Schleswig-Holstein problem. Although Bismarck agreed that action had to be taken against Denmark, he told the king that the policy advocated by German nationalists would invite serious dangers for Prussian foreign policy. Prussian intervention on behalf of Augustenburg, he warned the king, would constitute a violation of the London treaties and would turn its signatories (namely, Britain, France, and Russia) against Prussia. The British had already made it clear that they would not tolerate Prussian intervention on Augustenburg's behalf.[8] In the event that Prussia violated the London treaties by supporting Augustenburg, the British, who sympathized with the Danes despite their breach of the London treaties, would intervene against Prussia. This was a threat that Bismarck took seriously, and he therefore recommended that the London treaties, not Augustenburg, should serve as the basis for action against Denmark.

The minister-president also told the king, who was sympathetic to Augustenburg's claims, that Prussia stood to gain little in the event that the latter assumed leadership over the duchies. Bismarck warned the king that a new German state under Augustenburg would try to play Prussia and Austria off against each other, thereby threatening Prussia's drive for hegemony in German affairs.[9] Although the king did not accept Bismarck's arguments against Augustenburg's leadership over the duchies, he was wary of the possibility of foreign intervention in the event that Prussia supported the prince, and therefore he agreed that the London treaties should serve as the basis for action against Denmark.

Bismarck also strengthened Prussia's case against Denmark by persuading Austria to join Prussia in defending the London treaties.[10] In January 1864, the dual powers, Austria and Prussia, warned the German Confederation to abandon its efforts to act on Augustenburg's behalf or suffer the consequences, and the Confederation gave in.

During his discussions with the king, Bismarck concealed what he hoped to achieve by involving Prussia in the Schleswig-Holstein affair. The ultimate goal of his policy was to achieve a solution to the problem of the duchies that would increase Prussian power. By enforcing the London treaties, Prussia stood to gain prestige in the eyes of the treaty's signatories, but not power. Prussian power would also suffer in the event that a new German state under Augustenburg pursued an anti-Prussian policy. What Bismarck wanted was to incorporate the duchies into Prussia. As he himself put it, "Prussia's mission is to extend itself."[11] However, he was committed to pursuing this goal only under the most favorable of circumstances, which did not exist in late 1863. The king, the crown prince, and the liberals supported Augustenburg and did not give a thought to annexation. Further, any attempt by Prussia to annex the duchies would have met the hostility of all signatories of the London treaties and Austria as well.[12]

Bismarck's decision to stand by the London treaties angered the crown prince and the German nationalists. Frederick expressed his frustration with Bismarck's policy in a letter to his father in January 1864. He rejected Bismarck's argument that the duchies under Augustenburg would pursue an anti-Prussian policy. The crown prince admitted that the pro-Augustenburg course risked foreign policy complications but insisted that Bismarck's course was just as risky and would do nothing for the German national cause in general and Prussia in particular. He was also "convinced" that England would soften its stance toward revision of the treaties of London in the long run.[13] He recommended that Prussia release itself from its obligation to the London treaties, allow the duchies to be occupied by neutral troops, and recognize Augustenburg as the leader of the duchies.[14]

Once again, Frederick's letter had no effect on the king. When liberal deputy Vincke-Oldendorff encouraged the crown prince to continue his campaign against Bismarck's policy, Frederick admitted to his diary that any additional effort would be useless: "It is believed that I can arrange something with His Majesty; [he] has the right ideas, but Bismarck is spoiling everything. We are pursuing a headlong course to disaster."[15]

Shortly after he made this dim prediction, Frederick was stunned to discover that his lack of influence over the king stemmed from the ramifications of the Danzig episode. In January 1864 the king informed his son that he was forced to deny him access to government dispatches because he had made himself a member of the opposition with his Danzig speech. The king also suspected his daughter-in-law of divulging the contents of government dispatches to her mother, Queen Victoria. Frederick was incredulous about these accusations.[16] During a heated argument with his father, he tried to convince his father that he and his wife were innocent of any wrongdoing, but to no avail. Once again, Frederick found his ability to influence the king hampered by the latter's prejudice toward his son's liberalism.

In the midst of this turmoil between the king and his son, Prussia and Austria issued an ultimatum to Denmark. In late January 1864, the dual powers warned Denmark to withdraw its attempt to revise the London treaties by declaring its intention to incorporate Schleswig. The ultimatum was rejected by the Danes, and Austria and Prussia declared war on Denmark on 1 February 1864. Thanks to Bismarck's decision to abide by the London treaties, Prussia and Austria went to war as champions of international law and, as such, avoided the threat of foreign intervention on behalf of the Danes.

After the outbreak of hostilities, the crown prince served as an observer on the staff of General Ernst von Wrangel, the octogenarian commander-in-chief of the Austro-Prussian forces. The crown prince was denied his own command because the king did not wish to risk his son's life for the sake of a minor war. William also felt that his son would receive a first-rate education in military operations as an observer on Wrangel's staff.[17] There is no evidence showing that Frederick disagreed with his father's decision, and the crown prince enjoyed a cordial relationship with the old general. He was pleased to hear that Wrangel was not one of Bismarck's backers, and he wrote his wife that the general could even serve the liberal cause after the war. The crown princess replied, "I am so glad to hear about Wrangel's sensible views . . . if he could only exercise more influence over your Papa and pose a threat to Bismarck."[18]

Yet it soon became evident that Wrangel was of little use to the army, much less to an anti-Bismarck movement, for his robust physique belied his deteriorating mental faculties. However, he was kept on as head of the armies because the Austrians felt it would be improper to insult the famous veteran of the Wars of Liberation by insisting upon his resignation. Hence, a peculiar situation arose whereby the army chiefs of staff would duly consult with the general but make their decisions on the basis of separate meetings with the crown prince.[19] This made the crown prince the de facto head of the armies, and at the end of March, the king granted him an official position on the army staff.[20]

Although Frederick rejected the London treaties as the basis for Austro-Prussian intervention, he hoped that victory against Denmark would ultimately lead to victory for the Augustenburg cause, since the king supported the latter's claims to leadership over the duchies. The liberals, however, felt differently. Bismarck's adherence to the London Protocol only reinforced their view that a conservative government could do nothing for the national cause. When the government presented a bill on the eve of the war authorizing a credit of 12 million thaler to finance Prussian action against Denmark, liberals hoped that their rejection of the bill would cause the king to lose confidence in Bismarck and dismiss the unpopular minister-president.[21] Liberals also made it clear to the king that they would support any other minister as long as his policy was national. In the end, however, the liberals' intention to use their rejection of the bill to force Bismarck's dismissal came to nothing, since the military funds in question were not absolutely necessary.[22] Frederick chided the liberals for failing to share his optimistic belief that because the king supported Augustenburg, the latter, not Bismarck, would triumph. "The deputies have rejected everything . . . those good people have truly lost their sense of restraint and reason," he wrote in his diary.[23]

Unlike her husband, Victoria believed that Bismarck would persuade William to abandon his support for Augustenburg and was a determined opponent of the war. She wrote her husband: "If the war would ensure the protection of Germany from any foreign power which wished to humiliate the Germans in any way, how different things would be!"[24] She fumed at Bismarck's announcement that the purpose of the war was to restore the status quo ante in the duchies: "I'm not at all surprised that our troops do not feel more inclined towards us [Prussia]. . . . if only we had been the ones who had forced them to lay down their arms in 1848! This hasn't been forgotten, and now we are fighting so that they can be given back to the King of Denmark and be deprived of their legitimate leaders—all because this is what pleases Herr von Bismarck!"[25] Ultimately, she saw the war in general and Bismarck's leadership in particular as a threat to her dreams for a liberal Germany. Bismarck's power, she wrote, "embodies all that is evil and it ultimately seeks to promote reaction and to become the scourge of Germany. This pretty game will cost you your future happiness as well as that of your children which had such bright promise!"[26]

Victoria's complaints about the damaging effects of the war ceased after the Prussian army won a series of battles against Denmark. The performance of the Prussian army impressed many of Bismarck's enemies, and Victoria was no exception.[27] She now agreed with her husband that Augustenburg could triumph in the wake of Prussia's victory in the conflict; hence, she departed from her father's dictum that foreign policy victories were incapable of advancing the cause of liberalism in Germany. In the long run, she hoped that Augustenburg's victory would discredit Bismarck and his conservative regime, which had refused to go to war on Augustenburg's behalf in the first place.

Victoria now concentrated her efforts on facilitating Augustenburg's succession in the duchies. She knew that Augustenburg would have to reward Prussia for liberating the duchies from Denmark and handing them over to him. Victoria put pressure on her husband to serve as mediator between Augustenburg and King William and proposed terms of settlement between the two:

I thought it would be best if he [Augustenburg] were to ostensibly write a letter to your father, and if you would send this letter with an accompanying statement from you to Papa [the king]. I would think that Fritz [Augustenburg] would want to keep his aims limited so that it would not appear as if he was asking for too much, and then you could add a few more demands . . . for example, you could demand that Fritz assume responsibility for a part of the war debt, and transfer a fort and a port theoretically to the Confederation, but in reality to Prussia, [they could also agree to] a military and a naval convention, [and] entry of the duchies into the Zollverein . . . this seems such a simple solution, and has so many advantages which your Papa can't help but see.[28]

Frederick not only agreed with his wife's suggestions but also allowed Victoria and Stockmar to make corrections in his letters to his father on the matter. He added that he would send his letters only after they had received her seal of approval.[29] When Victoria received the copy of her husband's letter to the king, she wrote, "You can't imagine how happy your letter made me! Stockmar and I were very impressed by the way you expressed your ideas so clearly and correctly."[30] The letter was put to practical use: Augustenburg negotiated with the king precisely along the lines initially agreed upon by the royal couple and Stockmar.[31]

The British, however, wished to put an end to the conflict on the basis of the status quo ante. The Prussians and Austrians agreed to discuss proposals for peace at a conference in London. The dual powers offered to end the conflict if the Danes would give in to the idea of a personal union between the duchies and Denmark under King Christian, but the Danes refused.

As negotiations dragged on, Bismarck announced to his cabinet that Prussia was no longer willing to abide by the London treaties of 1851–1852. The cabinet considered two options: annexation of the duchies to Prussia or their admission into the German Confederation under Augustenburg. Frederick and Victoria vehemently opposed annexation. As they saw it, such a policy would only make Prussia seem avaricious and damage its reputation in the eyes of the other German states. In other words, Prussian annexation of the duchies would not be a moral conquest.[32] The royal couple therefore continued to support the succession of Augustenburg.

The crown princess now worked to overcome Austria's opposition to the succession of Augustenburg in the duchies. The Austrians had refused to support him, for a vote for Augustenburg was a vote in favor of national self-determination, and Austria could not afford to advocate self-determination abroad while denying it to its nationalities at home. However, Victoria insisted that the Austrians would abandon their opposition if Prussia and the German Confederation presented a united front in support of Augustenburg, and she tried to impress the king with her views:

I . . . asked Papa whether he intended to unite all German states and the German princes with the purpose of presenting a united front at the conference on the basis of the separation of the duchies from Denmark. He said that this would be a wonderful thing, but that Austria would probably refuse to agree to this and that Prussia could do nothing without Austrian aid. [I told him] I believed that Prussia and all the other German states could perhaps represent an adequate front, and that England and France would support our position. Even if France and England raised objections to Prussia's course of action, they would be less than likely to involve themselves in a purely continental matter—this is especially true of England.[33]

These ideas made no impression on the king, but the Austrians now agreed to support Augustenburg as a favorable alternative to Bismarck's idea of Prussian annexation of the duchies with vague promises of territorial compensation for Austria.[34] In May, the dual powers informed the London conference that they supported the succession of Augustenburg in the duchies. Although heartened by the dual powers' declaration in favor of Augustenburg, the crown prince suspected that Bismarck would try to sabotage his cause.

Frederick's suspicions were correct. When Augustenburg met with Bismarck in June to discuss his recognition by Prussia as leader of the duchies, Augustenburg found Bismarck's conditions unacceptable. Among other things, Bismarck demanded that Augustenburg give up his hope to rule the duchies according to liberal principles. He also hinted that Augustenburg should reward Prussia's military efforts on his behalf with territorial compensation. The duke refused to submit to this without consulting the ducal estates first.[35] Bismarck then proceeded to turn the king against Augustenburg. He told William that the prince preferred to consort with the Austrians and the ducal estates rather than accept Prussia's "just" demands. Bismarck's ploy worked.[36]

Despite the negative outcome of the Augustenburg-Bismarck interview, the royal couple remained hopeful that the former would somehow triumph. But they were distracted from the Augustenburg cause when the failure of the London conference signalled not only the resumption of hostilities but also the threat of British intervention after Prussia rejected British peace proposals accepted by the Danes.

The possibility that Britain would make war against Prussia horrified the royal couple. Since the crown prince and princess had reason to believe that the war would ultimately lead to Augustenburg's accession as leader of the duchies, they were quick to criticize British policy for even proposing intervention. Victoria wrote her mother that the threat of intervention from Britain only proved that its statesmen were incapable of comprehending the true aims of Prussian policy:

I see with regret that no one—not even Lord Clarendon—completely understands our position to the question at issue. The aim of this war is to preserve the rights and integrity of a German state. As the Danes wish rather to sacrifice their army than relinquish their unlawful hold on German territory, we as the first German power have no other means than to resort to arms and take it from them by force—that is, defend at all hazards that part of our German Fatherland which is in danger of being wrongfully swallowed up by another nation. That England should persist in turning the question upside down and in thinking that big Prussia wishes to eat up little Denmark is most lamentable.[37]

Once again, this quote shows Victoria's view that force was acceptable as long as it was used to defend the principle of self-determination of German peoples.

The royal couple was relieved when the British opted not to intervene on behalf of the Danes. After the collapse of the London conference in June, hostilities resumed, and without assistance from Britain, the defeat of Danish forces was inevitable. In early July 1864, King Christian formed a new cabinet, which announced its willingness to negotiate a peace settlement. A preliminary peace between Denmark and the dual powers was signed on 1 August, and the final peace signed two months later gave the duchies to the dual powers.[38]

The end of the war did not bring about the kind of victory that the royal couple desired, because the question of the disposition of the duchies remained unresolved and served to plague Austro-Prussian relations. To the dismay of Frederick and Victoria, Bismarck now insisted that Prussia annex the duchies, thereby ignoring the claims of Augustenburg. The Austrians rejected Prussian annexation of the duchies unless they would receive Hohenzollern enclaves in Silesia as compensation.[39] Bismarck replied that his king would never part with Hohenzollern soil.[40] When negotiations between Austria and Prussia on the disposition of the duchies reached an impasse, both powers engaged in an undercover battle to make their aims acceptable to the inhabitants of the duchies. Bismarck promoted annexation, whereas the Austrians did what they could to make the Augustenburg alternative acceptable to the Schleswig-Holsteiners.

The crown prince and princess expected the liberals to oppose Bismarck's annexationist aims but were disillusioned when the liberal front against Bismarck's anti-Augustenburg foreign policy began to unravel. Conservatives and right-wing liberals reversed their opposition to annexation, and the Progressive party split on the issue. Prominent leaders of the Progressive Party, such as Karl Twesten and Theodor Mommsen, now supported annexation. Although Mommsen still found Bismarck's domestic policy objectionable, he maintained that Germany's primary problem was unity and that this could be achieved only through the expansion of Prussian power and the creation of a strong executive.[41] More important, Mommsen declared himself willing to support the cause of a greater Prussia even if it strengthened the Bismarck cabinet. Opponents of annexation, on the other hand, accused their colleagues of willingness to sacrifice the Schleswig-Holsteiners' claims to self-determination—a cardinal principle of liberalism—to the greater glory of Prussian power.

In May 1864, Victoria wrote that she was shocked to hear that Frederick's trusted advisor Max Duncker also supported annexation and added that she could no longer trust his political judgment.[42] She also believed that Bismarck had tricked the king into supporting annexation: "One can only assume that Bismarck has so misguided the king that he no longer grasps the reality of the situation—or the negative feeling that annexation would arouse in Europe!! I can only take comfort in my fervent hope that it will never come to pass."[43]

Victoria feared that her husband, as a constitutional liberal, would be tempted to join the chorus of his colleagues who favored annexation. She warned him to be on his guard lest he, too, fall under Bismarck's "spell":

Bismarck may spin as many webs as he likes, but he must never catch you in them. . . . Whether Bismarck himself believes in the ridiculous lies he has entrusted his gullible young believers to spread, I do not know. . . . If you are granted the opportunity to see Bismarck, you should tell him quite calmly that you continue to hold the same views as you did last summer, and that your participation in the war hasn't changed them in the least![44]

Victoria's advice was heeded by her husband, who remained an ardent opponent of annexation. She also encouraged Frederick to make no secret of his feelings on the subject to Bismarck and suggested that he drop any pretense at courtesy in his correspondence with the minister-president: "With its friendly expressions and omission of certain intentionally caustic phrases, your letter, though excellent, was gentler in tone than my draft. I am afraid that it lacked the effect on Bismarck which was intended."[45]

The sharp tone of Frederick's letter to Bismarck of 27 April 1864 indicates that he followed his wife's wishes,[46] but it had little effect. Tensions between the dual powers mounted when Prussia announced its intention to establish a naval base at Kiel during the summer of 1865. The Austrians protested sharply, and war seemed imminent.

Frederick vehemently opposed the idea of war with Austria. By his lights, such a war had nothing to do with the idea of moral conquests, since it would be fought over territory that, in his opinion, belonged to a third party, namely, Augustenburg. He therefore made every effort to convince his father that war with Austria was highly undesirable and eminently avoidable. At a meeting of the crown council in May, however, Bismarck suddenly revealed that he was no longer determined to insist upon annexation and expressed the hope that a peaceful solution could be found.[47] Frederick did not attribute Bismarck's change of heart to any effort on his part, for up to that moment of the crown council meeting, he believed that Bismarck wanted war with Austria in order to prevent the succession of Augustenburg in the duchies.[48]

Frederick now took it upon himself to advise the king on a solution to the problem of the duchies that would fit within the framework of moral conquests. Without access to government dispatches, however, Frederick's advice revealed gaps in his knowledge of Prussian policy. In July 1865, Frederick told the king that the matter of the duchies could be settled if the ducal estates of the duchies were called together to make a choice between annexation by Prussia or Augustenburg. He added, "Austria has always been in favor of such a move."[49] Evidently, Frederick had no idea that Bismarck had tried precisely the same thing a few months before at the London conference. Bismarck's proposal to have the ducal estates vote on their own fate was rejected by Austrian foreign minister Rechberg, who was shocked by Bismarck's agreement to such a "revolutionary" proposition.[50]

The crown prince continued to criticize Bismarck's entire policy in the Schleswig-Holstein affair. In a letter to the minister-president, Frederick insisted that the crisis at hand could have been avoided had Prussia originally cooperated with the Confederation instead of Austria in the conflict over the duchies. Since the Confederation was slow to mobilize its troops, he wrote, Prussia could have quickly suppressed Denmark alone and could have presented the Confederation with a fait accompli. Such a policy, he added, would have precluded the need for an alliance with Austria, and, hence, the Austro-Prussian conflict could have been completely avoided.[51]

Frederick's tone in this letter was uncharacteristically sharp, and its contents so closely resemble Victoria's letter to him of 23 February 1864 that it is reasonable to assume it was composed by her and dutifully copied by her husband.[52] Bismarck was probably not at all impressed with the alternatives posed to his policy, for the plan proposed by the royal couple maximized the risk of Austrian and British intervention against Prussia. It has to be recalled that the British threatened to side with the Danes even when Prussia professed loyalty to the treaties of London and that Austria would have never tolerated a unilateral Prussian move into the duchies.

The crisis over the duchies was diffused by the Convention of Gastein of August 1865. In the end, the Prussian government rejected both the Augustenburg solution and annexation: the Austro-Prussian Convention of Gastein provided that both countries would maintain joint sovereignty in the duchies, with Prussia administering Schleswig and Austria administering Holstein. The Austrians viewed the agreement as a way to save the peace, but the agreement as such left room for the Prussians to cause their former allies trouble over the duchies.[53]

German patriots were shocked by the Gastein Convention, because it went against the grain of what they had been fighting for all along.[54] The crown prince and princess were disappointed and disillusioned by this turn of events and continued to insist that the strategy they had posed for the Schleswig-Holstein problem at the onset of the crisis, which, they believed, would have increased Prussian prestige and solved the constitutional conflict, had been the correct one. After the convention was concluded, the crown prince wrote in his diary, "I cannot understand what the far-reaching implications of this step will be."[55]

The crown prince and princess now turned their attention to the ramifications of the Schleswig-Holstein crisis on domestic affairs. Victoria tried to persuade her husband to support the opposition in the Prussian parliament, which refused to approve Bismarck's military budget for 1865. Although many liberals had supported Bismarck's desire to annex the duchies, they were far from willing to abandon their quarrel with him on the question of parliamentary rights. Progressive Party member Heinrich Bockum-Dolffs charged his colleagues to uphold the constitution, even at the risk of losing the duchies. Dolffs's colleague, Hermann Schultze-Delitzsch, echoed the feeling of many liberals when he declared that "the entire liberal party" would continue to fight "the Bismarck system without regard to the 'victory swindle.' "[56] The government, however, did not appear to be willing to make peace with the opposition, and the constitutional conflict continued. The cabinet submitted bills that had no chance of becoming law, and the opposition deliberated on amendments that had no chance of being accepted by the crown. In the meantime, the ministers governed the country without parliamentary influence.[57]

Since Prussia's military victories over Denmark had not quelled the fighting spirit of the opposition, ultraconservatives believed that the opposition would not give up until it achieved its goal to emasculate the powers of the crown. For this reason, they recommended a coup d'etat that would destroy the constitution and restore absolutism.

Victoria held that allegations of parliament's revolutionary intentions were false, and tried to persuade her husband that the government was responsible for the lack of peace between crown and parliament:

There are *no genuine* revolutionary elements in our parliament. According to my sources, there are only two or three radicals in parliament, and we have nothing to fear from them. But revolutionary feelings *must* be on the rise in the country because of the way in which the government rules. . . . I shudder to think about Lassalle[58] and his followers, because . . . their only goal is to cause upheaval and senseless destruction. The best way to combat this is to support the efforts of Schulze-Delitzsch.[59]

Frederick, however, was not inclined to support either Schultze-Delitzsch or the ultraconservatives. Once again, the crown prince found himself in a difficult position. On one hand, while liking their constitutionalist approach, he was alienated from right-wing liberals because of their support for annexation. On the other hand, while Frederick admired Schultze-Delitzsch's support for Augustenburg, he could not tolerate Delitzsch's agitation on behalf of the creation of genuine parliamentary government for Prussia. For this reason, Victoria's quest to induce her husband to lend support to Schultze-Delitzsch was unsuccessful.

Victoria was also very concerned about her husband's reputation and made every effort to counter rumors that her husband had joined forces with Bismarck. In April 1865, Frederick confided to his diary, "it has been said in court circles that I have been converted in support of annexation and Bismarck's principles. It is difficult to imagine how people could believe such nonsense."[60] Victoria attempted to destroy this rumor by putting pressure on her husband to dismiss Duncker. In December 1865 she wrote: "The liberal papers refer to Bismarck and Duncker in the same breath. . . . I am vexed that you continue to keep him on. As long as he remains with you, your position will remain unclear, and you should not allow people to perceive your position in a false light."[61] Evidently, Frederick was not eager to let political differences deprive him of a close friend like Duncker, who kept his position until June 1866.[62]

Thanks to Victoria's influence, however, Frederick did not reverse his negative opinions of Bismarck's policies.[63] As far as the crown prince was concerned, the minister-president had only made matters worse: his policies had abused the nationalist principle in foreign affairs and had done nothing to restore peace between the crown and parliament. Further, his annexationist aims had cost Prussia the support of south German liberals who interpreted Prussia's desire to annex the duchies as a harbinger of Prussia's intent to establish hegemony over all of Germany.[64]

Frederick's objections to Bismarck's policies increased when Austro-Prussian relations began to falter again over the question as to which power would have more influence in the duchies. In early 1866, Frederick was horrified when he learned that the king and Bismarck had concluded that the Austro-Prussian conflict could be resolved only by war.[65] He regarded the business of plunging Prussia into a war over a question that could have been easily resolved peacefully as a foolhardy enterprise. Moreover, military experts had predicted that superior Austrian forces would triumph over Prussia. Frederick expressed his opposition to the possibility of war with Austria in a meeting of the crown council in February 1866. He argued that the proposed struggle would constitute a civil war between German speaking people and recommended that the king resort to war only after all means to settle accounts peacefully with the Austrians had been exhausted.[66]

The impact of Frederick's antiwar comments may well have been diminished by his admission that he was not privy to government reports on the progress of negotiations with the Austrians. This meant that he was not sufficiently informed about the situation to argue a convincing case against war. His only source of information on this subject, he complained to the crown council, came from the newspapers.[67] Frederick's diary entries during the month of February 1866 show his frustration at being deliberately excluded from important meetings and policy-making sessions.[68] His disillusionment was corroborated by his wife, who wrote her mother: "We are more and more alarmed about the state of politics; officially we know nothing. Fritz is kept quite out of it all, the King does not speak to him on the subject, and the Ministers never communicate anything to him."[69]

Given their opposition to the war, the crown prince and princess were heartened when the British offered to mediate the Austro-Prussian conflict. In March, the crown prince happily reported to his mother-in-law that the king was interested in British mediation, adding that such mediation would probably make the difference between war and peace.[70] The crown princess also applauded British mediation in a letter to her mother, but she tactlessly implied that its success would compensate Britain's ill-timed threats of intervention in the Danish war: "You again, dearest Mama, may be the means of averting a European conflagration. . . . England's interference has often been so untimely and unlucky in Continental affairs, and her influence so much suffered, that I am doubly thankful to think she can now achieve a place—and the first place—among the great powers without any damage to herself, and most likely with every chance of success."[71]

Frederick, however, dimly predicted that the British demarche would be ultimately vetoed by Bismarck but the Austrians unwittingly aided him in blocking its success. In mid-March, the Prussians learned that the Austrians planned to mobilize regiments in Bohemia in preparation for war. Bismarck saw this move as evidence of Austria's warlike intentions. When British ambassador Loftus arrived in Berlin to discuss mediation, Bismarck replied that the British should begin mediation in Vienna, since it was the Austrians who threatened to disturb the peace.[72]

This turn of events ended the prospects for successful British mediation but did not signal the onset of hostilities. On 31 March, Austrian foreign minister Mensdorff announced that Austria did not harbor warlike intentions, and he challenged the Prussians to make a similar declaration. The Austrian announcement gave the opportunity for several influential people to convince William to abandon the thought of war with Austria. This antiwar group included the crown prince and princess, Queen Victoria, Queen Augusta, Counts Goltz and von Bernstorff, and the duke of Coburg. Their collective efforts to dissuade William from going to war became known as the "Coburg intrigue." Queen Victoria spoke for the feelings of the entire group when she advised William the war could be honorably avoided if the king dismissed Bismarck. In early April, she wrote, "You are deceived, you are made to believe that you are to be attacked, and I, your true friend and sister, hear your beloved name attacked and abused for the faults and recklessness of others—or, rather more, of *one* man."[73]

Although the queen's letter did not change William's opinion of Bismarck, he did momentarily reconsider the option of war. During the first week of April 1866, the king persuaded Bismarck to accept Mensdorff's challenge. But the Austrian reply to the Prussian dispatch was not satisfactory enough to make William drop the idea of war altogether, and Prussian preparations for war proceeded apace: on 8 April, Prussia concluded a defensive military alliance with Italy aimed against Austria.

Bismarck also gave a preview of his designs for Germany in the event Prussia defeated Austria: he announced Prussia's plans for reform of the German Confederation, including a parliament based on universal suffrage.[74] This move was meant to discredit Austrian policy and gain the support of national forces throughout Germany. According to Bismarck's biographer, Erich Eyck, "Bismarck hoped that Prussia would show by this proposal that she had the real interests and wishes of the German nation at heart, and that the nation would rally round her when she drew the sword for universal suffrage and national parliament against their adversaries."[75] Although Bismarck's declaration in favor of universal suffrage gave him the appearance of a revolutionary, what he ultimately hoped to achieve by this measure was to increase support for the government at the expense of the liberals. Bismarck held that the masses were essentially conservative and alienated from the liberal movement. Through universal suffrage, Bismarck ultimately hoped to avoid repetition of the constitutional conflict by returning parliamentary majorities that were conservative. As he himself put it, universal suffrage offered "greater guarantees for the conservative conduct of parliament than any of the artificial electoral laws that are calculated to achieve manufactured majorities."[76]

Bismarck's approval of universal suffrage was greeted with disdain by both sides of the political spectrum. Liberals objected on the grounds that it was intended to undermine their political power. The crown princess called universal suffrage "disgraceful,"[77] and this feeling was shared by many in England, who felt that Bismarck's announcement would undermine the English government's more modest plans for electoral reform.[78] Frederick himself was shocked that his father had agreed to such a radical reform measure.[79] Conservatives regarded the business of granting the vote to the politically inexperienced masses as a dangerous experiment and were incredulous at Bismarck's alliance with what they regarded as the "mob," the same people who had attempted to topple the crown in 1848.

Bismarck's wish to create a conservative all-German parliament did not, however, preclude his desire to find a basis for cooperation with the liberal movement. An alliance with the latter was absolutely necessary to effect the work of German unification, since the conservatives of the various German states who would sit in the German parliament were particularists. He knew that cooperation with the liberals could be secured only if he could assure them that he had no intention of dismantling constitutionalism in Prussia. Bismarck tried to prove this point by proposing a bill of indemnity in the event that Prussia won the war; the bill would ask parliament for retroactive approval of the funds spent by the government during the constitutional conflict.[80]

Bismarck's apparent willingness to do business with the liberals and his intention to use a major war with Austria to achieve leadership in German affairs attracted many members of the Progressive Party. Those same liberals who had reversed their opposition to Bismarck's intention to annex Schleswig and Holstein now agreed with him that no number of "moral conquests" would make the Austrians peacefully abandon their struggle for supremacy in German affairs. Further, they now believed that that the cause of liberalism would benefit by being associated with Bismarck's foreign policy. As prominent liberal Heinrich von Baumgarten put it,

We consider it to be our duty to do everything possible to make the liberals of northern Germany and Prussia aware of the danger and meaning of the current situation—to tell them that if they accept the war as a fact and support it, if they pull the power of the people on the side of Prussia, [then] the power of Prussia will emanate from the people. If Bismarck wins with the support of popular forces, a liberal Germany will be the victor. [But] if Bismarck wins while the people throw support to the sobbing of the *Kölnische Zeitung* and the Jewish *Volkszeitung,* the Prussian people will only turn their backs on the cause of liberalism.[81]

The sentiments of such liberals did not go unnoticed by the crown prince. He refused to accept the idea that Bismarck's course could ultimately lead to liberal reforms and believed that the liberals had been deluded by Bismarck:

Bismarck has tried to give the impression that he is dependent on the Progressive Party. On the other hand it seems clear that the Progressives are willing to be duped by Bismarck—he will exploit them until he achieves his aims and then he will drop them. It is rumored that he wants Roggenbach and Bennigsen as ministers—he will use their names and their beliefs as a cover for his swindles, and then he will throw them away like a used glove.[82]

Convinced that Bismarck's course would lead to disaster, the crown prince became even more determined to put a stop to the war plans. He was assisted in this task by Stockmar, who kept the crown prince abreast of French proposals for a great power conference to settle the Austro-Prussian dispute. In mid-May,

Stockmar advised the crown prince to deter the king from making further preparations for war until the conference had been arranged.[83] Unfortunately, plans for the conference fell through, as did an attempt by Napoleon III of France to mediate the conflict.[84]

The failure of the Coburg intrigue and proposals for a great power conference on the Austro-Prussian dispute made it clear that war was virtually inevitable. The crown prince now found himself in the uncomfortable position of being the only person in the crown council who was still opposed to the war. Moreover, he felt that a vast majority of Prussians shared his feelings. He believed that the Bismarck ministry was simply mistaken in its attempt to convince the king that the war would solve the constitutional conflict. As he confided to his diary: "The ministry has officially informed His Majesty that the current political situation is expected to produce a new breed of representatives who will be more willing to make concessions than their predecessors. I expect the opposite to be true, and believe that [the ministry] will be greatly disappointed, because no reasonable person in this country wants this war."[85]

Frederick's assessment of antiwar sentiment, however, was inaccurate with respect to the many liberals who supported the war. A vast majority of Constitutionalists advocated the war as the best means to solve the constitutional conflict,[86] and Progressives such as Baumgarten not only supported Bismarck's war policy but opposed Frederick's efforts to persuade the king to reject a military solution and dismiss Bismarck.[87] Baumgarten, in fact, thought that Frederick's accession prior to the outbreak of the Austro-Prussian conflict would be a setback to the cause of unification. As he told Sybel, "You must not forget in all these questions what is going to happen when the crown prince becomes king. If Prussia has not established her position in Germany by then, woe to us!"[88]

These sentiments were echoed by Sybel, who condemned an antiwar article that appeared in the *Kölnische Zeitung* on 28 May, which, he suspected, had its origins in the circle of the crown prince. Rudolf Haym also agreed and referred to the antiwar statements as the "unpatriotic, unreasonable, and sentimental resolutions of the Progressives."[89] Prominent liberals (including Bennigsen, Hans von Roggenbach, Bernhardi, and Duncker) also resented the efforts made by participants in the "Coburg intrigue." To discredit Bismarck at such a critical time, they argued, was tantamount to denying Prussia a future as a powerful and prominent nation. As Bernhardi put it:

Only Bismarck can conduct this war; a liberal ministry . . . could not! Such a ministry would only be thwarted by the opposition of the pro-Austrian party in the king's circle— the opposition of the Queen Dowager, her adherents and the Augustenburg agents. . . . A liberal ministry would only falter in the face of such opposition; it would not be capable of conducting a war and would only lead us to Olmütz. It is precisely for this reason that Bismarck must be retained and supported.[90]

But although the crown prince believed that liberals such as Baumgarten and Bernhardi had misjudged Bismarck's policy, he did not make his feelings against the war public despite the urgings of his mother-in-law. On 9 May 1866, Queen Victoria wrote the crown princess: "I wish Fritz would be firm and say that he refuses to take part in such an iniquitous war! It would raise him in the eyes of the world."[91]

Frederick ignored the queen's advice because he was preoccupied by the more immediate problem of how to conduct himself in a forthcoming meeting of the crown council devoted to war preparations. Stockmar noted that the meeting would put the crown prince in a difficult position because of his opposition to the war, not to mention the fact that any attempt to defend his position was bound to be hampered by his lack of knowledge concerning Bismarck's goals. Also, since Frederick had abstained from attending meetings of the council of ministers, he was unable to comment on the practical considerations of carrying out Bismarck's policies. Stockmar wrote the crown prince, "it would be as if you were in the position of a man who was ordered to put on blinders and give advice on continuing a game of chess which has already begun."[92] He advised the crown prince to save himself from embarrassment by stating his opposition to the war by opening the meeting with the following statement:

Since I have been asked to give an opinion concerning the possibility of war, I find myself in a rather strange position. The option of war has come about as the last resort of a policy in which I played no role—I have argued repeatedly against elements of this policy. More important, no information has been made available to me concerning the operations [Huelfsmitteln] and long-range goals of this policy. I feel I have no other obligation than to declare that I resign responsibility for a war which serves as an outcome of this policy.[93]

But the crown prince found himself involved in the war before he could make use of Stockmar's advice. On 17 May, the day before Stockmar's letter was written, the crown prince received command of the Second Army. Eight days later, a meeting of the war council took place, but the rationale for the war was not discussed. Hence the crown prince was deprived of the opportunity to make use of the antiwar statement that Stockmar had prepared for him.

The war of 1866 began just as Bismarck hoped it would when Austria unwittingly put itself in the position of aggressor. In early June, Austria announced plans to unilaterally enact reforms in Holstein. Bismarck declared that this act constituted a breach of the Gastein treaty, and Prussian troops were ordered into Holstein on 7 June. Since the Austrians had violated the treaty, Bismarck was able to argue that the Prussians were fighting a defensive battle. Although Bismarck was able to attract many Prussian liberals to his policy, the same was certainly not true of the majority of German states. Most of them sided with Austria in the war of 1866, for fear that Prussian victory would translate into Prussian domination over all of Germany.

The onset of hostilities precipitated a profound shift in the crown prince's views toward the war in general and Bismarck in particular. As we have seen, his political views prior to the war of 1866 were conditioned by his profound mistrust of the minister-president, his exclusion from affairs of state, and his firm belief that the future of constitutionalism was in jeopardy as long as Bismarck was at the helm. His disdain for Bismarck's policies was strongly supported by Victoria, who spared no effort in trying to isolate him from liberals such as Duncker who had become attracted to Bismarck's policies.

But two meetings with Bismarck prior to his departure for war changed Frederick's outlook. Although Frederick's diaries tell us nothing about their conversations, it is possible that Frederick's conversation with Bismarck resembled an exchange between Bismarck and liberal leader Bennigsen a few weeks earlier. Stockmar informed the crown prince about this conversation, in which Bismarck defended his policy as a means of solving the German question. When Bennigsen replied that this could have been accomplished by a liberal ministry, Bismarck argued that he had tried and failed to convince the king to appoint liberal ministers but that he was nonetheless willing to make concessions to the parliament in due course.[94]

Given Frederick's intense devotion to the war effort and his acceptance of Bismarck's views during and immediately after the conflict, it is likely that Bismarck was able to convince the crown prince that he had no intention of abandoning constitutionalism in Prussia and that his policy was superior to the idea of moral conquests with regard to the attainment of Prussian leadership in the German question. Frederick's partnership with Bismarck—which aroused the ire of Victoria, who continued to insist that she and her husband's original idea of unification via moral conquests had been right all along—is the subject of the next chapter.

NOTES

1. In 1848, the liberals of the Frankfurt parliament supported the abortive attempt of the Schleswig-Holsteiners to free themselves from Danish rule. The issue of the duchies was temporarily put to rest by the great powers in the London treaties of 1851–1852, which linked the duchies to Denmark through personal union with its king. But the Danes were forbidden to integrate the duchies into Denmark. This arrangement failed to satisfy any of the concerned parties. German nationalists insisted that both duchies rightfully belonged to the German Confederation, whereas the Danes wanted a closer union between the duchies and Denmark. See William Carr, *Origins of the Wars of German Unification* (London, 1991), pp. 46–47. The standard work on the Schleswig-Holstein crisis is L. D. Steefel's *The Schleswig-Holstein Question* (Cambridge, 1941).

2. King Frederick VII of Denmark died in November 1863, leaving no direct heir.

He was succeeded by Prince Christian of Glücksburg, who assumed the throne as king of Denmark and duke of Schleswig and Holstein. But the new king found his claims to the latter challenged by Prince Frederick of Augustenburg, who claimed to be the rightful ruler of the duchies. The laws of succession were complex. A Danish royal decree of 1665 stated that the line of succession to the Danish throne would fall to the female line in the event that the king died without issue. But this law of succession did not apply to the duchies of Schleswig-Holstein, where rulers could be descended only from the male line. Prince Christian of Glücksburg was descended through the female line. As a descendant from the male line, Augustenburg was, hence, the heir to the duchies. But his claim was complicated by the fact that his father had renounced his right to rule in the duchies in 1852, although he did not do so in the name of his son. See H. O. Meisner, ed., *Kaiser Friedrich III. Tagebücher von 1848 bis 1866* (Leipzig, 1929), p. 233 fn., and Ernst Rudolf Huber, *Deutsche Verfassungsgeschichte seit 1789* 4 Vols. (Stuttgart, 1957–1969), Vol. 1 pp. 460–461.

3. For liberals' commentaries on the Schleswig-Holstein problem, see Hans Rosenberg, ed., *Die Nationalpolitische Publizistik Deutschlands vom Entritt der Neuen Ära in Preussen bis zum Ausbruch des Deutschen Krieges.* 2 Vols. (Munich, 1935). Vol. 1, p. 312ff.

4. Otto Pflanze, *Bismarck and the Development of Germany. Volume 1: The Period of Unification, 1815–1871* (Princeton, NJ, 1990), p. 239.

5. Augustenburg's friendship with the royal couple may have led him to believe that his goals would be achieved sooner than he thought. He assembled a new government for the duchies in Gotha immediately after the death of King Frederick VII of Denmark, apparently unconcerned about the fact that the great powers did not recognize his claims to the duchies. See Carr, *Origins*, p. 48.

6. Meisner, *Tagebücher*, pp. 226–227.

7. Ibid.

8. W. E. Mosse, *The European Powers and the German Question* 3rd ed. (New York, 1981), pp. 157–160.

9. George O. Kent, *Bismarck and His Times* (Carbondale, IL, 1978), p. 48.

10. Ibid., p. 48.

11. Quoted in Pflanze, *Bismarck,* Vol. 1, p. 241.

12. But three years later, Bismarck got what he wanted. According to Otto Pflanze, "That Bismarck was able to maneuver his way through and over the obstacles to Prussia's acquisition of the duchies is one of the amazing feats in the history of politics." Ibid., p. 242.

13. "Von Einem bin ich überzeugt, dass nämlich die Macht, die jetzt sich hat verleiten lassen, die drohende Haltung anzunehmen, England, am ersten auch gelindere Saiten aufziehen würde, wenn Preussen eine entscheidene Richtung einschlüge." Crown Prince Frederick William to King William I, 3 January 1864. Meisner, *Tagebücher*, pp. 522–524.

14. Ibid., p. 524.

15. Ibid., p. 230.

16. Surprisingly, Frederick did not blame his father for this incident. Instead, he maintained that the entire episode was engineered by reactionary influences around the king, who were all too eager to see William and his son alienated from each other. Meisner, *Tagebücher*, p. 233.

17. Ibid., p. 237.

18. Hessische Hausstiftung (hereafter HH) Schloss Fasanerie, Fulda: Crown Princess Victoria to Crown Prince Frederick William, 4 February 1864.

19. Meisner, *Tagebücher*, p. 238.

20. Ibid.

21. Pflanze, *Bismarck*, Vol. 1, p. 269.

22. Ibid., p. 270.

23. Meisner, *Tagebücher*, p. 235.

24. HH: Crown Princess Victoria to Crown Prince Frederick William, Berlin, 31 January 1864.

25. Ibid., 4 February 1864.

26. Ibid., 31 January 1864.

27. Ibid., 21 February 1864. She told her husband, "It would be terrible if your father opted to retreat for fear of what the great powers would do—our time will be wasted unless we reach Jutland."

28. Ibid., Berlin, 23 February 1864.

29. HH: Crown Prince Frederick William to Crown Princess Victoria, 25 February 1864.

30. HH Crown Princess Victoria to Crown Prince Frederick William, 29 February 1864.

31. In April, Augustenburg assured William of his willingness to accept the inclusion of the duchies in the Zollverein, the erection of a confederate fortress in Rendsburg garrisoned by Prussia, and the organization of ducal armed forces along Prussian lines. Pflanze, *Bismarck*, Vol. 1, p. 264.

32. Eugen Wolbe, *Kaiser Friedrich: Die Tragödie des Übergangenen* (Hellerau, 1931), p. 131.

33. HH: Crown Princess Victoria to Crown Prince Frederick William, Berlin, 29 February 1864.

34. On 28 May, the dual powers astonished Europe by announcing to the London conference their support of the "complete separation" of the duchies from Denmark and "their union under a single state" under Augustenburg who, "in the eyes of Germany" had "the greatest right to succession." Pflanze, *Bismarck*, Vol. 1, p. 252.

35. Ibid.

36. Ibid., p. 253.

37. Crown Princess Victoria to Queen Victoria, 2 July 1864. Roger Fulford, ed., *Dearest Mama: The Private Correspondence of Queen Victoria and the Crown Princess of Prussia, 1861–1864* (London, 1968), p. 352. Victoria was highly critical

of British policy well before the threat of intervention in June. In April, she wrote her husband, "I am saddened by the entire conduct of British foreign policy! I am incensed about the way in which it meddles in affairs which are none of its concern. Children who stick their fingers into everything often end up with an unwanted surprise, and this stupid English foreign policy will earn itself a slap in the face! ... as a German, my sense of justice is violated by the idle talk printed in the newspapers and by the nonsense being discussed currently in Parliament, and as an Englishwoman, I feel humiliated and saddened that a country which is and always will remain the greatest in the world makes such a fool of itself in foreign policy!" HH: Crown Princess Victoria to Crown Prince Frederick William, 11 April 1864.

38. Pflanze, *Bismarck,* Vol. 1, p. 253.

39. Ibid., p. 259.

40. Ibid.

41. Ibid., p. 273. The *Preussische Jahrbücher*, which had endorsed the claims of Augustenburg in 1863, reversed this view a year later by claiming that annexation would be a "more national goal than the creation of a small state." Ibid., p. 272.

42. HH: Crown Princess Victoria to Crown Prince Frederick William, Berlin, 9 May 1864.

43. HH: Crown Princess Victoria to Crown Prince Frederick William, Berlin, 27 March 1864.

44. Ibid., 28 March 1864.

45. Ibid., 11 April 1864.

46. On the subject of annexation, the letter stated that: "the realization [of annexation] would invalidate our entire German policy and ruin our reputation in the eyes of the European powers. It would not be the first time that Prussia has tried to look more clever than all the other [powers] but has ended up falling between two stools." See Wolbe, *Kaiser Friedrich*, p. 131.

47. Pflanze, *Bismarck,* Vol. 1, p. 256.

48. 1 August 1866, Meisner, *Tagebücher*, p. 394.

49. Ibid., pp. 538–539, Crown Prince Frederick William to King William of Prussia, 17 July 1865. Frederick's letter to Bismarck on the same subject answers the question as to why he was proposing previously discarded solutions to the Schleswig-Holstein problem. The crown prince admitted that there were gaps in his knowledge of Prussian policy, but these he attributed to Bismarck. He hinted that the minister-president did not see fit to inform him about ongoing developments in the matter of the duchies because their views on the subject diverged so sharply. Crown Prince Frederick William to Otto von Bismarck, 17 July 1865. Ibid., p. 535.

50. Pflanze, *Bismarck,* Vol. 1, p. 250.

51. Meisner, *Tagebücher*, pp. 535–536.

52. HH: Crown Princess Victoria to Crown Prince Frederick William, 23 February 1864.

53. Carr, *Origins*, pp. 122–126.

54. Members of the diet as well as the Nationalverein registered protests about the Gastein Convention, which was called "a blow to the principles of justice and order in Germany." See Huber, *Verfassungsgeschichte*, p. 508.

55. 20 August 1864, Meisner, *Tagebücher*, p. 396.

56. Quoted in Pflanze, *Bismarck*, Vol. 1, p. 277.

57. Ibid.

58. Ferdinand Lassalle was a radical revolutionary in 1848 and a member of the left-wing opposition in the 1860s. He later became a socialist and a driving force in the creation of the German Social Democratic Party.

59. HH: Crown Princess Victoria to Crown Prince Frederick, Neues Palais, 28 June 1865. Apart from Schulze-Delitzsch's opposition to the Bismarck, the crown princess was also attracted to his hopes to "bind the working class to the liberal cause by promoting its economic needs within the limits of liberal economic doctrine." Schulze-Delitzsch's ideas were primarily geared toward the improvement of conditions for artisans and members of the lower middle classes, not the industrial workers. See Pflanze, *Bismarck*, Vol. 1, pp. 224–225.

60. Meisner, *Tagebücher*, p. 387.

61. HH: Crown Princess Victoria to Crown Prince Frederick William, 12 December 1865.

62. The crown prince and Duncker had a falling out because of the latter's support for the war of 1866. On the eve of his departure for the war, Frederick wrote Duncker: "My duty now calls me, as Heir to the Throne, to draw my sword in a quarrel arising from a system with which you sympathized, while I renounced it altogether. I can perfectly well understand that you have been oppressed by my recent reserve, and that you feel a desire for some other occupation." Quoted in Margarete von Poschinger, *Life of the Emperor Frederick* (New York, 1971), pp. 266–267. Historian Johannes Schulze claims that the two parted less cordially than this quote suggests: the crown prince blocked Bismarck's plan to make Duncker Staathalter of Kassel, and Duncker had to settle for a position as director of the Prussian state archives. Johannes Schulze, ed. *Max Duncker. Politischer Briefwechsel aus seinem Nachlass* (Osnabrück, 1967), p. xxii.

63. Frederick's opposition to the minister-president did not escape the notice of conservative cabinet member Edwin von Manteuffel. Ironically, he did not suspect that the crown princess was primarily responsible for influencing her husband against Bismarck. In June 1864, Manteuffel wrote: "Who is responsible for nurturing the crown prince's blind hatred of Bismarck? It is certainly not Duncker, there is sufficient proof of that. The only other logical suspects are Schleinitz and [Queen] Augusta. The second question is—why is he susceptible to these feelings [of hatred]? As far as I am concerned this stems from his lack of self-confidence and a lack of égards pour lui. I have made Bismarck repeatedly aware of this situation . . . one must take lead of the crown prince so that he will follow. [But] Bismarck is busy and neglects such important matters." H.O. Meisner, *Der*

Kronprinz im Verfassungskampf 1863 (Berlin, 1931), p. 48 fn. Bismarck did not accept Manteuffel's methods for dealing with the crown prince. Instead, he continued to make good on William's threat to withhold information on matters of state from his son as long as the latter opposed the policies of the government. This being the case, Frederick began to understand that the Gastein convention was a stopgap measure to camouflage Bismarck's plan to make war on Austria only when the crown council met in February 1866.

64. Pflanze, *Bismarck,* Vol. 1, p. 275.

65. The king argued that war was inevitable since the Austrians had refused to cease their efforts to alienate the Schleswig-Holstein population from the Prussian government. The council agreed that the army was ready for action, and that the Prussian population would not be hostile to the war effort. After the chamber rejected the military budget, Bismarck was able to raise funds for the army by selling the government's right to purchase stock in the Cologne-Minden railroad. The sale provided the government with funds to finance military operations against Austria. Bismarck's acquisition of funds was unconstitutional, since parliament was not consulted. Ibid., p. 280.

66. Frederick's account of this crown council meeting appears in Meisner, *Tagebücher*, pp. 543–544.

67. Ibid., p. 543.

68. On 19 February, Frederick wrote, "Graf Goltz [Prussian minister to Paris] is said to be en route from Paris to Berlin. Not one government official has said a word about this to me!" On 26 February, Frederick was informed that an important meeting had taken place in the foreign office in the presence of the king. Frederick's response: "How clever it was that the meeting was labelled unofficial so that I did not have to be invited!" Ibid., pp. 411–412.

69. Crown Princess Victoria to Queen Victoria, 9 March 1866. Roger Fulford, ed. *Your Dear Letter: The Private Correspondence of the Queen Victoria and the Crown Princess of Prussia, 1865–1871* (London, 1968), pp. 59–60. The crown princess also let her mother know that she and her husband were completely opposed to the idea of war against Austria: "I have no words to say what a calamity I would consider a war with Austria in every point of view, for Germany and for Europe. No one can tell where it would end and the only gainer by it would be the Emperor Napoleon." Ibid., p. 60.

70. Crown Prince Frederick William to Queen Victoria, 17 March 1866. Meisner, *Tagebücher*, pp. 544–545. Frederick also told the queen about the extent to which he was being kept in the dark about Prussian policy: "Im Vertrauen gesagt, glaube ich, dass Bismarck die Dinge übertreibt, um seinen dringenden Wunsch, Krieg zu führen, zur Ausführung zu bringen. Ich kann dies aber nur vermuten, denn ich habe seit sechs Monaten *nicht eine einzige Mittheilung offizieller Art von Bismarck erhalten.*"

71. Crown Princess Victoria to Queen Victoria, 19 March 1866. Fulford, *Your Dear Letter*, p. 65.

72. Queen Victoria thought otherwise. On 28 March she wrote Frederick that she blamed Bismarck for the escalation of the Austro-Prussian conflict, and added that it would be difficult for England to interfere with the course pursued by the Prussian government "under the influence of Count Bismarck." Queen Victoria to Crown Prince Frederick William, 28 March 1866. George E. Buckle, ed., *The Letters of Queen Victoria. Second Series. A Selection from Her Majesty's Correspondence and Journal Between the Years 1862 and 1878* (London, 1926), Vol. 1, p. 311.

73. Queen Victoria to King William I, 4 April 1866. Ibid., p. 317.

74. Pflanze, *Bismarck*, Vol. 1, p. 283.

75. Erich Eyck, *Bismarck and the German Empire* (London, 1968), p. 117.

76. Quoted in Pflanze, *Bismarck*, Vol. 1, p. 307.

77. In 1870, the crown princess wrote her husband of her hope that the new German empire would serve to "create a new and good constitution which would entail the elimination of that disgraceful universal suffrage." HH: Crown Princess Victoria to Crown Prince Frederick William, 9 December 1870.

78. Pflanze, *Bismarck*, Vol. 1, p. 308.

79. Meisner, *Tagebücher*, p. 419. "Papa bestätigt die Telegramme, dass in Frankfurt heute durch uns der Antrag auf Einberufung des deutschen Parlaments, aus direkten Wahlen hervorgegangen, eingebracht worden sei. S.M. meinte, es sei die blosse Fortsetzung des durch den Schleswig-Holsteinischen Krieg unterbrochenen Bundesreformwerkes!"

80. Eyck, *Bismarck*, p. 121.

81. Julius Heyderhoff and H. Wentzke, eds., *Deutscher Liberalismus im Zeitalter Bismarcks* 4 Vols. (Bonn, 1925–1926), Vol. 1, p. 282 (hereafter HW).

82. Meisner, *Tagebücher*, p. 421.

83. HH: Ernst von Stockmar to Crown Prince Frederick William, 14 May 1866. Stockmar also told the crown prince about a conversation between liberal leader Rudolf von Bennigsen and Bismarck, in which the latter expressed the fear that a great power conference would spoil his plans to go to war with Austria.

84. Napoleon III offered to mediate during the crisis by proposing the cession of Venetia to Italy, but the Italians did not want such an overture to be seen later as means by which France could meddle in Italian affairs. Kent, *Bismarck*, p. 57.

85. Meisner, *Tagebücher*, p. 422. On 10 May, the chamber was prorogued. In his diary, Frederick wrote that he was not officially informed of the government's decision to prorogue the chamber and that his source of information on the matter came from the newspapers.

86. HW, *Deutscher Liberalismus*, p. 282. Only a tiny minority of old liberals decried the war as "frivolous."

87. Ibid., Haym to Schrader, 16 May 1866, pp. 285–286.

88. Ibid., Baumgarten to Sybel, 11 May 1866, p. 283.

89. Ibid., Haym to Schrader, 16 May 1866. pp. 285–286.

90. Ibid., p. 283 fn.

91. Queen Victoria to Crown Princess Victoria, 8 May 1866. Fulford, *Your Dear Letter*, p. 72.

92. HH: Ernst von Stockmar to Crown Prince Frederick William, 18 May 1866.

93. Ibid.

94. HH: Stockmar to Crown Prince Frederick William, 21 May 1866.

Chapter 4

Unification by Force, 1866–1871

Frederick's frequent meetings with Bismarck during the war of 1866 upset Victoria. While Frederick fought the war against the Austrians, Victoria waged her own battle against Bismarck's influence on her husband. Her task outlasted the war, which was quickly decided in Prussia's favor. Thanks to the superiority of Prussian arms and military leadership, Prussian troops decisively defeated the Austrians in the Battle of Königgrätz (Sadowa) on 3 July, only three weeks after the war began. Prussia's speedy victory shocked European leaders, since it was expected that the war would be a long and drawn-out conflict.

Frederick's overall performance as leader of the Second Army during the war made him a war hero. His leadership over the Second Army in the Battle of Königgrätz earned him the decoration "Pour le merité," which was bestowed upon him by his grateful father.[1] After hostilities ended, the crown prince continued to suppress his grief over the death of his two-year-old son, Sigismund, who succumbed to meningitis shortly after his father's departure for the war.[2] As he confided to his diary: "I was obliged to remember that this was no time to give way to feelings of any kind; on the contrary, all our thoughts must be directed solely toward the beaten enemy and to the proper use to be made of our victory."[3]

Victoria acknowledged but resented Frederick's attitude. In a reference to her husband's absence from Sigismund's funeral, she wrote, "In you, of course, the soldier is uppermost." The longer her husband was away from her, the more she feared that his contact with Bismarck and conservative members of the military and the flush of victory would cause him to lose sight of his liberal constitutional beliefs. When she heard of the Prussian victory at Langensalza on 29 June, she wrote:

If you hope to gain anything in the future, do not forget that it is more important than ever to stay true to your principles. You should not give any hint that your views have changed in the slightest, even as you stand with the sword of victory in your hand. Forgive me for talking to you in this way—though I am a mother in mourning I nonetheless feel the ambition of a wife who cannot stand that her husband is being deliberately kept in the dark. If you wish to reap rewards in view of all the sacrifices you have made over the past two years and especially over these past two horrible weeks . . . people must know that you continue to oppose as usual an unscrupulous and evil policy. To fight when your country has been plunged into danger is quite another matter and must not be misunderstood.[4]

Yet Victoria's concern over her husband's vulnerability to conservative influence did not dampen her enthusiasm over Prussia's victory. Although she continued to insist that Prussian leadership in the German question could have been realized via moral conquests, that is, without a major war against Austria, she hoped that Prussia's victory would nonetheless lead to the unification of Germany:

We know too well how this war came about, and we know that our policy was unjust, brutal. . . . What has been brought about with blood and iron could have been achieved by moral conquests . . . a Prussia led by a powerful, good government could have achieved unification under its leadership; a bloodbath was not necessary. [But] we must accept this unfortunate fait accompli, but *as you say* Papa must compensate his people for their terrible sacrifices—I believe that this [compensation] should be the union of the German states, i.e. the new German Empire![5]

These sentiments were shared by prominent Progressives such as Eduard Lasker, who pleaded for national unification as the ultimate goal of the war. In an article that appeared in the *Nationalzeitung* after the battle of Königgrätz, Lasker wrote, "Let us vow in this great moment that Europe will never be quiet until Germany is united and strong in relation to its greatness and position."[6]

Like many Progressives, Victoria wished the new empire to be headed by a liberal government. In her mind, it was Bismarck's mission to serve as midwife to a new Prussian government that would eradicate the conservative power of old. But her ideas for the new government show that she wanted far more than someone like Bismarck—or her husband, for that matter—was willing to deliver:

Bismarck should put himself in contact with all the leaders of the democratic party [in Germany] and he must make concessions to the chamber at home—and replace his colleagues [in the cabinet]. If he was capable of persuading your father to go to war, he will be capable of making him do other things. Fate has decreed that Bismarck be called to create the Empire—now Bismarck should finish what he has begun and thereafter slip into obscurity so that we can forge ahead in good faith with a reasonable program and live in peace and freedom.[7]

Victoria insisted that her husband persuade the king and Bismarck to accept her ideas. She saw no obstacles in the path of her goals: "It would be so easy—the people expect it—we only have to take one small step and all will be well—the sickness which drove us into war (naturally, the disunity *within*) has been cured."[8] Victoria suggested that Bismarck's first order of business should be to end the constitutional conflict by confirming the chamber's budgetary rights. This confirmation would be presented with an indemnity bill whereby parliament would accept the budget of the past three years. She added, "Couldn't you bring this about? If I were there, I would press Papa and Bismarck to do so!"[9]

Bismarck and the crown prince already supported the idea of an indemnity bill, and their increasing agreement on other issues precluded any willingness of Frederick's part to accept any of his wife's other ideas, such as the unification of Germany under Prussian leadership.[10] The hesitancy exhibited by the crown prince and Bismarck on the question of unification stemmed from the consequences of an offer made by Napoleon III of France to mediate peace terms between Prussia and Austria. Bismarck feared that Napoleon's seemingly benevolent offer was merely a pretext to enable the French emperor to actively intervene in German affairs. Hence, Bismarck chose not to respond to Napoleon's offer and proposed, instead, to conclude a swift and lenient peace with Austria.

The crown prince and Bismarck were immediately confronted by conservative opposition to this idea from the king and his military advisers, who wished to make the most of Prussia's military victory by annexing Austrian territory and staging a triumphal march through Vienna. With difficulty, Bismarck tried to convince the king that Prussia's victory at Königgrätz had assured Austria's expulsion from German affairs and that any attempt to annex Austrian territory or proclaim German unity under Prussia would produce serious diplomatic complications, for it raised the threat of French and Russian intervention.[11] Instead of unification, Bismarck proposed to organize the German states north of the Main River into the North German Confederation, which would be dominated by Prussia.

None of these ideas impressed the crown princess. She wanted the peace settlement with Austria to spark the unification of Germany and the implementation of her more radical liberal reforms. Unable to see that her husband supported Bismarck, she asked her husband to impress her ideas upon the minister-president:

I am glad that Bismarck will present the indemnity bill in the opening speech to parliament . . . but that is not enough. You must demand more—the speech must also announce the confirmation of parliament's *budgetary* rights. . . . Our demands to Austria must be limited to the following: military supremacy in northern Germany, and everything associated with that; the ports, forts, war materials and possession of *Mainz, Frankfurt and Karstadt* as Prussian *cities*—with this we will be able to conquer southern Germany and we *must* do this. Bismarck's idea of the Main-line is awful. . . . It is of primary importance that Austria be suppressed [unterdrückt] and be made small and insignificant, and harmless. The minor princes can stay where they are but they should have no influence in German politics. . . . This plan should be acknowledged, refined and presented before the German parliament.[12]

The crown prince ignored these ideas. As a constitutional liberal who wished to preserve the status quo in constitutional affairs, Frederick was not interested in seeing the powers of parliament enhanced by a war that had been won by the crown and the army. Thanks to his sessions with Bismarck, the crown prince was also wary of the risks Prussia would incur in the event that it tried to make Austria "small, insignificant and harmless" as Victoria had suggested.

Frederick did not bother to explain his objections to Victoria's ideas. He simply told her that Prussia's peace terms were to be far more lenient than she hoped: "Austria will have to withdraw from the Confederation, give up the territories which we have occupied, and grant us power in the foreign affairs of the [North German] Confederation."[13] This reply frustrated Victoria, who chafed at her husband's apparent unwillingness to act upon her ideas: "What you tell me doesn't satisfy me in the least. It seems as if you have absolutely no influence in policy-making decisions at all. I was mistaken to believe that your views could make an impression on Bismarck. At the very least I hoped that you would make an attempt to do so. You have left him to do as he pleases, and I object to this heartily!"[14]

Frederick hid from his wife the fact that he was, indeed, exerting a great deal of influence as Bismarck's ally and that he considered the latter's views to be far more in line with his constitutional liberalism than those expressed by Victoria. He told Victoria only that Bismarck had left army headquarters before he had the opportunity to present her ideas to him, adding that he would "try" to abide by her wishes at the earliest opportunity. This elicited a forgiving response from Victoria: "I am . . . so happy that you wish to renew your attempt to exert your influence . . . for I know that Bismarck would be more than happy to throw us in the arms of France—I could imagine no worse fate than that."[15]

But over the days that followed, Frederick ignored his wife's demands. He continued to insist that he was "unable" to get in touch with the minister-president. Meanwhile, the crown prince tried to persuade the king to support Bismarck's policy. He mediated a conflict between Bismarck and the king when the latter insisted on a march through Vienna to dictate a conqueror's peace: "I have to admit that Bismarck's point of view is entirely correct, and I have tried to lend him significant support. My world is turned upside down. In the past three days Papa has said such awful things that Bismarck actually cried last night and was afraid to see Papa again. In the meantime, I had to calm both of them down!"[16] Frederick's role as mediator between the king and the minister-president was not an enviable task. Bismarck became so agitated that he threatened either to resign or to commit suicide. But his position was saved through the intervention of the crown prince, who for once managed to convince the king to change his mind.[17]

With misgivings, the king agreed to the terms of a lenient preliminary peace between Austria and Prussia drawn up in Nikolsburg in July and signed in Prague on 23 August 1866. Austria did not lose any territory but was permanently excluded from German affairs. Indemnities were imposed on those German states that had sided with Austria in the conflict, and in September, Prussia annexed

Hanover, Hesse-Kassel, Nassau, and the city of Frankfurt.

The crown princess was not satisfied with the peace settlement. She told her husband that the threat of French intervention was hardly grounds to stop the unification process: "I believe that we should still risk everything, even a war with France, to achieve the unification of Germany under Prussia!"[18] She heartily opposed the creation of the North German Confederation and saw it as "a justification for another civil war." She added: "the division is a disgrace; [it means] the *expansion of Prussia* with Napoleon's help—this is not a good result."

Once again, Frederick rejected his wife's views, for his alliance with Bismarck made him realize that her goals were untenable for several reasons. First, he knew that Victoria was mistaken in her assumption that particularism (the "disunity within," as Victoria put it) had been "cured" by the war of 1866. Hence Prussia and the rest of the German states were hardly ready to engage in a united struggle against France. He was more wary of the obstacles to German unification than was his wife and told her that he supported the creation of the North German Confederation:

God only knows that a confederation which only reaches the Main is not the goal we were trying to achieve, but now that we have gotten this much under challenging conditions, we do have an advantage in that we will be able to expand our gains at some time in the near future. The diplomats in Berlin are doing their best to quickly and secretly conclude treaties with the south German states which will bind them to the North German Bund and prevent them from allying with Austria.[19]

Second, the crown prince appreciated the power of conservatives opposed to liberal reforms that his wife advocated. For example, Frederick knew that the conservatives wanted the Prussian victory to serve as a pretext for the suspension or conservative revision of the constitution.[20] In Frederick's mind, Bismarck's indemnity bill was a sign that the minister-president wanted to preserve the constitutional process. Historian Otto Pflanze points out, however, that Bismarck's motives were opportunistic. Since he wanted to retain his position in the next reign (which appeared imminent in view of the king's advanced age), it was necessary for Bismarck to come to terms with the heir to the throne.[21] Although Frederick did not trust Bismarck, he supported the latter's wish to uphold the constitution in the face of conservative opposition:

I have taken it upon myself to insist on this matter when I speak to the king; strangely enough, Bismarck is likely to support me. Although I do not trust him and am suspicious about his plans for working with parliament, I consider him too intelligent to stir up any nonsense about this issue now. We will soon see whether or how he will attempt to label me as his "converted ally." I have reason to believe that my analysis of the current situation is accurate. Given the inclination of the king and his mood with respect to Bismarck's reasonable views, I have no choice but to be of service to advance the welfare of Germany under Prussian leadership.[22]

Thanks to Frederick's help, the king approved the indemnity bill, which asked the Prussian chamber to retroactively approve the government's unauthorized expenditures of the past four years.[23] Bismarck had little trouble getting parliament to accept the bill, for he had already exploited enthusiasm for Prussia's victory to his political advantage. Elections held on the day of the Battle of Königgrätz marked a defeat for many of those liberals who had been Bismarck's most bitter enemies: the Left Center and the Progressives, who had held 247 seats, reduced their numbers to 148, and the Conservatives gained 100 seats.[24] This new alignment reduced the influence of liberals who opposed the indemnity bill on the grounds that it "merely legalized the 'gap theory,' which had allowed Bismarck to defy parliament and did not offer any guarantees that this would not happen again."[25] The bill was passed by the Prussian chamber by an overwhelming majority on 3 September 1866. The indemnity bill precipitated a split in the liberals' ranks: those who supported the bill and Bismarck's policies resigned from the Progressive Party and formed the National Liberal party in 1867.

Passage of the bill signalled the end of the constitutional conflict. But liberals who hoped that their acquiescence to the bill would be rewarded with more political power in the North German Confederation were disappointed by Bismarck's constitution. Although the constitution recognized the existence and legislative competence of parliament and granted it control of the annual budget, the military budget still lay out of its jurisdiction.[26] Further, the constitution did not provide for positions that the Reichstag could attempt to hold responsible for the government's policies; hence, the crown once again denied the liberals a ministry responsible to parliament.[27] As before, the center of power was vested in the king, who controlled military and political power and retained the authority to use emergency powers as he saw fit.

As a constitutional liberal, Frederick had few reservations about the constitution and the powers granted to parliament. His wife, however, shared Progressives' disapproval of the constitution and hoped that the liberal majority in the new Reichstag would reject it. On 25 March 1867 she wrote her mother, "I have been to the Reichstag and heard some very good speeches but I fear that [they] will not please the Government as they showed very plainly that the people will not only keep their love of constitutional rights and liberty but care to express it, and will not accept this new, sham constitution without making their objections."[28]

But only a few weeks later, a crisis in foreign affairs between Prussia and France convinced Victoria and many other liberals that national solidarity against a foreign foe was more important than a more liberal constitution. After the war, the French had demanded compensation for their neutrality. In August 1866, the French ambassador to Prussia, Count Benedetti, asked Prussia to agree to French annexation of Belgium and Luxembourg. King William and Bismarck rejected the French demand for Belgium, since their acquiescence to such a move would incur the wrath of Britain, which regarded Belgium as a crucial sphere of interest. So far as Luxembourg was concerned, however, Bismarck informed Benedetti that he was prepared to be "obliging."[29] But over the next several months, Bismarck's stalling over the issue led the French to adopt a hostile attitude toward Prussia.

The crown prince and princess kept themselves informed about France's demands for compensation, and both saw that France's hostile attitude toward Prussia could result in another war. In November 1866, the crown princess wrote her husband: "the idea of a war with France . . . cannot be eliminated from the realm of possibilities."[30] The crown prince received this letter in St. Petersburg, where he was attending the wedding of the Czarevich Alexander to Princess Dagmar of Denmark. He replied, "There is much talk about the possibility of war, and this could well happen, but at this moment there is no real reason to initiate a new bloodbath."[31]

Tensions between Prussia and France mounted when the French, frustrated by Bismarck's stalling over the Luxembourg issue, put pressure on King William III of Holland to cede Luxembourg to France in March of 1867. But the king was reluctant to cede Luxembourg without the approval of Prussia. The news of France's efforts to acquire Luxembourg aroused the anger of German nationalists, who appealed to the government to prevent the cession of German-speaking territory to France.[32] Bismarck, in turn, was willing to use nationalist agitation to make a bold stand to the French; he declared to the French that his government would be "compromised" if it agreed to the cession of Luxembourg.[33]

The crown prince and princess sided with German nationalists who opposed the cession of Luxembourg. As Victoria told her mother: "People are in a wonderful state of excitement about Luxembourg, and I must say I think anything preferable than giving France a part of Germany . . . France has no right to interfere in our internal affairs . . . Should there be a war against France—which would be a dreadful calamity on the one side—the unity of Germany would be effected at once."[34] The recalcitrance of the Prussians in the Luxembourg question made the French scale down their demands. In April, the French declared their willingness to waive their claim to Luxembourg if Prussia would withdraw its garrison from the duchy and agree to its neutralization. But Bismarck refused to accept this arrangement. By his lights, the crisis presented an opportunity to fight particularism in Germany by encouraging the forces of nationalism. However, he did not want the crisis to explode into a war with France, for Prussia was not prepared for such a struggle. Army chief of staff Helmuth von Moltke thought otherwise; he wished to strike before French rearmament was complete. This view was shared by the royal couple, who felt that the time was ripe to strike against France.[35] As Victoria told her mother: "The aggression comes from France, and it is there they wish for war and not here. For my part, if the peace cannot be maintained I think it better the war should be now than later, horrible as it is . . . for the sake of Germany we must not hang back. This is my feeling and Fritz's and most people's here."[36]

The height of the Luxembourg crisis coincided with the crucial Reichstag debates on Bismarck's draft of the constitution for the North German Confederation. Feelings against France ran so high that liberal Reichstag members were willing to abandon their insistence on liberal reforms (such as ministerial responsibility and Reichstag control of the military budget) to the higher goal of solidarity between parliament and government against the foreign foe. The constitution was passed by a vote of 230 to 53 on 16 April 1867.

Victoria now approved of the Reichstag's adoption of the "sham" constitution. As she told her mother:

Prussia's language towards France in the Luxemburg question was decisive for Bismarck's position in Germany. This was the spirit that animated the interpolations of Monsieur de Bennigsen, and Bismarck's answer satisfied the Diet; and that was one of the reasons why the constitution was adopted so quickly, unsatisfactory as it was in its details and hard for many a one to accede to. All are united in coming to a conclusion so as not to put fresh difficulties in the way of the Government in case of a war with France.[37]

However, the crown princess still held out the hope that the French would agree to the unification of Germany without a war. She even took it upon herself to speak personally to Bismarck on the subject. Victoria told her mother that she had avoided discussing politics with the chancellor before because she considered him to be "such a dangerous person." But she overcame her trepidation and told him that her admiration for him would increase if he found a way of honorably preserving peace between France and the North German Confederation. Bismarck replied that peace did not depend on Prussia. Since France had increased its armaments, Prussia had no choice but to follow suit.[38] Victoria probably concluded from this conversation that war between France and Prussia was practically inevitable.

But contrary to Victoria's hopes, the Luxembourg crisis failed to provoke a war for the unification of Germany. The crisis ended when France and Prussia agreed to grant Luxembourg its independence.[39] Once again, like many liberals who reversed their opposition to the constitution during the crisis, Victoria gave in to the idea that national unity during this time of crisis was more important than liberal reforms, and she failed to see that Bismarck had deliberately exploited the Luxembourg issue to speed the deliberations of the constituent Reichstag to a favorable conclusion.[40] After the Luxembourg crisis failed to provoke a war for unification, however, Victoria made it clear that she was still dissatisfied with the constitution and resumed her criticism of Bismarck and his policies.

Victoria also resumed her campaign to draw her husband away from Bismarck. She felt that Frederick's image as a liberal would be best preserved if he played no active role in the new German government as long as Bismarck was at the helm. Frederick accepted her advice: though he supported Bismarck's policies during the war and was far more satisfied with the outcome of the recent war with regard to the new constitution and the creation of the North German Confederation than was his wife, he was wary of being labelled as Bismarck's ally.[41]

Thanks to Victoria's influence, Frederick was conspicuous by his absence from the political limelight after his return from the war of 1866. Apart from his military duties and attendance at meetings of the crown council, his only job was to represent his father on politically insignificant missions abroad. Although Frederick traveled widely as his father's representative, his letters to his wife from Russia, Italy, France, and Egypt (where he attended the opening of the Suez Canal in 1869) resemble travelogues and are devoid of political commentary. When the crown prince visited Vienna in 1869, he spent an hour with Emperor Franz Josef "without mentioning a word about politics."[42]

The crown prince's lack of political activity aroused the concern of his close friend and advisor Albrecht von Stosch, who was the crown prince's quartermaster general during the war of 1866. Despite his conservative military background, Stosch was regarded as a liberal.[43] But Stosch's approach to liberal reform was far too conservative for Victoria's tastes. Stosch told the crown princess that her political views were far too "radical" and that her "stormy struggles for reform" were the result of her extreme youth. He added that lasting innovation in Prussia could be produced only slowly, "doubly slowly" if one wished not to destroy, but to reform.[44] But although Stosch and Victoria argued frequently about politics, they had a mutual admiration for each other.

Stosch urged the crown prince to involve himself in political affairs by supporting Bismarck in his battle against particularism, the major obstacle to the unification of Germany, and warned him against letting his personal differences with Bismarck stand in the way of more important goals for Germany:

At the moment a considerable opposition to Count Bismarck is asserting itself in the Prussian State Ministry . . . Prussian particularism is especially noticeable. . . . Since it is of greatest importance for our progress that Count Bismarck remains the *victor* of this battle, I would like Your Royal Highness to support him vigorously, and by no means to take steps against him because of his "tactlessness" in Your Royal Highness' house, about which Your Royal Highness writes so ill-humoredly. Count Bismarck is the only one who can help us forward.[45]

But, for the most part, Stosch's efforts were blocked by Victoria, who felt that if Frederick allied himself with Bismarck, he would have had to share credit for the achievement of unification with him.[46] But Victoria wanted her husband, not Bismarck, to be responsible for the work of unification, which, she believed, could be achieved by reinvigorating the policy of moral conquests. After the war of 1866, Victoria wrote:

You have the right instincts for this task [unification] and your father does *not*. . . . The right people will fly to your side, and you will do the right thing and you will be able to do it *without Bismarck* . . . your Papa wants nothing more than to be the king of Prussia in the

narrowest sense of the word, and he casts himself in the mold of kings of centuries gone by
. . . you can achieve a higher goal for Prussia, but without the sword![47]

Victoria's efforts to isolate her husband from Bismarck and the government did
nothing to further the work of unification. On the second anniversary of the Battle
of Königgrätz, the crown prince wrote his wife:

Two whole years have passed since the grand event—but how much farther have we come
since that turning point, and what progress have we made to do justice to this German
victory?! We must satisfy ourselves by saying that our efforts [toward unity] must and
will bear fruit—but we do not know how to exploit our advantageous position, and it is
unfortunate that we have not compensated for the sacrifices made. I only hope that you
and I will be able to find a way . . . to finish the work of unification, and finally bring
Barbarossa to life![48]

On the same day, the crown princess wrote her husband:

May you emerge just as victorious from your battle to relieve Germans of the ignorance
which stifles them, along with their lack of political and religious freedom—you must
never doubt that this is possible! You will take on the larger task of unification with the
same energy and endurance which enabled you to survive those difficult days [in 1866] . . .
you will summon loyal and honest men to your side and follow their sound advice. The
work [of unification] must be completed . . . and the evil spirits of reaction and confusion
must be eliminated . . . and I know that you can do this.[49]

A comparison of these letters reveals that while the crown prince groped for
answers as to how unification could be achieved, his wife assumed that her husband would somehow be able to find them, seemingly oblivious to the fact that by
isolating her husband from the government, she had made him politically impotent.

By 1868, Bismarck had also become increasingly concerned about the progress
of unification. He was well aware of official and popular opposition in many German states to the idea of the extension of Prussian authority, which would be the
inevitable result of unification. The elections to the Customs Parliament
(Zollparlament) of February 1868 produced a sizable bloc of deputies opposed to
unification, and these results were viewed as a setback to the unification cause.[50]
A year later, Bismarck was informed that the king of Bavaria had grown cool to the
subject.

A number of German princes argued that German unification could be achieved
by a war with France. Pressure for war came from other areas as well. In December
1869, Bismarck admitted to his aide Keudell that pressure for war was evident in
German business circles. The news from Berlin bankers was particularly disquiet-
ing: they declared that another six months of armed uncertainty would ruin Ger-

many.[51] There was a great deal of official and popular opposition in many German states to the idea of the extension of Prussian authority, which would be the inevitable result of unification.

Despite such bad news, Bismarck was not eager to accept the necessity of a war with France to achieve unification. He told his advisers to concentrate on progress already made toward unification: since 1866, Austrian interference in German affairs had been eliminated, and the south German states were bound to Prussia by a series of economic and military treaties. Bismarck did not see any reason why the obstacles to unification could not be eliminated peacefully, and he told his advisers that the time was simply not ripe to involve Prussia in a major war with France.

Bismarck was nevertheless deeply concerned about the lack of progress toward unification, and, as usual, he kept several options open. If peaceful means of achieving unity failed, Bismarck knew it could still be achieved by exploiting the patriotic sentiments emanating from a national war against France. There was yet another option: if the position of France in Europe were weakened through a diplomatic defeat, unification could be achieved without French interference.

The possibility of weakening French prestige came about when the throne of Spain was secretly offered to Prince Leopold of Hohenzollern-Sigmaringen, a member of the Catholic branch of the family of the king of Prussia. The Spanish throne was originally offered to Prince Leopold in 1868. The prince was not enthusiastic about the offer, but the Spaniards refused to give up their quest to put him on the throne. Bismarck became attracted to the project in February 1870. In his mind, the installment of a Hohenzollern on the Spanish throne would constitute a serious blow to French prestige. Such a blow could precipitate a domestic crisis that could prevent French intervention in German affairs for some time to come. The question as to whether Bismarck intended to use the Hohenzollern candidacy for the Spanish throne as a diplomatic weapon against France or as a means to incite the French to declare war against Prussia remains a matter of historical debate.[52] What is clear is that Bismarck took up the candidacy in earnest after February 1870, and he put a great deal of pressure on Prince Leopold to accept the offer and on King William to sanction it as head of the Hohenzollern family.[53]

Bismarck saw to it that these negotiations were kept secret. "He reasoned that if he failed to take the French by surprise by putting a Hohenzollern on the Spanish throne as a *fait accompli,* the whole action would have to be covered up in such a way that Prussia would appear as if it had nothing to do with what was essentially a dynastic matter."[54] But the parties concerned were not enthusiastic about the Spanish offer. In March 1870, the king wrote Bismarck that he opposed the idea of putting his relative on the Spanish throne because such a move would provoke a negative reaction from France. This refusal did not persuade Bismarck to abandon the project. Negotiations between the Spaniards and the Sigmaringen Hohenzollerns continued in secret.

Bismarck also asked the crown prince and princess to help him overcome the king's opposition. The crown prince was interested in the project. If successful, it would increase Prussian prestige at what appeared to be a critical stage in the unification process. At the same time, however, he was wary of possible negative ramifications of the project with regard to Prussia's position in foreign affairs.[55] This concern was shared by Bismarck, who asked the crown princess to tell her mother about the candidacy in order to determine discreetly England's attitude toward a project that could well result in war with France. On 12 March, only three days after the king was informed about the Hohenzollern candidacy, the crown princess asked her mother to give some indication concerning England's attitude toward the matter.[56] Queen Victoria duly broached the subject to her foreign minister, Lord Clarendon, who replied that it would not be "expedient" for the queen "to give any advice upon a matter in which no British interest is concerned." He added that the matter could be decided only according to the interests and feelings of the Hohenzollern family.[57] The tone of Clarendon's remarks must have indicated to Bismarck that the British had no serious reservations about what they considered to be essentially a family matter.

Although the news from England was encouraging, the crown prince remained hesitant to support the project. He was ultimately swayed in favor of the candidacy by Roon (the minister of war) and Delbrück (the minister of finance), who argued that Prussian prestige would be increased in the event that a Hohenzoller sat on the Spanish throne. Two days after the crown council meeting, the candidate himself, Leopold von Hohenzollern, noted the change in Frederick's attitude toward the project: "It becomes more and more difficult to bring forward those reasons of the heart which have hitherto been preponderant . . . even the Crown Prince, who up to present has concurred in my views against acceptance, now thinks the more deeply one ponders over the question, the more decidedly reason comes down on the side of acceptance."[58] Once the crown prince overcame his doubts about the Spanish project, he willingly assisted Bismarck in his efforts to assure the king and the Sigmaringen Hohenzollerns to do the same.

In discussing the Hohenzollern candidacy with Major von Versen, a member of the Prussian general staff, the crown prince commented that, "the new king will have no bed of roses, only a bed of thorns." But Versen noted in his diary that the crown prince seemed very concerned "about the greatness of his house."[59] From this Versen concluded that the crown prince saw the candidacy as a means to enhance Prussian prestige.[60] Yet Frederick also made it clear that he saw the enhancement of Prussian prestige as a crucial part of the unification process. As he told Bismarck:

I have been in favor of the candidature of the Hereditary Prince of Hohenzollern ever since it came under discussion this spring as I assumed it would meet with no serious difficulties and could in no way lead to the danger of conflict with France. . . . On this assumption it seemed to me that the accession of a Hohenzoller to the Spanish throne would not be without advantage to German interests and to the position of the dynasty, and therefore deserved acceptance rather than rejection.[61]

Thanks to agitation from the crown prince and Bismarck, along with favorable reports on conditions in Spain from Major von Versen, the king and the Hohenzollern Sigmaringen family decided to accept the Spanish offer, and news of Leopold's acceptance was dispatched to Madrid.[62] On 8 June, the crown prince wrote Bismarck: "I regard the whole matter as settled; should difficulties of any kind arise they will not be attributable to members of the Hohenzollern house but to the Spaniards."[63]

Having secured Leopold's acceptance of the Spanish offer, Bismarck's next task was to keep the matter secret until the prince was formally elected as king by the Spanish parliament so that European cabinets could be presented with an accomplished fact. But this plan failed when news of the candidacy leaked out before the Spanish parliament was summoned to elect Leopold. Contrary to Frederick's predictions, the news caused an uproar in France, where anger was directed not against Spain but against Prussia. France's response to the candidacy was dictated by its anti-Prussian foreign minister, Gramont, who wished to exploit the incident to humiliate Prussia and thereby bolster the sagging prestige of the French government.[64]

Although the crown prince believed that the French response to news of the candidacy was exaggerated, he strongly urged Bismarck to abide by France's demand to withdraw Leopold's candidacy.[65] Initially, the French campaign to humiliate Prussia was successful when the king and the Sigmaringen Hohenzollern family agreed to withdraw Prince Leopold's candidacy. After the candidacy was withdrawn, Frederick felt that the Franco-Prussian crisis had been put to rest. But on 13 July, he was informed that the French ambassador to Prussia, Benedetti, planned to meet with the king at Ems. Since France had already scored a diplomatic victory by securing withdrawal of the candidacy, the crown prince assumed that the purpose of Benedetti's visit was to place new demands on Prussia. The crown prince wrote Queen Victoria that his country would not tolerate a French move to use a defunct candidacy as a pretext to meddle in Prussian affairs:

Should fresh demands be made upon us . . . he [Napoleon III] will meet with a unanimous expression of German feeling and anger which will cost him dear. Already German feeling is wounded, as I have seldom seen amongst peaceful people; but I say that, after the events of 1866, we can well afford to take a step which proves our love of peace, without laying us open to the charge of fear and cowardice, as was the case in 1850 at Olmütz![66]

The crown prince was perfectly correct in assuming the nature of Benedetti's mission to Ems, which was to obtain from the king a guarantee that the candidacy never be renewed. The king knew that acceptance of these demands would incur serious humiliation for his country; hence, he politely dismissed Benedetti after hearing him out and resisted his subsequent attempts to discuss French demands.

However, the king's demeanor did not satisfy Bismarck. He edited the king's telegram from Ems in order to give the appearance that Benedetti had been rudely
dismissed by the king, and he released this embellished version of events at Ems
to the press. With the release of the Ems telegram to the press, Bismarck was able
to turn the tables on France's attempt to humiliate Prussia, for the telegram infuriated the French and provided them with a pretext to declare war on Prussia. This
suited Bismarck, for France's declaration of war on 2 July 1870 put Prussia on the
defensive, as had been the case in 1866.

Although many historians have alleged that the Hohenzollern candidacy was
part of Bismarck's larger plan to instigate war with France, it is interesting to note
that the crown prince and princess never brought up Bismarck's name in connection with the origins of the war of 1870. In their minds, Bismarck had been the
instigator of the "unnecessary" wars of 1864 and 1866, but this view did not apply
to the war of 1870. As far as they were concerned, the French alone were responsible for the outbreak of the conflict. Also, as much as the royal couple abhorred
the idea of war and bloodshed, they knew that this war, unlike the others insti-
gated by Bismarck, would complete the unification process if German troops
emerged victorious.

This feeling was shared by many prominent liberals. Shortly after the war broke
out, National Liberal leader Eduard Lasker wrote Bismarck that his party considered the unification of Germany as one of the foremost objectives of the war.[67] But
members of the National Liberal Party also knew that particularism was still a major
obstacle to unification. In spite of the fact that all the German states were united in
the struggle against France, National Liberal leaders knew that there was bound to
be opposition to any extension of Prussian authority that would result from the
war. Joining Bismarck at Prussian headquarters, Ludwig Bamberger proposed to
propagandize the cause of unification among the masses.

Thinking along similar lines, the popular novelist and liberal Gustav Freytag
embarked upon a grandiose plan to launch a publicity campaign to popularize the
crown prince in southern Germany. Since the crown prince, as head of the Third
Army, commanded south German troops, Freytag proposed to endear them to the
idea of unification and to their future sovereign.[68] Freytag's concern over Frederick's
popularity in southern Germany was unnecessary. The crown prince was warmly
received in southern Germany en route to the front, and the quick string of victories won by united German troops proved the willingness of all Germans to unite
against a common foe.

The German victories in the war of 1870 were primarily the result of superior
military leadership of Prussian army chief of staff Helmuth von Moltke and by the
organizational talents of war minister Albrecht von Roon. Yet the military leadership of the crown prince also earned him praise when French troops were defeated
in the battles of Wörth and Weissenburg in August 1870. In September, German
troops decisively defeated French troops at the Battle of Sedan, which forced the
capitulation of the French army and the surrender of Napoleon III. But although

the war was over for Napoleon, the same was not true of the French people. On 4 September, a republic was proclaimed in Paris, and its leaders vowed to continue the war until the Germans were defeated. Two weeks later, German troops lay siege to the city of Paris.

The continuation of the war after Napoleon's surrender did not dampen Frederick's hopes for the unification of Germany. After the Battle of Sedan, his war diary entries were dominated by his thoughts on the remaining obstacles to unification and the organization of the new empire.

Before entering into a discussion of Frederick's observations during the war of 1870–1871, it is necessary to examine his war diary more closely as a historical document. The original can be found at the Geheimes Preussisches Staatsarchiv in Merseburg. The archive contains not one but three versions of the war diary, ranging in size from 366 pages to 761 pages.[69] In his preface to the final version of the diary, the crown prince explained the reason for revision of his work:

The daily impressions received during the campaign of 1870 and 1871, only cursorily jotted down in my Diary under the stress of the military duties, I have supplemented and completed since my subsequent return home by extracts from my correspondence regularly maintained between my wife and myself. On principle, however, I was firmly resolved to set down only my actual, personal experiences and feelings from day to day; consequently no improvement or alteration has been made under the influence of later events.[70]

It is generally agreed that the crown prince wished to have his diary serve as historical proof of his patriotism and his appreciation of the liberal movement. But if the crown prince was "firmly resolved" to set down only *his* "actual experiences and feelings," it is evident from a close examination of the original diary that Frederick lost an important argument with his wife. A comparison between Victoria's wartime correspondence with Frederick and the final diary revision of 1872 reveals that entries indicating his sympathy with progressive as opposed to constitutional liberalism were written by his wife and later included in the final version.[71] This discrepancy occurs several times throughout the war diary.[72]

For example, Frederick's diary entry for 24 October 1870 gives the impression that the crown prince supported his late father in law's views with regard to the establishment of British-style parliamentary government for Germany:

I cannot help myself . . . from thinking a great deal of the plans my late father-in-law, as also the King of the Belgians . . . entertained for a united Germany under a monarchical head. God so willed that those men should conceive the notion of a free German Imperial state, that in the truest sense of the word should march at the forefront of civilization and be in a position to develop and bring to bear all the noble ideas of the modern world. . . . In such a state we should gain a bulwark against socialism, while at the same time the nation would be delivered from the oppression of bureaucracy, despotism, and priestly domination.[73]

But this entry closely resembles Victoria's letter written to her husband three days earlier: "Alice (Victoria's sister, wife of the Duke of Hesse-Darmstadt) and I ... revel in the idea of a free German imperial state that in the truest sense of the word should march at the forefront of civilization ... this state should serve as a bulwark against socialism, [and] deliver the nation from the oppression of bureaucracy, despotism and priestly domination."[74]

The diary entry that is most often cited as evidence of Frederick's liberalism because of its critique of Bismarck's policies is his so-called Silvesterbetrachtung of 31 December 1870: "I still hold fast to-day to the conviction that Germany, without blood and iron, simply by the justice of her cause, could make 'moral conquests' and, united, become free and powerful. ... The insolent, brutal 'Junker' willed it otherwise. In 1864 his schemes and intrigues spoilt the victory of the good cause; in 1866 he broke up Austria without making Germany one."[75]

Yet this, too, was penned by Victoria on 27 December:

I insist that Germany could have become *united, free and powerful without* blood and iron, [and,] simply by the justice of her cause, could have made moral conquests, and united, could have become free and powerful. But the insolent, brutal Junker willed it otherwise. In 1864, *against* the wishes of the German people, he conquered Schleswig-Holstein for Prussia with Austria's help, in 1866 he smashed Austria without making Germany one.[76]

The crown prince's reflections on the place of the united Germany in the family of European nations were also written by his wife. His diary entry for 23 February 1871 reads:

Our next duty in peace-time is the solution of the social question; on this lofty aim must all the treasures of German erudition and German intellect be concentrated. France is disqualified by lack of mental balance, England by the too wide severance to be found between rich and poor, but Germany, where no similar colossal fortunes exist, offers a productive field for a thorough solution of this question.[77]

But on 20 February, Victoria wrote her husband: "My *dream* is that *all* the treasures of German erudition and intellect will be concentrated on the solution of the social question. *France* cannot do this because [the French] lack mental balance. England cannot do this because the contrast between rich and poor is too great. But in Germany, where no similar great fortunes exist, the way to the solution [of this question] is open."[78] Victoria's "contributions" to her husband's diary attest to her view that the liberalization and unification of Germany had to be accomplished simultaneously. If one deletes Victoria's contributions from her husband's war diary, it is evident that the crown prince was primarily concerned with unifying Germany and securing the imperial title for the house of Hohenzollern. Unlike

Victoria, he held that Germany could be liberalized—within the framework of the constitutional status quo—only after unification.

The question that arises from these discrepancies is: Why did Frederick allow his wife to pass off her thoughts as his own in an important historical document? The answer may have a lot to do with the fact that the diary was meant to be published fifty years after Frederick's death: he may not have been concerned about Victoria's entries, since his record as emperor, not necessarily his war diary, would speak for itself. He may have also wished to include reflections on both the constitutional liberal and left-liberal points of view to indicate that he, as Victoria once put it, "stood above all political parties." In other words, he was sympathetic toward elements of both points of view, but he himself would pursue a unique course as German emperor.

After the Battle of Sedan, the crown prince worked energetically to secure unification and the imperial title for his house. One remaining obstacle was the unwillingness of some of the south German states to join the union. Representatives from Württemberg, Bavaria, and Saxony told Bismarck they opposed a united Germany under Prussian hegemony but were willing to consider a loose federal organization of German states in which each state retained a wide margin of sovereignty.[79]

While Bismarck was willing to make certain concessions to the sovereign rights of the south German states, the crown prince opposed the idea of concessions altogether. He told his friend Gustav Freytag that Prussia had sufficient power to obtain the agreement of recalcitrant south German rulers to union by force, if necessary.[80] Then Frederick reconsidered the option of force when he asked Bismarck to proceed with the proclamation of the new German empire without Bavaria and Württemberg.[81] But Bismarck was unwilling to do this, since a united Germany without Bavaria would weaken the empire and make it vulnerable to French or Austrian influence.[82] Bismarck overcame Bavarian opposition through bribes and concessions to particularism. The kingdom was granted special privileges in the empire, and King Ludwig was paid a subsidy in exchange for his agreement to offer the imperial crown to King William.[83]

Once the obstacles to unification had been overcome, Frederick expressed his desire for liberal reforms, and entries on this subject reflect his constitutional liberal point of view. By his lights, it was the government, not parliament, that needed to be reformed. On 7 March 1871 he wrote in his diary, "A noble task lies before our government, if it is firmly resolved to strive earnestly for the internal development of the Empire on liberal lines in accord with the spirit of the age, and by so doing give the world a guarantee for lasting peace."[84] His constitutional liberal point of view is particularly evident in his wish to see the monarchy, as opposed to parliament, adapt to the needs of the day: "Personally, I am for a monarchy which will independently, in the truest sense of the word, face the claims and questions of the day, by immediate introduction of a free system of elections by districts, as also by granting the laity a share in Church government."[85]

These were fine liberal notions, but Frederick also had a rather archaic idea regarding the character of the new empire:

Furthermore, the re-establishment of the Empire must be reformed root and branch and be freed from all connection with the principles and traditions of the erstwhile "Holy Roman Empire," the very nature of which was essentially rotten, hollow, and utterly effete. Otherwise and barring this difference, I regard the empire of to-day as identical with that which existed in Germany for over a thousand years and which has only been in abeyance since the abdication of Emperor Francis II in 1806 until the present moment when, after a sixty-five years' interregnum, it is re-established, purged of its defects and made heredi-tary.[86]

While Victoria no doubt approved Frederick's sentiments with regard to monar-chical reform, she found little favor with his comments on the Holy Roman Empire and put pressure on her husband to abandon his attempt to draw any ties between the old empire and the new. Her disapproval of her husband's outdated concep-tion of the empire was evident when she rejected his draft of a proclamation announcing the creation of the new empire:

The new German Empire is something completely *new, regardless* of whether we approve of its government or the way in which it came to be. . . . Your draft does not show me that you share this view. Only a small minority will approve of the way in which the draft is worded, whereas practically all members of the liberal and national parties of the land see something new and original in the new Empire, and hope that this new creation will bear no similarity to its outdated predecessor.[87]

Upon receipt of this letter, the crown prince told his wife that there was no reason for disagreement on this point:

Our opinions on this matter are far more similar than they appear to be; perhaps I can prove this to you by telling you that *just as in 1848, the old Prussian kingdom died and was buried, straightaway, thank God, to rise again fundamentally changed as a constitu-tional monarchy, while keeping its titled and external forms unaltered, and this should be the case to-day with the newly founded Empire.* . . . what I desire is that the present Empire should preserve only in its outward manifestations any close and clear connection with the old empire of a thousand years or more, whereas its inward constitution, framed on entirely new lines, must be something essentially different and adapted to meet the claims of the day.[88]

Frederick's efforts to conjure up a relationship between the new empire and the Holy Roman Empire may have been motivated by his desire to distinguish what he hoped to accomplish during his coming reign from the former, which had been created by Bismarck and had increased his power and influence to a remarkable degree. Frederick may have wished to use his imagery of the Holy Roman Empire—albeit in a modernized, constitutional form—to lend credence to the idea that it would be he, and not Bismarck, who would determine how the monarchy would respond to the needs of the day during his coming reign.

Despite Frederick's effort to reassure his wife that he was not dwelling on outdated political institutions,[89] his addiction to the traditions of the Holy Roman Empire was evident in his abortive effort to persuade his father to wear coronation robes worn by Holy Roman Emperors.[90] Bismarck thought that Frederick's fixation on imperial titles was absurd: "The crown prince is a most stupid and vain individual, and one day he'll die from this emperor madness," he said.[91]

The hope of liberals and Victoria that the new empire would be established along the lines of the British constitution was dashed by Bismarck's constitution for the new German empire.[92] As far as Victoria and the liberals were concerned, the constitution only extended the evils of the Prussian government to the rest of Germany. The Progressives attempted to redress the faults of the constitution by demanding amendments to increase the power of parliament and guarantee fundamental civil rights. When the government refused to include such amendments, the deputies tried to force the issue by prolonging their debate on passage of the treaties with the south German states.[93] The delay infuriated Bismarck, who warned the deputies that their stalling could result in the failure of unification.[94]

The following entry in Frederick's war diary gives the impression that he opposed the constitution drawn up by Bismarck for the new empire:

The best guarantee for peace would be an alliance with England and Austria; after that, resistance to ultramontane activities, and lastly unceasing efforts to further the work of German unity, the external structure of which is finished, but whose internal completion will have endless separation, disunion, mistrust, jealousy and confusion to contend against. The new Constitution unfortunately favors the development of all these evils, which are nothing more or less than elements of future weakness.[95]

But this entry does not reflect Frederick's true feelings with regard to the constitution for two reasons. First, the entry was penned by Victoria, who wrote:

It seems to me that the best guarantee for a lasting peace is an alliance with Austria and England, resistance to ultramontane activities, and effort must be made to consolidate German unity. On the surface, [Germany] is one, but in reality disunity, particularism, mistrust, jealousy and confusion prevail, and the constitution sanctions the further development of these things, which are sources of future friction.[96]

Second, the crown prince agreed with Bismarck that the Progressives' opposition to the constitution could jeopardize unification. As he confided to his diary, "It would be too dreadful, on the eve of the consummation of the great work of

Unification, spoiled and stunted as it may be, [if] the people's representatives ruined the harvest the War has ripened so rapidly, and to which 'Emperor and Empire' is actually the assured sequel."[97] Frederick acted on his feelings by urging Eduard Simson (the speaker of the Prussian chamber) to accept the treaties with the south German states and the new constitution. The pressure from Bismarck and the crown prince bore fruit. On 10 December 1870, the Reichstag approved the treaties with the south German states and the extension of the north German constitution to the rest of the empire.[98]

The crown princess did not appear to be aware that her husband was partly responsible for blocking a new constitution for the empire. Instead, she fumed at Grand Duke Frederick of Baden, who, for all his sympathy with the liberal movement, did not insist on a new liberal constitution as a prerequisite for his country to join the new empire:

It was such a comfort to hear Roggenbach's opinions concerning German matters. He, along with all other reasonable people I've spoken to lately, blames Baden for the extension of the North German constitution to all of Germany as opposed to the utilization of the opportunities of the present time to create a new and good constitution which would entail the elimination of that disgraceful universal suffrage. . . . [The people of] Baden have done a disservice to the great liberal German party in Prussia, for they are responsible for retaining and having perpetuated the old ways which we had hoped to get rid of at such an opportune time.[99]

Once again, Victoria persuaded her husband to refrain from associating his name with the creation of a nonliberal empire. She urged him to stop work on his draft for the proclamation of the empire: "It would be better for you to relegate responsibility for drafting the proclamation to Bismarck alone . . . the creation of the Empire will bear Bismarck's stamp, but your mark will be made on a new era."[100] Frederick agreed: "You are quite right; Bismarck's stamp belongs on *his* creations, but my mark will be made on what I hope to achieve later . . . in time, you and I will consecrate anew that which has sprung from Bismarck's cabinet."[101]

The new German empire was formally proclaimed at Versailles on 18 January 1871. On that day, the crown prince confided to his diary:

So Emperor and Empire would seem at last an acknowledged fact. . . . God grant that this league may never be broken, and [that] more and more princes arise who seem worthy to devote themselves to such a task! My own opinion is that from now on my duties and my wife's will become twice as heavy, important and responsible, because I shrink from no difficulty, because I feel I have no lack of fresh courage to set about the task fearlessly and steadfastly.[102]

But only four days after the crown prince declared his intention to serve unified Germany, he told his wife, "The events of the past several days have made a terrible impression on me. I will have to pull back into my shell. I cannot be seen as a silent contributor or accomplice [to these events]."[103] Frederick's diaries and correspondence do not supply the reason he chose to resume passive resistance. He may have become aware of the underhanded methods Bismarck used to secure unification—such as concessions to particularism and the bribing of King Ludwig of Bavaria. Hence, he may have meant that he had no intention of associating himself with the questionable methods Bismarck used to create the new empire. It is also possible that he resented the way in which the resolution of a recent conflict between Bismarck and Moltke over peace terms for France served to increase the influence of the former.[104]

Frederick's decision to renew his policy of passive resistance put him in a difficult position since he was once again isolated from the government and vulnerable to his father's disapproval.[105] But he remained hopeful that he could usher in a new liberal era when he came to the throne. As he told his wife:

We can only hope that the immediate future will be devoid of domestic upheaval—until you and I can begin a new era. I will then rise up to its challenges, and I look forward to this task, for I am now a complete man, and I hope to return home free of my annoying little faults. All that I have learned over the past ten years could not have been for naught, and I feel I have made progress in my ability to judge human character. Yet it is best to carry on as a silent observer and take advantage of every learning opportunity.[106]

Victoria did not share her husband's optimism. She failed to see how a "new era" would be possible since the government of the new empire was hostile to liberalism. In January 1871, she wrote her husband: "I see confusion everywhere. Our political judgement, our interest in social progress and in the progressive development of our own country has diminished because of the war! I fear that an era of reaction will ensue—I can already see its dark shadows hovering over us!"[107]

By Frederick's lights, however, Bismarck's policies during the first years of the empire's existence—which corresponded to the liberal views of the crown prince—contradicted his wife's dim predictions. However, Frederick's optimism about his coming reign faded rapidly at the end of the 1870s as Bismarck dismantled liberal policies in order to form an alliance with conservative parties and forces in the empire. Frederick's journey from optimism to disillusionment is the subject of the next chapter.

NOTES

1. See Eugen Wolbe, *Kaiser Friedrich: Die Tragödie des Übergangenen* (Hellerau, 1931), p. 149.

2. The crown princess was stunned by her son's death; her lengthy letters to her husband and mother give evidence of her intense grief. Yet her husband's

response was far more controlled. Upon receiving news of Sigismund's death, the crown prince wrote only one sentence in his diary: "Thy will be done!" H. O. Meisner, ed., *Kaiser Friedrich III. Tagebücher von 1848 bis 1866* (Leipzig, 1929), p. 427. When the king granted his son leave to attend Sigismund's funeral, the crown prince refused to leave his post. He explained, "I am in the service of the fatherland. I would never forgive myself if we were attacked when I was absent from my post." Georg Schuster, ed., *Briefe, Reden und Erlasse des Kaisers und Königs Friedrich III* (Berlin, 1907), p. 85.

3. Meisner, *Tagebücher*, pp. 448–449.

4. Hessische Hausstiftung, Schloss Fasanerie, Fulda (hereafter HH): Crown Princess Victoria to Crown Prince Frederick William, Neues Palais, 29 June 1866.

5. Ibid., 30 June 1866.

6. James F. Harris, *A Study in the Theory and Practice of German Liberalism. Eduard Lasker, 1829–1884* (New York, 1984), p. 54.

7. Ibid., 4 July 1866. Later, however, Victoria acknowledged that Bismarck and Roon had to be kept on because of their popularity with the people.

8. Ibid., 4 July 1866.

9. Ibid., 4 July 1866

10. Frederick suggested that the Prussian victory could be rewarded by its annexation of territory from some of the defeated German states, but he stopped short of suggesting the unification of Germany under Prussian leadership. Meisner, *Tagebücher*, p. 547.

11. Otto Pflanze, *Bismarck and the Development of Germany. Volume 1: The Period of Unification 1815–1871* (Princeton, NJ, 1990), pp. 311–313.

12. HH: Crown Princess Victoria to Crown Prince Frederick William, 10 July 1866.

13. HH: Crown Prince Frederick William to Crown Princess Victoria, 19 July 1866.

14. HH: Crown Princess Victoria to Crown Prince Frederick William, 19 July 1866.

15. Ibid., 22 July 1866.

16. HH: Crown Prince Frederick William to Crown Princess Victoria, 24 July 1866.

17. Pflanze, *Bismarck,* Vol. 1, p. 308.

18. HH: Crown Princess Victoria to Crown Prince Frederick William, Heringdorf, 26 July 1866.

19. HH: Crown Prince Frederick William to Crown Princess Victoria, 29 July 1866. This quote is also reproduced in Frederick's diaries of 1848–1866. See Meisner, *Tagebücher*, p. 480–481.

20. Ernst Ludwig von Gerlach and Edwin von Manteuffel both put pressure on the king to use the army to beat the "hidden enemy," that is, the parliamentary process, into submission. They also recommended abrogation of the constitution and the installation of a reactionary ministry. See Ernst Huber, *Deutsche*

Verfassungsgeschichte Seit 1789 4 Vols. (Stuttgart, 1957–1969), Vol. 3, p. 348.

21. Ibid., pp. 328–329

22. Meisner, *Tagebücher*, p. 481, 1 August 1866.

23. George O. Kent, *Bismarck and His Times* (Carbondale, IL, 1978), p. 62.

24. H. W. Koch, *A Constitutional History of Germany in the Nineteenth and Twentieth Centuries* (London 1984), p. 101.

25. James J. Sheehan, *German Liberalism in the Nineteenth Century* (Chicago, 1978), p. 124.

26. The Reichstag was initially denied the right to control the military budget, but in 1874, after a lengthy struggle between government and the Reichstag, the latter was granted the right to vote on the budget every seven years. Kent, *Bismarck*, p. 65. See also Huber, *Verfassungsgeschichte*, pp. 649 ff.

27. Sheehan, *German Liberalism,* pp. 130–131.

28. Crown Princess Victoria to Queen Victoria, Berlin, 26 March 1867. Roger Fulford, ed., *Your Dear Letter: The Private Correspondence of the Queen Victoria and the Crown Princess of Prussia 1865–1871* (London, 1968), p. 127.

29. Pflanze, *Bismarck,* Vol. 1, p. 372.

30. HH: Crown Princess Victoria to Crown Prince Frederick William, Neues Palais, 12 November 1866.

31. HH: Crown Prince Frederick William to Crown Princess Victoria, St. Petersburg, 15 November 1866.

32. Pflanze, *Bismarck,* Vol. 1, p. 373.

33. Ibid., p. 380.

34. Crown Princess Victoria to Queen Victoria, 2 April 1867. Fulford, ed. *Your Dear Letter,* p. 122.

35. Ibid., 20 April 1867, p. 129.

36. Ibid.

37. Ibid., 27 April 1867, p. 132.

38. Ibid., p. 133.

39. Though the French suffered a humiliating diplomatic defeat, Franco-Prussian relations recovered quickly. Only a few months after the crisis was resolved, King William and the crown prince were invited to the Paris Exhibition. The crown prince made no political observations about the recent crisis in his letters to his wife from Paris apart from the statement, "In der Politik hat sich hier Alles befriedigend gelöst." HH: Crown Prince Frederick William to Crown Princess Victoria, Paris, 20 June 1867.

40. Pflanze, *Bismarck,* Vol. 1, p. 379. At first, Victoria refused to place any truth in the rumor that Bismarck had engineered the Luxemburg crisis for his own benefit. She was reassured by the king on this point, and she, in turn, reassured her mother: "I said [to the king] I thought that people in England had the notion that Bismarck had encouraged the Emperor [Napoleon III] to think that he could have Luxembourg upon which the King replied, 'That is not true; Bismarck, Goltz and I have always said that if a proposal came to us for an arrangement by which we

could honorably withdraw our troops from the garrison [in Luxembourg] we should have no objection to treat on the subject with France; it is the French who made propositions to us we cannot accept.' I give you the king's words." Fulford, *Your Dear Letter*, p. 132.

41. HH: Crown Prince Frederick William to Crown Princess Victoria, 1 August 1866. Victoria also may have convinced her husband that the day-to-day details of political affairs were simply not important. She told her mother: "You are quite mistaken if you think I like politics. . . . The course of daily, political events or rather diplomatical, small talk—I think the greatest bore in the world. I am anxious that . . . dear England may sometime or other may look upon us as fit to share her position in the world. . . . I do not know whether this is being fond of politics." Crown Princess Victoria to Queen Victoria, Berlin, 2 February 1867. Fulford, *Your Dear Letter*, p. 119.

42. HH: Crown Prince Frederick William to Crown Princess Victoria, Vienna, 7 October 1869.

43. Frederic B. M. Hollyday, *Bismarck's Rival; A Political Biography of General and Admiral Albrecht von Stosch* (Durham, NC, 1960), p. vii.

44. Hollyday, *Stosch*, p. 42.

45. Ibid., p. 63.

46. Frederick's biographer Werner Richter defends the crown prince's absence from the political limelight by asserting that his political activity was purposely limited by Bismarck, who had "no further use" for him after the peace of Nikolsburg. Werner Richter, *Friedrich III: Leben und Tragik des Zweiten Hohenzollern Kaisers* 2nd ed. (Munich, 1981) p. 173. But the nature of Victoria's influence over her husband at this time suggests that it may well have been Frederick who had no use for an alliance with Bismarck.

47. HH: Crown Princess Victoria to Crown Prince Frederick William, 29 July 1866.

48. HH: Crown Prince Frederick William to Crown Princess Victoria, Treptar, 3 July 1868.

49. HH: Crown Princess Victoria to Crown Prince Frederick William, Reinhardsbrünn, 3 July 1868.

50. Pflanze, *Bismarck,* Vol. 1, p. 433.

51. Josef Becker, "Zum Problem der Bismarckischen Politik in der Spanischen Thronfrage" *Historische Zeitschrift* Vol. 23 (1971), p. 605. Bismarck dismissed the pressure from businessmen for a war with the following: "Diese Ansicht sei doch verwerflich. Man müsse fortfahren, die Ursachen eines unmöglichen Kriegsfalles wegzuräumen und der beruhigenden Wirkung der Zeit vertrauen. Niemand kann die Verantwortung fuer den Ausbruch eines Kampfes übernehmen, der vielleicht nur der erste einer Reihe von Rassenkriege sein würde." Quoted in Ibid., p. 591.

52. Historians such as Josef Becker have come to the conclusion that Bismarck promoted the candidacy with the specific goal of achieving German unification by instigating a conflict with France. They believe that the process of German unifi-

cation was in a "Stagnationsphase" by 1870. Therefore, Bismarck needed a war against France lest the unification process fall through altogether. On the other hand, historians such as Jochen Dittrich have concluded that in promoting the candidacy, Bismarck sought nothing more than to weaken the position of Napoleon III, thus peacefully facilitating the unification process. Dittrich concludes that the candidacy was simply a "diplomatic weapon," a policy designed to avoid war with France. Otto Pflanze, ed., *The Unification of Germany* (New York, 1968), p. 85. In a similar vein, Rolf Wilhelm argues that the situation with regard to unification was far from desperate by 1870, and that Bismarck embarked upon the candidacy to "nudge the inevitable unification along." See Rolf Wilhelm, *Das Verhältnis der süddeutschen Staaten zum Norddeutschen Bund 1867–1870* (Husum, 1978).

53. Georges Bonnin, ed., *Bismarck and the Hohenzollern Candidature for the Spanish Throne: Documents in the German Diplomatic Archives* (London, 1957), p. 27.

54. Helmut Böhme, *The Foundation of the German Empire: Select Documents* (London, 1971), p. 206.

55. Initially, the crown prince and his wife were wary of supporting the Hohenzollern candidacy for the Spanish throne. Shortly after Frederick wrote to Queen Victoria on the subject, he asked Bismarck for more information on the matter. Crown Prince Frederick William to Count von Bismarck, 14 March 1870. Bonnin, *Bismarck and the Hohenzollern Candidature,* p. 76.

56. Crown Princess Victoria to Queen Victoria, 12 March 1870, George E. Buckle, ed., *The Letters of Queen Victoria. Second Series. A Selection from Her Majesty's Correspondence and Journal Between the Years 1862 and 1878* (London, 1926), p. 10.

57. Earl of Clarendon to Queen Victoria, 14 March 1870, George Buckle, *Letters of Queen Victoria,* p. 11.

58. Bonnin, *Bismarck and the Hohenzollern Candidature,* p. 294.

59. Ibid., p. 293. Major von Versen was sent to Spain by the king to counterbalance the optimistic reports on conditions in Spain that were relayed by Bismarck's envoy, Lothar Bucher. In the king's eyes, the mission backfired, since Versen became an ardent supporter of the candidacy. The crown prince agreed, for he wrote Leopold that Versen was "zu sanguinistisch" about the whole matter (Bonnin, p. 295). However, Martin Philippson, one of Frederick's biographers, wrote that the crown prince had no doubts about Versen's reports on conditions in Spain and that he supported the candidacy without knowing that Bismarck had ulterior motives in the project. Martin Philippson, *Das Leben Friedrichs III* (Wiesbaden, 1900), p. 219.

60. His preoccupation with Prussian prestige is also evident in his negative response to the possibility that the Spanish throne would be offered to a Bavarian prince in the event of Leopold's refusal. Frederick believed that a Bavarian prince would only increase the prestige of Bavaria at the expense of Prussia. Bonnin,

Bismarck and the Hohenzollern Candidature, p. 247.

61. Ibid.

62. Leopold's father, Prince Karl Anton, expressed his willingness to accept the Spanish offer only on the condition that the crown prince and Bismarck assume responsibility in the affair. The crown prince and Bismarck agreed to this condition, and on 31 May, Frederick wrote Leopold, urging him to accept. Karl Anton viewed this intervention by the crown prince and Bismarck as a substitute for the king's declaration that acceptance of the candidacy was in the interests of the Prussian state (Bonnin, p. 172). The king and Prince Leopold were reluctant abour the candidacy to the very end. Pflanze, *Bismarck,* Vol 1, p. 457.

63. Bonnin, *Bismarck and the Hohenzollern Candidature,* p. 172.

64. Apart from its defeat in the Luxembourg crisis, French prestige also suffered when Napoleon III sponsored the installation of the brother of the Austrian emperor, Grand Duke Maximilian, as emperor of Mexico. The new emperor was overthrown by the Mexicans and executed in 1867.

65. Bonnin, *Bismarck and the Hohenzollern Candidature,* p. 247.

66. Buckle, *Letters of Queen Victoria,* pp. 29–30.

67. Andreas Dorpalen, "Frederick III and the Liberal Movement," *American Historical Review* Vol. 54, No. 1 (1948), p. 19.

68. Ibid., p. 20.

69. A. R. Allinson, trans., *The War Diary of Frederick III* (London, 1957), p. vii. The originals of the war diary can be found at the Geheimes Staatsarchiv Preussischer Kulturbesitz, HA Rep. 52 (Nachlass Friedrichs III), FI Nr. 21: Redaktion B1 des Tagebuches Friedrichs III 1870–1871; HA Rep. 52 FI Nr. 22 Redaktion C des Tagebuches Friedrich III 1870–1871; HA Rep. 52, FI Nr. 23 Redaktion D des Tagebuches Friedrich III 1870–1871.

70. Allinson, *War Diary,* p. 1.

71. Otto Meisner, who originally edited Frederick's diaries in the 1920s, most likely did not have access to Victoria's personal correspondence. Hence, he had no way of knowing that Victoria had included her letters in the completed version of the diary that he prepared for publication. Heinrich Otto Meisner, *Kaiser Friedrich III. Kriegstagebuch 1870–1871* (Leipzig, 1926).

72. HH: Crown Princess Victoria to Crown Prince Frederick William. Portions of the following of Victoria's letters were added to her husband's diary: 26 September 1870 (matches Frederick's entry for 22 September); 27 December 1870 (matches Frederick's entry for 31 December); 10, 28, 29, 30 January 1871 (matches Frederick's entries for 29 December, 29 January, and 2 February); 1, 8 February 1871 (matches Frederick's entries for 8 February 1871); 2 March 1871 (matches Frederick's entry for 7 March 1871).

73. Ibid., p. 168.

74. HH: Crown Princess Victoria to Crown Prince Frederick William, 21 October, 1870. "Alice und ich schwärmen beide in gleicher Weise, (und ich seit meiner *Kindheit)* für den einigen Deutschen Kaiserstaat, der im wahren Sinn des Wortes

an der Spitze der Civilisation [sic] marshieren soll . . . Dieser Staat soll ein Bollwerk gegen den Socialismus [sic]—aber die Nation von dem Druck des Despotismus . . . befreien."

75. Allinson, *War Diary*, p. 241.

76. HH: Crown Princess Victoria to Crown Prince Frederick William, 27 December 1870: "Ich bleibe dabei, Deutschland hätte *einig, frei* und *mächtig* werden können, *ohne* Blut und Eisen, bloss indem es auf seinen guten Recht füssend moralische Eroberungen machte und Deutschland hätte einen anderen Präponderenz als die der Waffen gehabt . . . Der Gewalthätige kühne Junker [Bismarck] hat es aber nicht gewollt—1864 hat er *gegen* das deutsche Volk Schleswig-Holstein mit Österreich für Preussen erobert, 1866 hat er Österreich zerschlagen ohne Deutschland zu einigen."

77. Allinson, *War Diary,* p. 312, 23 February 1871.

78. See HH: Crown Princess Victoria to Crown Prince Frederick William, Berlin, 20 February 1871: "Mein *Traum* wäre, dass *alle* Schätze deutscher Bildung und seines Geistes dazu verwerthen solle, die Lösung der socialen [sic] Frage zu fördern: Frankreich kann es *nicht* denn es fehlt ihm den geistigen Grundlage dazu. England kann es nicht weil der Contrast [sic] zwischen Reich und Arm zu gross ist. In Deutschland aber, wo keine so grosse Vermögen existiren, ist das Feld dazu offen."

79. Kent, *Bismarck*, p. 74.

80. See Gustav Freytag, *The Crown Prince and the German Imperial Crown* (London, 1890), p. 21: "The objection that the South German kings would hardly be content with such an arrangement he [the crown prince] met by the assumption that the power to compel recalcitrants already existed." According to Pflanze, Bismarck ruled out the thought of coercing the south German states into joining the empire because "he was aware that the expansion of the north German system over so many millions of people could be successful only if approved. Coercion was not enough. To endure as the government of Germany, the Prussian system had to be based upon a moral consensus." Pflanze, *Bismarck, Vol 1*, pp. 486–487.

81. Dorpalen, "Frederick III," *AHR,* p. 21.

82. Kent, *Bismarck,* p. 75.

83. Bavaria retained control of its own army in peacetime and a postal system separate from the rest of the empire.

84. Allinson, *War Diary*, p. 239.

85. Ibid.

86. Ibid., p. 228. This quote matches Frederick's letter to his wife of 18 December 1870. See HH: Crown Prince Frederick William to Crown Princess Victoria, Versailles, 18 December 1870.

87. HH: Crown Princess Victoria to Crown Prince Frederick William, 10 January 1871.

88. HH: Crown Prince Frederick William to Crown Princess Victoria, 13 January 1871. This letter duplicates Frederick's diary entry for 29 December 1870. See Allinson, *War Diary*, pp. 237–238.

89. Frederick's admiration for the Holy Roman Empire was outdated as well. According to historian John Gagliardo, many influential Germans admired the Holy Roman Empire at the beginning of the nineteenth century "because it offered a unique alternative to the power state and because its balance between imperial and territorial levels of government precluded a use of force that could stifle the cultivation of the individualism so central to enlightened German ideals." See John Gagliardo, *Reich and Nation: The Holy Roman Empire as Idea and Reality 1763–1806.* (Bloomington, IN, 1980), p. 12.

90. HH: Crown Prince Frederick William to Crown Princess Victoria, 15 December 1870: When the king refused to wear robes worn by Holy Roman Emperors, Frederick wrote: "I will not dwell on this any more, since I can see how many oppose the idea, and [although] I have always dreamed of gracing the German people with a *restoration* of emperor and empire, I never considered a recreation [of the old empire]." Frederick also told his father that Prussia would do well to deprive the south German kings of their titles, since these titles did not have any connection with the Holy Roman Empire. Because their titles had been bestowed upon them by the foreign invader, Napoleon I, Prussia was now "compelled" to assert its supremacy over the south German kings. See Allinson, *War Diary*, pp. 142–143. Historian Erich Eyck condones Frederick's fixation on the Holy Roman Empire: "His [Frederick's] critics assert that he sought for himself alone the pomp and the splendour of the Imperial purple robe. That may be so. But it is only natural that he considered himself the representative of Germany's future, the more so as he knew perfectly well that his aged and old-fashioned father did not care in the least for anything that was outside the old Prussian tradition." Erich Eyck, *Bismarck and the German Empire* (London, 1968), pp. 175–176.

91. Ernst Feder, ed., *Bismarcks Grosses Spiel: Die Geheimen Tagebücher Ludwig Bambergers* (Frankfurt am Main, 1932), pp. 243–244.

92. Huber, *Verfassungsgeschichte,* p. 766 ff.

93. Pflanze, *Bismarck,* Vol. 1, p. 501

94. Ibid.

95. Allinson, *War Diary,* p. 287.

96. HH: Crown Princess Victoria to Crown Prince Frederick William, 29 January 1871: "Das *beste* Garantie für dauerende Frieden scheint mir eine Allianz zwischen Österreich und England-ein *resolutes* bekämpfen aller Catholischen [sic] Tendenzen, und ein *Arbeiten* an dem Einigungswerk Deutschlands. Äusserlich ist es eins aber in Wirklichkeit blühend Uneinigkeit, Partikularismus, Mistrauen, Eifersucht und Confusion [sic], die neue Verfassung begünstigt die Entwickelung dieser schlimmen Dinge—die Elemente der Schärfe sind."

97. Allinson, *War Diary*, pp. 213–214.

98. Pflanze, *Bismarck,* Vol 1, pp. 501–502.

99. HH: Crown Princess Victoria to Crown Prince Frederick William, 9 December 1870.

100. Ibid., 10 January 1871.

101. HH: Crown Prince Frederick William to Crown Princess Victoria, Versailles, 13 January 1871.

102. Allinson, *War Diary,* pp. 268–269, and HH: Crown Prince Frederick William to Crown Princess Victoria, 18 January 1871: This statement once again attests to Frederick's constitutional liberalism. By his lights, the creation of a unified Germany and the maintenance of that union were the work of the princes, not of the people. Indeed, he was disappointed when Bismarck rejected his idea to have the rulers of the separate German states sit in the upper house of the German parliament. Margarete von Poschinger, *The Life of the Emperor Frederick* (New York, 1971), p. 345.

103. HH: Crown Prince Frederick William to Crown Princess Victoria, 22 January 1871.

104. The proclamation of the empire took place against the backdrop of ongoing negotiations for peace with France, and Frederick soon found himself mediating a conflict between the Moltke and the king, on one hand, and Bismarck, on the other. When the French refused to accept a number of Prussia's peace terms, Moltke and William advocated renewed hostilities against France. This was opposed by both Frederick and Bismarck, who feared renewed hostilities would increase the likelihood of foreign intervention in France's favor. In the end, Bismarck overrode the king's point of view on the matter, and it was Bismarck alone who "conducted the crucial surrender negotiations with Jules Favre, the General Staff being called in only for subsequent consultations on whether the agreed terms were to be accepted or rejected." See Gerhard Ritter, *The Sword and the Scepter. The Problem of Militarism in Germany* 2 Vols. (Coral Gables, FL, 1969), Vol. 1, p. 223.

105. Frederick's biographers claim that his lack of political activity after unification was involuntary. In her biography of Frederick, Margarete von Poschinger writes that the crown prince was "prevented by circumstances from having any active part in political affairs." Poschinger, *Emperor Frederick,* p. 355. Other biographers have made attempts to elucidate these "circumstances." Martin Philippson claims that the kaiser was primarily responsible for his son's political inactivity. "The kaiser abided faithfully by the dictates of the divine right of kingship, which dictated that he and he alone was to be the sole vessel of political authority. This being the case, he was not about to risk jeopardizing the welfare of his country by granting political authority to his liberal-minded son who did not share his political outlook." Philippson adds that Frederick's exclusion from affairs of state pleased Bismarck, since this meant that his influence over the emperor was not rivalled. Philippson, *Kaiser Friedrich III,* p. 288. Werner Richter supports this argument, noting that the crown prince's "hands were tied by the emperor and Bismarck." Richter, *Friedrich III*, pp. 239 ff.

106. HH: Crown Prince Frederick William to Crown Princess Victoria, 8 March 1871.

107. HH: Crown Princess Victoria to Crown Prince Frederick William, 6 January 1871.

Chapter 5

From Optimism to
Disillusionment, 1871–1879

Although his position was just as difficult in the new empire as it was before, the early 1870s were happy years for Frederick William. He was a popular war hero and earned praise even from a French journalist who wrote: "The Crown Prince has left the memory of countless traits of kindness and humanity in the land that he fought against. . . . He and his subordinates showed esteem for the unfortunate defeated enemy, and paid a tribute of respect to their bravery."[1] The London *Times* heralded Frederick's visit to England in July 1871 with the following tribute:

The Prince has won as much honour for his gentleness as for his prowess in the war. . . . He comes among us, the hero of military exploits unsurpassed, if equalled, in the world's history. . . . The Prince is known to have been the consistent friend in Prussia of all mild and liberal administration, so far as was consistent with the paramount objects which his father had in view. He has gathered around him by tendency the general confidence of his future subjects, and the fact that he is the heir to the resuscitated throne is one of the most reassuring circumstances in the prospects of the Empire. His influence in any position has been exerted, and will, we believe, be exerted, in behalf of a peaceful and unaggressive policy.[2]

After suffering criticism from both sides of the political spectrum in the wake of his Danzig speech and his opposition to the war of 1866, such praise was a tonic for the crown prince. During a tour of Swabia in August 1872, Frederick happily noted to his wife: "Massive crowds of people greeted me at every stop on the tour. At every station, I was asked to hear speeches that were not only patriotic, but very flattering to me personally. I wish that you could have been with me to experience the wonderful impact which the achievement of emperor and empire has had on the people of Swabia."[3]

Such approbation made the crown prince look forward to his reign, which appeared imminent in view of his father's advanced age and precarious health.[4] His enthusiasm about his coming reign was also based on his belief that he would be allowed to rule according to his liberal principles. As he told his wife, "You and I will have to do the [imperial] title justice in a contemporary, progressive fashion, while Papa will enjoy the honor emanating from the title during the twilight of his life."[5]

Frederick had good reason to be optimistic, for the new empire was ruled according to liberal dictates during the first years of its existence. The first several years of the empire's existence were, indeed, known as the "liberal era." The National Liberals were the majority party in the Reichstag, and Bismarck relied heavily on their support to consolidate the empire against the forces of particularism.[6] The Prussian cabinet included three liberal ministers, and the economic prosperity that the new German empire enjoyed during the first few years of its existence was accredited to the liberal policy of free trade.[7]

Indeed, German liberalism was a confident movement in the wake of unification. Despite the defeats that liberals had suffered during the constitutional conflict, they relished the successes they had achieved during the late 1860s and early 1870s. Constitutionalism had been preserved, unification had been achieved, and liberal agitation in favor of measures to consolidate unification bore fruit: the early 1870s saw the establishment of a national bank, the creation of national offices, and a national press law. Further, given the advanced age of the emperor and the precarious health of his chancellor, liberals felt that they would soon see the day when "politicians of ordinary dimensions" would lead the liberal state.[8]

Liberals regarded these political victories as but a prelude to further liberal reforms[9] but were once again divided on the question as to whether they should include increasing the powers of parliament. Frederick, along with liberals such as Heinrich von Treitschke, Heinrich von Sybel, and Rudolf Haym, regarded the foundation of the Reich as the fulfillment of the liberal program, and questioned the desirability of transferring English institutions to Germany.[10] Other National Liberals and Progressives, on the other hand, hoped that the future course of liberal reform would see the establishment of a government responsible to parliament that would control the budget of the military, the strongest support of the monarchy.[11]

The crown prince was not disturbed by the divisions in the liberal ranks; Bismarck's attitude toward the future appeared to be more important. On this score, he had good reason to believe that Bismarck looked forward to the coming reign. This impression was not lost on the British ambassador to Germany, Odo Russell, who made the following report to British foreign secretary Granville in 1873:

Prince Bismarck ... went on to repeat his grievance against his Imperial Master for resisting the introduction of a system of administration under a responsible Premier, which he [Bismarck] considered the best method of developing the political education of the Germans, and teaching them the art of self-government. If, however, he should have the misfortune of outliving William I, he foresaw no difficulty in persuading the Crown Prince to follow the good example of England, which His Imperial Highness understood and appreciated as the best for Germany.[12]

Russell also quoted Bismarck as saying that "the Emperor was too much of a particularist and stood in the way of the administrative unification of Germany." Russell added that Bismarck was "only awaiting His Majesty's death to destroy particularism at a blow," and that Bismarck's intentions were fully supported by the crown prince.[13]

In the meantime, Frederick supported efforts undertaken by Bismarck and the liberal majority to combat particularist forces in the empire. The most controversial aspect of this policy was the campaign conducted by Bismarck and the liberal majority against the Roman Catholic Church in Germany. Bismarck and the liberals suspected that German Catholics owed more allegiance to Rome than to the government of the empire, and they therefore wished to temper the power of an institution perceived to be an antinational and potentially disruptive force in the new empire. Their hostility toward Catholics increased after the founding of the Catholic Center Party in Prussia in 1870. Within the space of only one year, the Center Party had amassed enough support to become the second largest party in the Reichstag.[14]

Bismarck and the liberal parties viewed the growing strength of political Catholicism with alarm. Bismarck thought that German Catholics, supported by their counterparts in Austria and France, could compromise the unity of the empire. His feelings seemed confirmed by France's animosity toward Germany and by the fact that the Center Party was most popular in areas that had not acceded willingly to unity with Germany.[15] The liberals also opposed the Roman Catholic church since it propounded a philosophy that placed restraints upon the freedom of the individual.[16] The liberals dubbed the struggle against the Catholic Church the Kulturkampf, or the struggle between modernity and medievalism.

During the early 1870s, Bismarck and the liberals passed measures designed to combat what they regarded as the Catholic threat. The Catholic section of the Prussian ministry of ecclesiastical affairs (the Kultus-Ministerium) was dissolved following the accusation that ministry officials supported particularist interests of Poles and Catholics. In March 1872, the liberals achieved an important victory in the field of secular education when a law was passed eliminating ecclesiastical supervision in schools. Several months later, the antiliberal Jesuit order was disbanded. The Kulturkampf reached its zenith in May 1873, when Adalbert Falk, the minister of education and ecclesiastical affairs, passed a body of anti-Catholic laws for Prussia, known as the May-Laws, which placed restrictions upon the training and employment of priests, limited the disciplinary powers of the church, and made civil marriage obligatory. By supporting these measures, the liberals hoped to root out the federalist and particularist tendencies of the Center Party. More important, "they also believed that their support of the Kulturkampf would ultimately increase the power of the Reichstag against Bismarck's semi-autocratic policies in other fields."[17]

The crown prince supported these measures, for he had long been an advocate of the liberal ideal of a secular state. In fact, the Kulturkampf saw the realization of many ideas that Frederick himself had proposed earlier to control Catholic influence in Germany.[18] During the 1860s, he tried to make his father and Bismarck wary of what he regarded as Rome's attempts to overextend its clerical authority in Germany,[19] and he supported the dissolution of the Catholic section of the Prussian ministry of culture as early as 1865.[20] In 1869, the crown prince asked minister of justice Friedberg to pursue his plan to grant the German Catholic church a status similar to that of the Hungarian Catholic church, which had looser ties with Rome.[21] This plan resembled Bismarck's goal in the struggle, which was to bring the German Catholic Church under state control, so that it would serve as a unifying, as opposed to a divisive, force in the empire. So closely did Kulturkampf legislation resemble Frederick's goals that the British ambassador to Germany, Odo Russell, suspected Bismarck's support of the campaign was part of a larger plan to make himself indispensable to the future emperor.[22]

In April 1873, Stosch wrote the crown prince that the struggle against the Catholics had gone too far: "Up to now the conflict has served state interests. I therefore believe that we should content ourselves with that, for we shall not obtain a positive success. The struggle remains theoretical and embitters minds. Both state and religion are harmed. I would make peace and sacrifice Falk."[23] By the late 1870s many protagonists of the Kulturkampf, including Bismarck, had come to the same conclusion, for it was patently obvious that the struggle had failed: German Catholics' hostility to the government only increased, as did the power of the Center Party in the Reichstag. Some liberals also turned against the struggle on the grounds that the discriminatory nature of Kulturkampf legislation undeniably went against the liberal philosophy of individual liberty.[24]

Frederick, however, along with a majority of liberals, suffered no such pangs of conscience. He told liberal leader Bamberger that the deputies to the Reichstag from the Center Party were not Germans but "aliens," whose influence was intolerable.[25] Although the crown prince described some of the discriminatory legislation of the Kulturkampf as "lamentable," he concluded: "since the struggle has been undertaken, we must see it through."[26] He did not believe that the Kulturkampf was turning German Catholics against the monarchy: a few months after the controversial May laws were passed, he told his wife that he had received a rousing reception in the heavily Catholic hinterland of Ulm, where even the Catholic priests gave him a warm welcome.[27] In late 1873, Stosch commented that a continuation of the Kulturkampf would be inevitable during Frederick's coming reign.[28]

Frederick's support of Bismarck's policies during the early 1870s left little room for doubt that the chancellor would be retained after the kaiser's death. When the crown prince fell seriously ill with an intestinal inflammation in 1872, the *Rheinische Courier* reported that the crown prince wished the following message relayed to his wife: "The physicians say my illness is dangerous. . . . My father is old, Prince

William is still a minor, and it is therefore not unlikely that you may be called upon to act as Regent for a time. You must promise me to do nothing without Prince Bismarck, whose counsels have raised our House to un-dreamed of power and greatness."[29] Although no such statement appears in Frederick's letters to his wife during his illness, the sentiment expressed in the statement rang true.

Many liberals, however, were displeased with the rapprochement between the chancellor and the crown prince since they feared that Bismarck was exaggerating the threat of particularism in order to increase his own powers as chancellor. As Karl von Normann, chamberlain to the crown prince, explained to Gustav Freytag:

He [the crown prince] appreciates the importance of the progressive development of German affairs. But he is far too inclined to believe in rumors of German particularism in places where it does not exist, and a clever . . . minister who is aware of the weaknesses and preferences of his master would have little difficulty in misleading him onto a dangerous new course. The only thing that will protect him [the crown prince] is not so much his knowledge of this situation but his prevailing and possibly instinctive mistrust of the Chancellor.[30]

As we have seen, Frederick's "prevailing mistrust of the Chancellor" was nurtured by Victoria, who was far more reserved in her approval of Bismarck's policies than her husband.[31] But by the late 1870s even she had come to the conclusion that Bismarck's services would be indispensable during her husband's coming reign because she supported his foreign policy. As she told her mother:

You know I look upon him [Bismarck] as a misfortune for Germany and for the development of liberties, our trade, etc., and certainly a danger for the Crown but I cannot shut my eyes to the fact that he is entirely for England, and that England's power should on all occasions rise superior to Russia's. . . . I hardly think we have one statesman in Germany half as anxious to be well with England as Bismarck. . . . This you may rely upon as being the truth.[32]

Victoria also blamed the British government, not Bismarck, for stifling negotiations toward a possible alliance between Germany and England.[33] More important, she did not appear to believe that Bismarck would stand in the way of liberal reforms when she and her husband came to the throne. On 1 October 1876, she wrote her husband:

The war *united* all the German states in defense against the enemy; they were inspired solely by the *power* of Prussia—*you* were lucky enough to be responsible for one victory after another. The fruit of these efforts was the creation of a unified entity under the leadership of Prussia and the elevation of its king to leadership over the entire empire. The responsibility for elevating the new creation to serve as an example of *culture,* freedom, and peace, of progress in every field so that [Germany] will fulfill its mission in Europe and the world lies with the *German people* [and] with the prince who will lead them and that is *you*.[34]

However, in his reply to this letter it was clear that Frederick did not share his wife's optimism. He wrote, "it has become clear to me that our mission will be a very difficult one. . . . But with you at my side I am sure that we will succeed."[35]

Frederick's doubts may well have stemmed from Stosch's prediction that Bismarck was planning to abandon his alliance with the National Liberals in order to make peace with the Center Party and the conservatives.[36] Such a step would make the royal couple's quest for a continuation of reforms pursued in the "liberal era" difficult, if not impossible.

By the late 1870s, there was good reason to believe that Stosch's prediction was correct. Bismarck had several reasons for abandoning his alliance with the National Liberals. First, the chancellor's relations with the liberal majority were not always harmonious during the liberal era: the liberals opposed his military budget[37] and his plan to use discriminatory legislation to curb the growth of the socialist movement. Liberals also refused to approve a number of economic measures proposed by the chancellor for fear that they would reduce Reichstag control over the empire's finances. Finally, Bismarck was disturbed by left liberals' demands for constitutional changes.[38] These struggles made it clear to the chancellor that it would be impossible for him to convert the liberal majority into a an obedient pro-government party, as he had originally hoped.

Bismarck's growing disillusionment with the National Liberals must also be seen against the backdrop of serious economic problems in the new empire. In 1873, the economic boom that the empire enjoyed during the first years of the decade ended. The ensuing economic depression made it difficult for the German states to make their annual contributions (Matrikularbeiträge), which, in turn, deprived the empire of a major means of financial support. The depression also created a budget deficit and strained textile and iron industries.[39]

This situation made Bismarck eager to find a way of solving the Reich's financial difficulties. One way to do this, he believed, would be to heed the demands of industrialists and businessmen and create a system of protective tariffs and state monopolies to alleviate the effects of the depression.[40] Such a program required assent from the Reichstag, but Bismarck could hardly expect enough support from liberal parties to ensure passage of such an economic program. The liberals were divided on the issue of protectionism,[41] and were uniformly opposed to any measures—such as state monopolies—that would reduce the Reichstag's budgetary powers. Given his differences with the liberals on political and economic issues, Bismarck was determined to construct a new conservative parliamentary majority.

The motive for Bismarck's creation of a conservative parliamentary majority has been subject for historical debate. Some historians argue that Bismarck intended to refound the empire on a conservative basis, and crush liberalism once and for all,[42] whereas others see that Bismarck's conservative legislation was a pragmatic response to the crisis facing the empire.[43] But neither of these explanations takes into account the possibility that Bismarck's shift was motivated by his wish to stay in power after the accession of the crown prince. Bismarck suspected that he could lose his job if the crown prince came to the throne while the chancellor was at loggerheads with the liberal majority in the Reichstag, for he knew that Frederick would be most likely to appoint a chancellor who had the backing of the majority in the Reichstag. This scenario may have compelled Bismarck to put together a conservative parliamentary coalition that would support him, so that the next emperor would have little choice but to retain the chancellor.

Bismarck's willingness to abandon his alliance with the liberal majority was evident in February 1878, when he delivered a speech announcing the introduction of protective tariffs and an imperial tobacco monopoly. The speech constituted a challenge to the liberals' budgetary powers as well as their free trade policy and was accompanied by the resignation of minister of commerce Camphausen, who rejected Bismarck's abandonment of free trade.[44]

As defenders of the Reichstag's budgetary powers and free trade, the crown prince and princess viewed this turn of events with dismay. They knew that a debate to secure passage of protectionist legislation would most likely split the liberal parties in the Reichstag, which, in turn, would allow a resurgence of conservative parties. In other words, as they saw it, passage of tariffs would reverse many of the gains liberals had made during the early years of the decade. Further, protectionism would also alienate German economic policy from that of England and most likely decrease the chance that the two could form the alliance that the royal couple had always dreamed about. Victoria's sense of alarm about the declining fortunes of the liberal majority was evident after an attempt was made on the life of the emperor by an alleged socialist in May 1878. She assumed the worst, namely, that the government was going to use the assassination attempt as a pretext to enact reactionary legislation. She wrote her husband, "Your . . . letters have confirmed my fear that the reactionary movement is gaining the upper hand in Berlin!"[45]

Victoria's alarm was not unfounded. Although Bismarck believed that antisocialist legislation was necessary to protect Germany from a dangerous movement, he also wished to use it to divide the liberal majority in the Reichstag.[46] But liberal parties did not split over the issue. They agreed that Bismarck's antisocialist bill violated the principle of equality before the law, and, to Bismarck's dismay, it was defeated in the Reichstag by a large margin.

Bismarck's humiliation over the defeat of the bill did not last long. On 2 June 1878, another attempt was made on the life of the kaiser. This time the emperor was seriously wounded and was unable to resume his duties for several months. As before, the gunman was an alleged socialist, and the event gave Bismarck a golden opportunity to proceed with his plans against the liberals. He dissolved the Reichstag, and during the election campaign that followed, the government press blamed Social Democrats and their alleged left liberal allies for the assassination attempts.[47] The election results showed that voters agreed with this propaganda: the conservatives made gains at the expense of the liberal parties; National Liberal representation declined from 127 to 99 seats, and the Progressives lost 9 seats, while the Conservatives and Free Conservatives each gained 19 seats.[48] Further, there was a shift within National Liberal representation toward the right: many of the newly elected deputies represented heavy industry and agriculture and hence favored protectionism.

When the antisocialist bill came up for debate in the Reichstag for the second time in the fall of 1878, it was rejected by the Progressive and Center parties, but support from the Conservatives, Free Conservatives, and National Liberals ensured its passage. The antisocialist law upset its liberal opponents since it clearly violated liberal principles of equality before the law and freedom of assembly: the Social Democratic Party was outlawed, party assemblies and meetings were forbidden, and socialists deemed guilty of breaking the law were driven into exile.

Some of the National Liberals who reversed their previous opposition to the law appear to have been convinced by Bismarck's argument that the law was necessary to suppress a movement that posed a threat to public order. The crown prince, who signed the bill into law while serving as regent during his father's convalescence, shared this view. As he wrote to his friend and distant relative King Carol of Rumania, "We can only hope that the law against the Social Democrats will be a tool with which we can defeat this evil [socialism]. It will take a lot of effort on our part to get rid of this unhealthy movement, which has recently gained such popularity."[49] This statement shows that unlike his wife, the crown prince did not see the antisocialist law as part of the growing reactionary trend in German politics.

Although Frederick and Bismarck supported the antisocialist law, the relationship between the two was strained during the regency. After the kaiser was wounded, he stipulated that his son could only represent him—this meant that Frederick would be allowed to rule only according to his father's principles, as opposed to his own. When the crown prince summoned Bismarck to discuss the form that his representative functions were to take, the chancellor immediately presented a document (Stellvertreter Urkunde) that denied Frederick a decisive role in important matters of state, even as his father's deputy. Frederick was indignant because this document made it clear that his decisions would be either ignored or subject to approval of the Chancellor. The meeting degenerated into a shouting match, but as Bismarck prepared to leave the room in disgust, Frederick said, "If nothing more, I am the delegated representative of my father and I therefore demand of you a report concerning the status of the affairs of state!"[50] Although Bismarck complied grudgingly with this wish, Frederick sensed that Bismarck was determined to ignore his opinions on domestic and foreign policy for the duration of the regency.

Frederick's prediction was correct. When a congress of the great powers met in Berlin to revise the harsh peace imposed by the Russians on the Turks after the war of 1877–1878, Frederick served only as the dinner host to the plenipotentiaries. Although there is no record as to how Frederick felt about the outcome of the congress, it is safe to assume that he approved of the limitation of Russian gains. When the emperor later blamed his son and not Bismarck for Russia's humiliation at the congress, Frederick denied his father's charge by insisting that the Chancellor did not consult him about such matters.[51] As he wrote King Carol of Rumania: "You can imagine that I thought a lot about you during the congress and during the difficult time when the separation of Bessarabia [from Rumania] was being negotiated. But I purposely wrote you nothing about this since I did not know how to express myself about the issue."[52]

Nor did Bismarck deem it necessary to provide the crown prince with an explanation as to why he was turning away from the liberals. When Frederick asked to meet with the chancellor to discuss the abrupt changes in his domestic policy, the chancellor replied that he was "too busy" to comply with his wishes. Frederick noted sarcastically, "Of course, if three Ministers are dispensed at one blow, and a compromise effected with the Center Party in order to raise the price of food to produce protective tariffs and pursue a reactionary policy in Church and State so that the Crown Prince will one day have difficulty in ruling, then possibly there may be little time for anything else."[53]

If Frederick expected sympathy from his father because of Bismarck's high-handedness, none was forthcoming. As he told his wife, "Papa's behavior toward me hasn't changed a bit. He was criticizing everything and ordering people around at the maneuvers as if it were he who was in charge. . . . This is all fine and good for a couple of days, but for no more than that; we just cannot be at the same place at the same time as long as I am in charge of things."[54] He showed his ambivalence toward his regency when he wrote Carol of Rumania: "It isn't easy to bear all the burdens of the monarchy without being able to . . . carry out my duties to the best of my ability."[55]

While it is perfectly understandable that Frederick had mixed feelings about his "promotion" to the position of "deputy to the emperor," it is surprising that he did no more than complain about Bismarck's limitation of his political responsibilities. However, Victoria's attitude toward the regency sheds light on her husband's lack of resistance. Surprisingly, the crown princess viewed the check on her husband's powers as a good thing. Because of the political unrest that characterized the weeks immediately following the two assassination attempts, she knew that repressive measures would have to be undertaken to restore order. Since such measures were bound to be unpopular, Victoria felt that they should not be her husband's responsibility.[56] In other words, it was better to have it known that Frederick had no power to oppose the conservative policies enacted during his regency.[57]

Shortly after the emperor resumed his duties, Frederick learned that Bismarck was willing to go so far as to remove him from Berlin to prevent him from interfering with his new conservative program.[58] In early 1879, Bismarck renewed an offer to make the crown prince the governor (Statthalter) of Alsace-Lorraine through Prussian minister of justice Friedberg.[59] According to Friedberg, Bismarck wished to provide the crown prince with some useful activity. He added that it was almost "scandalous" that the emperor could "ignore his capable son who had proven his ability to rule" during his tenure as regent. The crown prince was quick to see through Bismarck's flattery and was astonished that Bismarck had even dared renew the offer. As he told his wife, his tenure as regent had confirmed the extent to which the chancellor controlled not only the affairs of the empire but the emperor as well. From this he came to the conclusion that many of his decisions as Statthalter would be subject to Bismarck's approval. Informing his wife that he was refusing the offer, he added, "This [refusal] should show him once and for all that I will never see fit to be subordinated by him or dependent on him."[60]

Frederick was more than simply insulted by Bismarck's renewal of the Statthalter offer: he had been informed through reliable sources that Bismarck wished to get the crown prince out of Berlin so that he could proceed more smoothly with the implementation of his conservative policies. Frederick and his wife had suspected this during the previous year, but the fact that Bismarck's renewal of the offer coincided with a heightening of his protectionist campaign only served to confirm their suspicions.[61]

It is more than likely that Frederick's suspicions concerning Bismarck's motives were correct. Although Bismarck was ready to relinquish some of his own responsibilities in Alsace-Lorraine as of 1878, it was still within his power to reconsider decisions made by the Statthalter "if they endangered national security in any way."[62] This being the case, Frederick could hardly have declared his independence from Bismarck by accepting the Statthalter offer. More important, had the crown prince accepted the offer, he would have filled many of the posts in the administration of the imperial province with his liberal friends, thereby further undercutting liberal opposition to protectionism in Berlin. As it turned out, Bismarck was, indeed, later to use Alsace-Lorraine as a "dumping ground" for liberal-minded economic bureaucrats whose services were no longer desired in Berlin.[63]

The worst fears of the crown prince and princess concerning the abandonment of free trade were confirmed in January 1879 when the chancellor announced that he would seek tariffs on iron and grain. Yet even after he tried to split the National Liberal Party with the antisocialist law, the party remained intact and was bound to reject his measures. Consequently, Bismarck turned to the pro-protectionist Center Party for the support that he needed. In late March, he met with Center Party leader Windthorst. Bismarck intimated that he would be willing to sacrifice some of the Kulturkampf legislation in exchange for support from the Center for his economic program. No agreements were made, and in the course of the months that followed, a good deal of negotiating was required on both sides before a compromise could be reached.[64]

The royal couple resented Bismarck's attempted accommodation with the Center Party. Victoria wrote her husband: "Is it even possible that Bismarck would give in to Hanoverian demands because he wishes to reach an agreement with the Center Party? He can do anything if he puts his mind to it, and all objections to his plans will come to naught. The means always justify the ends . . . dishonesty and betrayal are at the root of all of his policies!"[65] Frederick agreed with his wife: "Can you believe that Windthorst was present at Bismarck's soiree? One hardly knows any more what to make of the methods he uses to obtain party loyalties! Bismarck will go along with Windthorst, Lasalle and anyone else if it serves his purposes, but no one is aware how high the price for such friendships will be"[66]

Victoria hoped that opposition from liberal parties to the proposed protection- ist legislation would thwart Bismarck's plans. She noted, "As long as I can remem- ber it has always seemed to me that free trade should be the only policy of a good national economy; [it is] the only way that nations can get to understand each other, get closer and united as one. . . . Adam Smith, Cobden, Michel Chevalier have always been my heroes."[67] Victoria also believed that the growing trend toward protectionism not only in Germany but also in Britain and France was the work of "ignorant individuals such as communists and conservatives." In Victoria's mind, "true liberals" invariably and without exception supported free trade, and she accused those National Liberals who supported tariffs as a means to prop their economic interests of "betraying" the liberal cause.[68]

The efforts of Victoria's "true liberals" failed to save the policy of free trade. When the Reichstag convened in the spring of 1879, the abandonment of free trade was a foregone conclusion. The passage of tariffs had a particularly damag- ing effect on the liberals, for it showed that economic interests had gained influ- ence in the political decision-making process. According to historian Dieter Langewiesche, "This victory of economic interests in turn undermined the liberal ideal of the nation state as a guarantee of political, economic, social and cultural progress. With the spread of interest politics, political liberalism was no longer seen as a necessary ingredient of economic progress."[69] To make matters worse, Bismarck accepted a Centrist proposal on allotment of revenues gained from the new tariffs, making it clear that the chancellor no longer had use for the National Liberals.[70]

These developments depressed the royal couple, and Victoria repeatedly pressed her husband to state publicly his opposition to the new policies. But Frederick refused, arguing that his input would do no good since the political scene was in a state of upheaval and confusion. He added that there was nothing he could do to even attempt to reverse the political trend until he came to the throne. Frederick tried to compensate for his lack of activity by assuring his wife that she would be granted a great deal of political influence during his coming reign: "wait a bit longer until you obtain a higher position than your present one! Then all of your knowledge, talent and all of your abilities and experience will be acknowledged, and all of your critics will be silenced."[71] Frederick also told his wife that she would play a prominent role in re-instituting free trade when he came to the throne.

Unlike the crown prince, Max von Forckenbeck, the National Liberal president of the Reichstag, chose to act. On 18 May he protested against Bismarck's new policies at a banquet for members of the Berlin municipal diet. Two days later, he resigned from his post as president of the Reichstag to create a new liberal party that would fight against Bismarck's measures. Several days later, the liberal vice-president of the Reichstag, Franz von Stauffenberg, followed suit. Forckenbeck and Stauffenberg's daring gestures did not, however, benefit the liberal cause: their posts were assumed by a Conservative and a member of the Center party, respectively.[72]

One would think that Frederick would have viewed the creation of a new liberal party as an omen of hope and that he would have supported it in some way. Instead, he told his wife that Forckenbeck's party was doomed to failure. Recent events, he said, had convinced him that his hopes for a liberal Germany had been shattered by Bismarck, whose triumphs had succeeded in chipping away the strength of German liberalism. The masses, he believed, had been so dazzled by Bismarck's successes that they no longer saw the need to oppose him. Under these conditions, Frederick failed to see how he, as emperor, could dismantle the political machinery that Bismarck had put into place, because all those capable of challenging the chancellor had come under his spell: "Think back to the times when you and I considered who should fill the ministerial posts during my reign! Look at what we have now! The graduates of schools of civil service are used up, drained and thrown out like old lemons—they mimic Bismarck's gestures and inflate themselves with false pride."[73] The crown prince begged his wife's forgiveness for painting such a bleak picture and hoped that Forckenbeck's efforts would prove him wrong, but the day-to-day progression of political events only increased his sense of resignation. His response to the election of Baron von Franckenstein, whom he called a "zealot from the Center Party" to the position of Reichstag vice president was so negative that he told his wife the best thing to do was to remove his family to a remote corner of the world so that they all could be shielded from the political chaos in Berlin.[74]

Although the crown princess certainly shared her husband's fears, she refused to give up all hope. She tried to assure him that their future was not necessarily doomed by recent political events. She wrote: "I never get discouraged; I only try to understand events for what they are, and try to see through them as well as the men who make them. In this way one has nothing to fear."[75] Unlike her husband, she clung to the hope that Bismarck's deeds could be undone and that there were many capable men available who had not been "spoiled" by his influence.

Victoria's rather optimistic attitude failed to relieve her husband's depression. He said that he was past the prime of his life and prophetically assumed that his reign would be brief: "I am comforted by the hope that after a Bismarckian regime, with the little time on this earth that we may have left (this applies to me more than you), it will be possible to rule according to different methods."[76] But this brief glimmer of hope was overshadowed by Frederick's statement that recent events deprived him of any ability to look forward to his reign. He told his wife that when he came to the throne, he would do his best to rule according to his principles, but he would do so without enthusiasm. He added that his experiences as regent had given him little encouragement to look forward to the road that lay ahead. Frederick concluded these observations with the alarming declaration that he considered himself henceforth retired from political life.[77]

Victoria was no doubt shocked by this declaration. She had no interest in seeing her husband "retire" from political life. While she was willing to accept the fact that her husband did not look forward to his reign, she did what she could to rouse a willingness on his part to challenge Bismarck. She encouraged him to retain his liberal political contacts and keep looking for ways to turn the political tide when he came to the throne.[78]

Several months after Frederick's "retirement," new developments in German foreign policy gave the royal couple hope that the political tide could be turned after all. In the fall of 1879, Bismarck perceived the need for a decisive shift in German foreign policy because of the deterioration in Russo-German relations since the Congress of Berlin. The Russians believed that Germany had been responsible for their losses at the congress. The tsar felt that the Congress of Berlin had been "a European coalition against Russia under the leadership of Prince Bismarck, whose aim had been to secure all possible advantages for Austria."[79] After the congress, the Russian press vented its frustration at Germany and suggested that Russian interests would be best served through an alliance with France. Bismarck knew too well that Germany could not afford to be surrounded by hostile neighbors, and by the spring of 1879, he also realized that he could not afford to antagonize the other great powers, especially England and Austria. Bismarck's reply to Russian hostility was a defensive alliance with Austria against attack by Russia (or a power supported by Russia). The chancellor was interested in attracting Britain as an alliance partner.[80]

The emperor, however, was opposed to the chancellor's plans. William was committed to maintaining good relations with Russia, which, he feared, would be destroyed by an Austro-German alliance. Bismarck therefore asked the crown prince to help him convince the emperor of the desirability of the alliance.

Frederick was more than happy to cooperate with the chancellor, since he and his wife felt that the alliance could turn the conservative political tide and breathe new life into German liberalism. In their minds, Bismarck's proposed alliance was the first step toward the creation of an anti-Russian coalition that would isolate Russia and compromise conservative pro-Russian influence in the Prussian government, and the alliance with England would make Germany more open to British political influence. As Victoria told her husband:

The Russians seem to understand nothing but murder, theft, and duplicity, and display nothing but all the wicked spirits of the underworld. They are champions in the art of lies and intrigues . . .if Germany truly allies with Austria, England, France and Italy, I fail to see how world peace can ever be disturbed. Such a union will bring great advantages and blessings to all of its members and commercial differences will disappear and it will signify the return of the trust [between nations] which is currently non-existent.[81]

When Victoria noted that the alliances under discussion would "cause all commercial differences to disappear," she meant that the coalition would naturally accept Britain's lead in the formulation of its economic policies, and the policy of free trade would thereby be restored not only in Germany but also in the rest of Europe. In the long run, the alliance held out the possibility of reversing Bismarck's economic policies, which would, in turn, restore liberal influence in Germany.

According to Frederick's report on the negotiations for the Austro-German alliance entitled, "The Political Situation of 1879," Bismarck led the crown prince to believe from the onset that the proposed Austro-German alliance would include England.[82] More important, he believed that such a combination was not only possible but imminent. Despite the fact that Bismarck was having tremendous difficulty in convincing the emperor of the necessity of the Austro-German alliance, the crown prince wrote his wife: "There is really reason to trust in the possibility that the g[rea]t powers together with your native land [England] could join to oppose the pretensions of Russia. Should this be realized, then certainly R[ussia] must remain quiet."[83]

Frederick's optimism did not wane even after his father, who bitterly opposed the alliance, met with the tsar at Alexandrovno. On 14 September, he wrote his wife in halting English, indicating his appreciation of the secrecy of the negotiations:

I think that there is every reason to expect that what is reasonable for the empire's welfare together with that of other western g[rea]t powers will be gained against Russia. I tried to do my best in proposing measures, [but] could not satisfy both parties without interfering directly and I believe that the result will be a good one. You must permit me to write in such strange terms because I am to [sic] anxious to tell anything of importance to the post.[84]

Frederick became directly involved in alliance negotiations when he learned that Bismarck did not wish to confront the emperor personally on the issue. Instead, Bismarck sent Count Stolberg (the vice-president of the Prussian ministry of state) to argue the merits of the alliance in his place. Frederick could not comprehend why Bismarck chose not to meet with the emperor during such a critical time: "The Chancellor finds it much more to his liking to send a young and inexperienced man who is in awe of the emperor to do battle with him at a time when the most important issue involving the future of the Reich is at stake! This incident clearly illustrates the quality of management here, and also the type of behavior that Bismarck is able to extract from his men!"[85] Frederick also told his wife: "the great man prefers to avoid exciting discussions, and all is done by correspondence."[86] The crown prince was incensed enough by what he considered to be Bismarck's "carelessness" to ask the emperor if he could be present at the conference with Stolberg. The emperor agreed, albeit grudgingly.

The crown prince and Count Stolberg certainly had their share of "exciting discussions" with the emperor. He stubbornly refused to see anything good about the Austro-German alliance and maintained that it would do irreparable damage to Russo-German relations. Stolberg countered that Saburov, the Russian ambassador to Constantinople, saw no harm in the alliance at all.

Frederick must have been surprised to discover that "secret" negotiations for an alliance that he perceived to be a stepping-stone toward formation of an anti-Russian coalition had been leaked to—of all people—the Russians. Evidently, Frederick did not know that throughout the course of negotiations for the dual alliance, Bismarck held out hope for reconciliation with Russia and saw to it that the Russians learned about the alliance before the treaty was signed. Frederick also did not realize that Bismarck was prepared to expand the alliance to include England only in the event that the Russians maintained their bellicose attitude toward Germany after learning about the Austro-German alliance.[87] But the reaction of the Russian leaders was just what Bismarck hoped it would be. They realized that an alliance of the two central European powers that could also include Britain was a dangerous prospect, and that their anti-German attitude since the Congress of Berlin had been pointless. They were therefore ready to appeal to Bismarck for a renewal of the Three Emperors' League.

On 2 October, Bismarck telegraphed the emperor clarifying Saburov's position. According to Saburov, Russia still considered itself part of the Three Emperor's League and believed that its long-term foreign policy interests would not clash with Germany. The emperor was still not convinced. The crown prince and Stolberg tried a different line of approach, stressing that the dual alliance could serve as a means to effect reconciliation with France; they argued that French foreign minister Waddington favored a moderate, non-revanche policy. Again, the emperor was not impressed. Bismarck, he said, was relying too much on the "pretty words" of one foreign minister. At that point the meeting degenerated into a shouting match. The emperor declared that he would rather abdicate than make a disgrace of himself by consenting to such a dangerous alliance. The crown prince was not surprised by this outburst, since the emperor had repeatedly made such threats in the past. He calmly suggested that his father write the tsar, stressing the point that the dual alliance was the logical culmination of the Austro-German rapprochement since 1866 and hence represented no direct threat to Russia. The emperor gave in on this point only.[88]

On the following day, the protagonists met again, and the emperor drew up a fresh list of objections to the alliance. The alliance, William argued, was unfair to Germany since it stipulated that Austria could anticipate German help in the event of an attack by Russia, whereas Austria would only remain neutral in the event of a French attack on Germany. The crown prince replied that this would be mitigated by the fact that France would not attack Germany without allies, and the dual alliance, with the added strength of England, would prevent France from concluding a separate alliance with Russia.[89] This remark did more harm than good, for the crown prince made it clear that he wished to see the creation of an anti-Russian coalition. This, of course, did not please the emperor, who was convinced that Bismarck wanted war with Russia. Stolberg and the crown prince hastened to assure him that this was not true, but to no avail. The final push had to come from Bismarck, who threatened to resign with his entire ministry unless his master sanctioned the alliance.

Having done his part to convince the emperor to accept the Austro-German alliance, the crown prince expected that England's adherence to it was forthcoming. But he was to be bitterly disappointed. In his report to the crown prince of 14 October, Count Münster, the German ambassador to England, was able to report only that British prime minister Beaconsfield and foreign minister Salisbury responded favorably to news of the dual alliance. In short, there was no indication that negotiations toward an Anglo-German alliance were taking place or would take place in the near future.

Frederick was not pleased with Münster's response and wrote to Stolberg requesting more information on the subject. It was only then that Frederick learned that Bismarck had, indeed, instructed Münster on 27 September to make discreet inquiries as to what England's response would be should Germany refuse to sanction unjustified Russian claims in the eastern question. Münster learned that in this event Britain would do no more than guarantee French neutrality.[90] Stolberg told the crown prince that this assurance was insufficient to serve as a basis for an Anglo-German understanding. He added that as England's ally, Germany would also be forced into foreign policy conflicts outside its sphere of influence. Hence, the British guarantee of French neutrality in the event of a Russo-German conflict was a meager reward.[91] The overall implication of Stolberg's letter was that an Anglo-German alliance was not only unnecessary but also possibly dangerous.

Frederick refused to give up all hope of an Anglo-German agreement. He instructed Stolberg to obtain information from the German embassy in St. Petersburg on Russia's reception of what he stubbornly referred to as "our new-found friendship with Austria *and* England." He also reported that he had spoken to the king of Italy on the subject of "our peace league" and that influential members of the Italian court favored the inclusion of their country in the alliance system. He also told Stolberg to pursue his idea for a trade treaty between Germany and England. "Such a step would not be difficult," he said, "because German policy is currently popular in England." More important, he insisted that the trade treaty would provide a good basis for a future alliance.[92]

Stolberg was either unable or unwilling to fulfill his master's wishes. While he agreed that it was necessary to preserve friendly relations with England, he could find no compelling reason to begin negotiations for a trade treaty. Stolberg insisted that Germany's new protectionist trade policy would make negotiations for a trade treaty with England—a country that adhered to the policy of free trade—difficult if not impossible. He added that even if Germany opened up its trade borders, it was more than likely that German industry would suffer from British competition in the long run.[93]

As we have seen, Frederick and Victoria hoped that an agreement with England would reverse Bismarck's protectionist policy, which, in turn, would help stage a comeback for the liberal parties. But when the treaty with England failed, the crown prince became more than ever convinced that there was no hope for a liberal Germany. Conservative Party victories in the fall Reichstag elections, the replacement of Falk with the conservative Puttkamer in the Ministry of Public Worship and Education (Kultusministerium), and growing Russo-German rapprochement in the wake of the signing of the Austro-German alliance only served to confirm this view. Frederick's advisers did what they could to raise his spirits, arguing that the situation was not as bleak as it seemed. Stolberg held out hope for a trade agreement with England once Germany emerged from the economic depression. The crown prince's chamberlain and friend Karl von Normann pointed out that the Center Party's position in the Reichstag was tenuous and that there was no reason the National Liberals could not stage a comeback.

None of this had any effect on Frederick, who threatened to withdraw completely from political life for the second time in the space of a single year. Once again, Victoria refused to give up all hope. She encouraged her husband to maintain contact with their political allies and told him that Bismarck's conservative policies could be undone. She gently urged him on:

Why don't you arrange some meetings with a few nice men sometimes? I think that you would get a lot out of it. You could meet with Normann or Mischke! . . .You could see political and non-political people. Unfortunately, you have too little contact with too few people and it would be so nice to hear about many different points of view! Maybe [you should see] Lasker, Bennigsen, Bamberger, Bunsen, Stauffenberg or Lindau . . . or even my valued railway director Schrader, among others. In this pleasant and pressure-free atmosphere you could learn so much about the things which are being covered up in official circles![94]

The crown prince was quick to abide by his wife's wishes and met with Bennigsen, Delbrück and Forckenbeck separately during the weeks that followed. Surprisingly, Bennigsen was not alarmed by the implementation of Bismarck's conservative policies. By his lights, the success of Bismarck's conservative measures was bound to be temporary, and the liberals would again rule the Reichstag. Like Bennigsen, Delbrück saw no reason for alarm.[95]

Forckenbeck was less optimistic than his liberal colleagues. He admitted that Bismarck's economic policy posed a serious threat to liberal parties. Although Forckenbeck agreed that protectionism was necessary given Germany's economic situation, he never dreamed that Bismarck would go so far as to press for indirect taxes on consumer goods. In his opinion, passage of this measure would be the "kiss of death" for the National Liberal Party. In any case, Forckenbeck felt that divisions within the National Liberal Party destroyed their potential as a strong opposition party. But he quickly added that his new Progressive Party could and would challenge the vagaries of the Bismarck system.[96]

The crown prince and princess were not comforted by these statements. Victoria told her husband that she was "amused" by Delbrück's optimistic opinions and labelled him a "Bismarckian protagonist who ignorantly preaches that all indeed is well in order to justify the superiority of the German people over all others on the earth." She added, "How can he be so blind!"[97]

The events of 1878–1879 had a tremendous impact on the political views of the royal couple. As we have seen, Frederick failed to see how the liberal movement could be revived after the passage of conservative legislation and the conservative realignment in the Reichstag. Frederick had good reason to exhibit such pessimism. First, Bismarck's shift in policy provided the basis for additional revisions in the government's social and economic policy, all of which "deviated from the ideal of liberal-state cooperation pursued during the early years of the decade."[98] Second, the emperor recovered not only his strength but his vitality after the assassination attempts of 1878, and the succession of his son did therefore not appear to be imminent. The longer the emperor reigned and allowed Bismarck to continue his conservative course, the less likely it appeared that it could be revised along liberal guidelines in the future.

Frederick's grim views on Germany's future were shared by many members of the liberal elite.[99] National Liberal Franz von Stauffenberg believed that the entire future of liberalism was in danger. He wrote, "*Only* personal interest still has weight with the people. Our part seems to be over and done with, and I am becoming less and less able to do anything against the increasingly powerful feeling that that for which I have worked for half my life amounts to nothing. . . . . The very thought of party politics disgusts me beyond belief."[100] The crown prince's views on the impact of the events of 1878–1879 have found an echo in the works of many German historians, who hold that Bismarck's shift to the right initiated a lengthy period of reaction that destroyed German liberal aspirations.[101]

The view that a liberal resurgence was impossible after 1879 has been challenged by historians who argue that Bismarck's shift to the right in politics did not prevent his political enemies from making impressive gains during the Reichstag elections of the 1880s.[102] A strong case has also been made suggesting that conservative changes in politics and bureaucracy were not as pervasive as they seemed.[103] Yet no one has attempted to assess the impact of anti-Bismarck agitation at court nurtured by crown princess Victoria. Unlike her husband, Victoria did not believe that the events of 1879 had destroyed the possibility of a liberal Germany. Her letters to her husband during the 1880's show her lively interest in the possibility of liberal reforms during her husband's coming reign. Such reforms, she told her husband, could be achieved by supporting minority liberals who refused to accept the chancellor's policies.[104] Victoria's efforts to sway her husband against the chancellor were supported by anti-Bismarck members of Frederick's entourage, who encouraged the royal couple's hatred of Bismarck in order to secure powerful positions for themselves in the next reign.

Theories suggesting that the shift to the right after 1879 was irreversible also fail to take into account the fact that in the process of creating his coalition, Bismarck alienated the only person who had the power to dismiss him—the future emperor. Thanks to Victoria's efforts, Frederick became more critical of the chancellor, and admitted that he had been wrong to support a number of the chancellor's policies in the past: "I am now obliged to agree with your long-held view that policies such as the Kulturkampf and universal suffrage, though hailed upon their initiation, have meant nothing but trouble for Germany in the long run, and I must admit that Bismarck's policies resemble a clumsy accumulation of hasty ventures that have little to do with common sense."[105] At the same time, however, Frederick was also confronted with pressure from Bismarck's adherents, who spared no effort in attempting to convince the crown prince that the chancellor's services would be indispensable during the coming reign.

Once again, the crown prince found himself in a difficult position. On one hand, he was hesitant to mend fences with Bismarck because of his opposition to the chancellor's policies. On the other hand, Frederick's constitutional liberalism made him equally hesitant to join forces with left-wing liberals. The response of the crown prince to these conflicting pressures is the subject of the following chapter.

NOTES

1. Margarete von Poschinger, *Life of the Emperor Frederick* (New York, 1971), p. 350.

2. The London *Times*, 6 July 1871. The crown prince attached this article to his diary. Geheimes Staatsarchiv Preussischer Kulturbesitz, Abteilung Merseburg. (hereafter GStAPK Merseburg) HA Rep. 52 (Nachlass Friedrich III) FI, Nr. 7k Diary, 1871.

3. Hessische Hausstiftung, Schloss Fasanerie, Fulda (hereafter HH): Crown Prince Frederick William to Crown Princess Victoria, Ulm, 19 August 1872.

4. In June 1873, Odo Russell, England's ambassador to Germany, predicted that the end was near for the emperor: "Emperor William's symptoms are in reallity [sic] the beginning of the end. . . . like his brother the King he is threatened with softening of the brain . . . his [Bismarck's] allusions to a regency were very clear." Russell to Granville, 7 June 1873, Public Records Office, Kew, England (hereafter PRO) PRO 30/29 #93 (Granville Papers). The emperor rallied, only to fall ill again in December. Again, Russell saw the beginning of the end: "An impression is gaining ground at Court that Emperor William's powerful constitution is breaking up and that his increasing want of decision will seriously impede the work of the administration." Russell to Granville, 5 December 1873. Paul Knaplund, ed., *Letters from the British Embassy, 1871–1874, 1880–1885* (Washington, D.C., 1944), p. 119.

5. HH: Crown Prince Frederick William to Crown Princess Victoria, 3 December 1870. See A. R. Allinson, *War Diary of Frederick III* (London, 1957), p. 212.

6. Frederick appears to have underestimated the fragility of German unity. During a tour of south German states in 1872, he wrote his wife: "My soul is stirred by the warm feelings expressed toward me by the South German people! I cannot begin to tell you just how much my heart rejoices at the thought that all the German tribes now see each other as equals and see me as their Crown Prince and that most of the borders of the Reich . . . have fallen! May it remain so!" HH: Crown Prince Frederick William to Crown Princess Victoria, Ingolstadt, 26 August 1872. In her reply, Victoria correctly pointed out that the forces of particularism had not been eradicated by German unification. "It was good to hear that you received such a wonderful reception in Württemburg," she wrote, "[but] I believe that the people were much more enthusiastic about your achievements as a war hero than they were about the idea of emperor and empire." HH: Crown Princess Victoria to Crown Prince Frederick William, Berchtesgarten, 21 August 1872.

7. Dieter Langewiesche, "German Liberalism in the Second Empire," in Konrad H. Jarausch and Larry Eugene Jones, eds., *In Search of a Liberal Germany: Studies in the History of German Liberalism from 1789 to the Present* (New York, 1990), p. 222.

8. Ibid.

9. Ibid.

10. James J. Sheehan, *German Liberalism in the Nineteenth Century* (Chicago, 1978), pp. 132–133, and Alan Kahan, "The Victory of German Liberalism? Rudolf Haym, Liberalism, and Bismarck." *Central European History,* Vol. 22 (March 1990), p. 61.

11. Langewiesche, "Liberalism in the Second Empire," p. 220.

12. Odo Russell to Lord Granville, 11 February 1873, Knaplund, *Letters from the British Embassy*, p. 81. In 1872, Russell wrote: "If the Emperor, whose health was said to be fading, were to die, the enlightened constitutional tendencies of the Crown Prince would lend him to select popular administrators, and then Bismarck, the most powerful man, would be indispensable." Odo Russell to Lord Granville, 24 February 1872. PRO, FO 64 /742, Nr. 12 (Granville Papers).

13. "I notice an impression that Bismarck is paving the way to a future war which will enable him to sweep away the smaller German states and complete the unity of the German empire. These people (members of the National Liberal Party) believe he is acting with the full knowledge and consent of the Crown Prince." Odo Russell to Lord Granville, 31 January 1874, Knaplund, *Letters from the British Embassy*, p. 124.

14. George O. Kent, *Bismarck and His Times* (Carbondale, IL, 1978), p. 84. Historians writing from the liberal perspective have condemned the Center Party's clericalism and conservatism, and have concluded that it had a negative impact on the political development of Germany. This view has, however, has been revised within the past two decades. Margaret L. Anderson's biography of the Center

Party leader Windthorst, holds that the party supported political reform and worked to "deabsolutize" the state. Margaret L. Anderson, *Windthorst: A Political Biography* (Oxford, 1981). This view is supported by Ellen Lovell Evans, whose survey of the history of the Center Party shows that many party members cooperated with the political left. Ellen Lovell Evans. *The German Center Party, 1870–1933: A Study in Political Catholicism* (Carbondale, IL, 1986).

15. Kent, *Bismarck*, p. 84.

16. Gordon Craig, *Germany: 1866–1945* (New York, 1978), p. 70.

17. Kent, *Bismarck*, p. 86.

18. Frederick's letters to his wife during the late 1860s show his fear of growing ultramontane influence in Germany. He told Victoria that ultramontane influence could block the progress of German unification: "I get the impression that the Catholic movement is making remarkable progress in Schleswig; the mothers allow their children to be confirmed in the enemy Catholic faith or they intimidate their husbands until they too convert; this is quite tragic and will have dangerous consequences for us." HH: Crown Prince Frederick William to Crown Princess Victoria, Koeppitz, 24 October 1868. Frederick believed that growing Catholic influence could be fought by a reformed Protestant Church: "there should be an immediate movement toward recruitment of ministers from the upper classes, but it is difficult to see how this would be possible under present circumstances." Ibid., Promnitz, 28 October 1868.

19. In 1864, the crown prince strongly opposed Rome's bid to induce the Prussian government to sanction the election of the ultramontane bishops of Trier and Cologne. He convinced his father and Bismarck that Rome had overextended its clerical authority and thereby blocked the election of ultramontane bishop Kettler to the archbishopric of Cologne. Martin Philippson, *Das Leben Friedrichs III* (Wiesbaden, 1900), p. 320.

20. In a memorandum to his father, Frederick accused the Catholic section of working in the interests of Rome at the expense of the Prussian state. HH: Crown Prince Frederick William to William I, "Die katholische Abtheilung in Cultus=Ministerium, November, 1865" (Copy).

21. He wrote, "As far as I know, the concordat is ignored in Hungary, and the head of their Church recommends candidates for bishops to the Emperor [Franz Josef] without consulting Rome." HH: Crown Prince Frederick William to Justice Minister Friedberg, 20 October 1869. The crown princess liked the idea but suspected correctly that it would not succeed. As she told her mother, "Perhaps at some future time . . . the German Catholics [may] become an independent church on their own, but I doubt that happening in our day." Crown Princess Victoria to Queen Victoria, 4 September 1869. Roger Fulford, ed., *Darling Child: The Private Correspondence of Queen Victoria and the German Crown Princess, 1871–1878* (London, 1976), p. 246.

22. Winifried Taffs, *Lord Odo Russell, a Biography* (London, 1954), p. 13.

23. Frederic B. M.Hollyday, *Bismarck's Rival. A Political Biography of Gen-*

eral and Admiral Albrecht von Stosch (Durham, NC, 1960.), p. 119.

24. Craig, *Germany,* p 78.

25. Philippson, *Friedrich III,* p. 320. Frederick objected to having his views on the ultramontane movement made public. In 1874, the crown prince refused to permit Bismarck to publish Frederick's letter to him of 14 July, which gave strong evidence of the crown prince's hatred of the ultramontane movement. He told the Chancellor that publication of his letter would give the false impression that the crown prince supported the violation of the civil rights of Catholics. Crown Prince Frederick William to Bismarck, 29 July 1874. GStAPK Merseburg, HA Rep. 52 (Nachlass Friedrich III) EIII, Nr. 2.

26. Crown Prince Frederick William to King Carol of Rumania, March 1874. Poschinger, *Life of the the Emperor Frederick,* p. 367. Even when he considered protesting elements of Kulturkampf policy, Stockmar advised him against it. In 1875, Stockmar convinced Frederick to refrain from lodging a protest against the dissolution of monasteries devoted to the care of the sick. HH: Stockmar to Crown Prince Frederick William, 22 April 1875.

27. HH: Crown Prince Frederick William to Crown Princess Victoria, Ritissen bei Ulm, 8 September 1873.

28. Stosch did not relish this prospect. He wrote: "No one can hope more than I that we will keep the old ruler. He is so necessary to win peace with the Church. If Germany is to be powerful, we cannot carry on the civil war between Church and State to the knife, for we cut off our own muscles. Right now the [reign under the] young Prince would weaken our political situation." Stosch to Holtzendoff, 29 December 1873. Hollyday, *Stosch,* p. 119.

29. Poschinger, *Life of the Emperor Frederick,* p. 361. Frederick did make an ominous observation to his wife during the illness: "I am so accustomed to suffering from colds in the throat, hence this departure from my usual pattern is rather strange." HH: Crown Prince Frederick William to Crown Princess Victoria, Karlsruhe, 14 November 1872.

30. Karl von Normann to Gustav Freytag, Neues Palais, 6 July 1873. Julius Heyderhoff and Paul Wentzke, eds., *Deutscher Liberalismus im Zeitalter Bismarcks* 4 Vols. (Bonn, 1925–1926), Vol. 2, pp. 81–82.

31. The crown princess expressed her doubts about the Kulturkampf in a letter to her mother: "I do not believe that such a struggle belongs to our age." Crown Princess Victoria to Queen Victoria, 12 October 1874. Frederick Ponsonby, *Letters of the Empress Frederick* (London, 1929), p. 239.

32. Crown Princess Victoria to Queen Victoria, 14 April 1877. Fulford, *Darling Child,* p. 248.

33. As Victoria told her mother: "This spring he [Bismarck] would have given anything for a hearty response to his overtures. He wanted to know what British policy was going to be, and he would have backed it up—he got no answer, or only what was so very vague—that he said himself as many a German does, 'Oh! there is no use in reckoning on England or going with England, she has no policy,

will do nothing, will always hang back so there is no help for it but to turn to Russia . . . the only strong power–willing to stand by Germany . . . is Russia, therefore we must . . . keep on best terms with her. . . . Surely Prince Bismarck is not to blame for this." Crown Princess Victoria to Queen Victoria, 25 October 1876. Ibid., pp. 227–228.

34. HH: Crown Princess Victoria to Crown Prince Frederick William, Neues Palais, 1 October 1876.

35. HH: Crown Prince Frederick William to Crown Princess Victoria, Baden-Baden, 29 September 1876.

36. Stosch to Crown Prince Frederick William, 13 March 1876. Hollyday, *Stosch,* p. 121.

37. In 1874, Bismarck asked the Reichstag to approve an Äternat, a military budget that would run indefinitely. This proposal was rejected by the National Liberals, for it would significantly reduce Reichstag control over military expenditures. National Liberal leader Rudolf von Bennigsen proposed a seven-year budget (known as the Septennat) whereby the Reichstag retained the right to approve the budget every seven years, and the proposal was grudgingly accepted by Bismarck.

38. James J. Sheehan, *German Liberalism in the Nineteenth Century* (Chicago, 1978), p. 137.

39. Otto Pflanze, *Bismarck and the Development of Germany. Volume 2: The Period of Consolidation, 1871–1880* (Princeton, NJ, 1990), pp. 313–316.

40. Sheehan, *German Liberalism,* p. 181.

41. Kenneth Barkin, *The Controversy over German Industrialization, 1890–1902* (Chicago, 1970), p. 34.

42. See Helmut Böhme, *Deutschlands Weg zur Grossmacht. Studien zum Verhältnis von Wirtschaft und Staat während der Reichsgründungszeit 1848–1881* (Cologne, 1973), Hans-Ulrich Wehler, *Krisenherde des Kaiserreiches, 1871–1918* (Göttingen, 1970), and Gordon Craig, *Germany, 1866–1945* (New York, 1978).

43. Kenneth Barkin holds that the shift to protectionism was the only way that Bismarck could "preserve the union of merchant and Junker and fill imperial coffers." Barkin, *Controversy,* p. 36. See also Lothar Gall, *Bismarck, The White Revolutionary* (London, 1986), p. 96: "We are tempted. . . to see a politician at work here who, feeling that he was isolated . . . reacted in a thoroughly emotional manner. Bismarck simply took the bull by the horns . . . without looking too closely into where this course might lead him."

44. Pflanze, *Bismarck,* Vol. 2, p. 384.

45. HH: Crown Princess Victoria to Crown Prince Frederick William, 15 May 1878. The crown prince wrote his wife that Bismarck and Falk wished to punish those responsible by legislating strict controls against the social democratic press. He added that Berlin was engulfed in an atmosphere of disorder and confusion over the assassination attempt. Evidently he was besieged with questions as to how the government would respond to the assassination attempt; as he told his

wife, "I am twice as happy to be able to leave this place soon, so that no one can ask me about anything." HH: Crown Prince Frederick William to Crown Princess Victoria, 9 and 13 May 1878.

46. Sheehan, *German Liberalism*, pp. 182–183.

47. Ibid., p. 183.

48. Kent, *Bismarck*, p. 90.

49. Crown Prince Frederick William to King Carol of Rumania, 19 October 1878. Georg Schuster, ed., *Briefe, Reden und Erlasse des Kaisers und Königs Friedrich III* (Berlin, 1907) p. 273. Frederick's biographer Wolbe claims that he was compelled to sign the antisocialist law, even though he was convinced of its negative consequences. Wolbe, *Kaiser Friedrich*, p. 222.

50. Richter, *Kaiser Friedrich III*, p. 248.

51. Ladislas Farago, *Royal Web* (New York, 1982), p. 220.

52. Crown Prince Frederick William to King Carol of Rumania, 2 August 1878. Schuster, *Briefe, Reden und Erlasse*, p. 273.

53. Norman Rich, *Friedrich von Holstein* (Cambridge, 1965), p. 132.

54. HH: Crown Prince Frederick William to Crown Princess Victoria, 23 September 1878.

55. Crown Prince Frederick William to King Carol of Rumania, 19 October 1878. Schuster, *Briefe, Reden, und Erlasse*, p. 275.

56. Crown Princess Victoria to Queen Victoria, 4 June 1878. Farago, *Royal Web*, p. 219.

57. Stosch also viewed the check on the crown prince's powers as a good thing, but for different reasons. Stosch hoped that Bismarck's shabby treatment of Frederick during the regency would goad him into being less vulnerable to the chancellor's wiles in the future. When he told Freytag that Bismarck had forbidden the crown prince to make any changes in personnel during his regency, he added, "He feels this chain, and that, I hope, will strengthen the powers of his resistance." Stosch was also happy to report that Frederick's duties as regent forced him to finally take an active interest in affairs of state. As he told Freytag, "The Crown Prince works vigorously and is serious and industrious beyond expectation." Stosch hoped that the regency would counteract Frederick's vulnerability to the influence of stronger personalities and his lack of interest in affairs of state. Stosch to Freytag, 8 June 1878, Hollyday, *Stosch*, p. 129.

58. Ibid., 22 February 1879. Frederick was also informed that Bismarck wished Frederick's tenure as regent to be ended at the earliest possible moment so that he could push his protectionist programs under the aegis of the more pliable kaiser: "deshalb müsste es gemacht werden, dass der Kaiser den Winter in Berlin residire und wider regiere!"

59. Bismarck originally offered the post to the crown prince in 1878. Initially, Frederick was enthusiastic about the offer since it provided him with the opportunity to rule on his own, free from the stifling political atmosphere of Berlin. Moreover, Bismarck made the offer especially attractive by assuring the crown prince

complete control over the selection of his administrators. Bismarck to Crown Prince Frederick William, 14 March 1878. GStAPK Merseburg HA Rep. 52 (Nachlass Friedrich III), Nr. 11. The emperor, however, heartily objected to the idea. Due to his advanced age, he felt that his son and heir was obliged to stay by his side. Additional opposition to the project came from the National Liberals, who objected to the exploitation of Alsace-Lorraine as a "training ground for future German emperors" and they pointed to several factors that would make implementation of the project difficult at best. PRO: F.O. 64/905, Odo Russell to Lord Salisbury, 11 May 1878.

60. HH: Crown Prince Frederick William to Crown Princess Victoria, 22 February 1879.

61. Ibid., 22 February 1879.

62. Dan P. Silvermann, *Reluctant Union: Alsace-Lorraine and Imperial Germany, 1871–1918* (State College, PA, 1972), p. 44.

63. Silverman, *Reluctant Union*, p. 46

64. Anderson, *Windthorst*, p. 228.

65. HH: Crown Princess Victoria to Crown Prince Frederick William, 25 February 1879. This statement illustrates that the crown princess was misinformed about Bismarck's willingness to placate the Center Party. Although Windthorst had supported the cause of the particularist Hanoverian Guelphs, this subject was not brought up in his negotiations with the chancellor in 1879. The royal couple also mistakenly assumed that Bismarck's negotiations with Windthorst meant that the former was ready to end the Kulturkampf. This was something that Bismarck was not prepared to do, and he was also concerned about the Center Party's cooperation with their fellow political pariahs, the Social Democrats. On the other hand, Windthorst was by no means ready to give in to all aspects of Bismarck's economic reform program—especially any plan that would make the empire's finances totally independent of the Reichstag. Anderson, *Windthorst*, p. 230.

66. HH: Crown Prince Frederick William to Crown Princess Victoria, 7 May 1879.

67. HH: Crown Princess Victoria to Crown Prince Frederick William, 8 May 1879.

68. Ibid., 12 May 1879.

69. Langewiesche, "Liberalism in the Second Empire," p. 225.

70. Windthorst suggested the adoption of the so-called Clausula Franckenstein, which concerned itself more with the preservation of the rights of the separate German states than the budgetary powers of the Reichstag. The clause not only thwarted Bismarck's original intention of freeing the empire from parliaments and particularism, but also had the advantage of being totally unacceptable to the National Liberals because of its federalist character. Anderson, *Windthorst*, p. 230.

71. HH: Crown Prince Frederick William to Crown Princess Victoria, 21 May 1879.

72. Anderson, *Windthorst*, p. 230–231.

73. HH: Crown Prince Frederick William to Crown Princess Victoria, 22 May 1879.

74. Ibid., 24 May 1879.

75. HH: Crown Princess Victoria to Crown Prince Frederick William, 25 May 1879.

76. HH: Crown Prince Frederick William to Crown Princess Victoria, 27 May 1879.

77. Ibid., 27 May 1879.

78. HH: Crown Princess Victoria to Crown Prince Frederick William, 28 May 1879.

79. William L. Langer, *European Alliances and Alignments* (London, 1950), p. 172.

80. "The identity of British and Austrian interests, shown by their recent collaboration in the Congress of Berlin, made Britain the logical third partner." Pflanze, *Bismarck*, Vol. 2, p. 501.

81. Ibid., 22 September 1879.

82. Friedrich Wilhelm, Kronprinz, "Zur politischen Sachlage 1879." Auswärtiges Amt, Bonn (hereafter AA) Asservat 2b #28. Bismarck told the crown prince that political unrest in Russia was weakening the very fabric of the empire, and German security would therefore be best served by an alliance with Austria and England.

83. HH: Crown Prince Frederick William to Crown Princess Victoria, 3 September 1879. This letter was written in English.

84. Ibid., 14 September 1879.

85. Ibid.

86. Ibid., 30 September 1879.

87. Pflanze, *Bismarck,* Vol. 2, p. 508.

88. Zur politischen Sachlage, 1879," AA, Asservat 2b, #28.

89. Ibid.

90. Historian William Langer has suggested that Münster may have departed from the letter of his instructions. What Bismarck wanted was a statement of British policy in the event of a Russo-German conflict. Münster deviated from this question and discussed only the general state of Anglo-German relations with special reference to France. Bismarck's response to Münster's report was that the English statement was inadequate. Langer, *European Alliances and Alignments,* p. 176.

91. Münster to Crown Prince Frederick William, 14 October 1879. AA Asservat 2b, #12.

92. Crown Prince Frederick William to Count Stolberg (draft) 20 October 1879. AA, Asservat 2b, #13.

93. Stolberg to Crown Prince Frederick William, 27 October 1879. AA, Asservat 2b, #14.

94. HH: Crown Princess Victoria to Crown Prince Frederick William, 8 December 1879. Victoria also suggested that her eldest son, Prince William, establish ties with these men, since she wished to extricate him from the ultraconservative influence of the "Potsdam crowd."

95. HH: Crown Prince Frederick William to Crown Princess Victoria, 24 December 1879.

96. Ibid., 30 December 1879.

97. HH: Crown Princess Victoria to Crown Prince Frederick William, 28 December 1879.

98. Sheehan, *German Liberalism*, p. 188.

99. Ibid., p. 189.

100. Langewiesche, "Liberalism in the Second Empire," p. 226.

101. This view is held by historians such as Hemut Böhme, Hans-Ulrich Wehler, James Sheehan and Gordon Craig.

102. As early as 1881, "the Reichstag elections produced the worst defeat of the government since 1863, with the National Liberals losing 52 seats, and the Free Conservatives 29, whereas the left liberals and Progressives enjoyed massive increases, and the Center, Socialists and Poles each gained a few places." Paul Kennedy, *The Rise of Anglo-German Antagonism, 1860–1914* (London, 1987), p. 102. See also Lothar Gall, *Bismarck, The White Revolutionary* (London, 1986), pp. 96–97. According to Ernst Huber, "Die Lage der Regierung gegenüber dem Reichstag war 1881–1887 geradezu katastrophal." See *Deutsche Verfassungsgeschichte seit 1789* 4 Vols. (Stuttgart, 1957–1969), Vol. 4, pp. 146–150.

103. An article by Kenneth Barkin and M. L. Anderson "The Myth of the Puttkamer Purge," *Journal of Modern History,* Vol. 54, #4 (December 1982), also argues that the purge of the liberal bureaucracy initiated by Minister of Interior Robert von Puttkamer in 1879 was not as effective or pervasive as previous scholarship on the problem has suggested.

104. In 1885, Victoria told her husband that she had no use for the liberals who supported Bismarck's conservative policies: "The National Liberals and Free Conservatives have done Germany a great disservice! They became the lackeys of the great man [Bismarck] and they caved in to all of his policies instead of building themselves up as a large, independent middle party which he [Bismarck] would have had to do battle with . . . but now, party politics are, as usual, insane." HH: Crown Princess Victoria to Crown Prince Frederick William, 21 August 1885.

105. HH: Crown Prince Frederick William to Crown Princess Victoria, 16 May 1879.

Chapter 6

The Succession Crisis, 1880–1887

Frederick's sense of resignation about his coming rule increased during the 1880s as he saw the chancellor obtain stronger conservative consensus for his policies by achieving greater control over the executive branches of the imperial and Prussian government. In 1881, Bismarck tried to bring the working classes into his conservative coalition at the expense of the Social Democratic Party by securing passage of a social welfare program.[1]

The crown prince and his wife shared the views of those opposition liberals who rejected the social welfare legislation. Liberals predicted it would repress individual initiative and ultimately decrease productivity.[2] Frederick agreed with this assessment. As he confided to his diary in November 1884, "The monarchy has been put into an awkward position since Bismarck has declared 'social kingship' as his weapon against socialism. . . .We are faced with a [new] year that will be full of unwelcome developments, which will arise from the government's false position toward the workers."[3]

The royal couple also witnessed with dismay the growing factionalism among the liberal parties, which they attributed to the movement's inability to block the chancellor's conservative policies. They bemoaned the resolution of the Heidelberg Conference of National Liberals in 1884, which made it clear that the National Liberals were closer to the conservative rather than the opposition parties on decisive contemporary issues such as social welfare legislation. The party deemed cooperation with the government as a necessary means to combat its enemies in the Center Party, who were attempting to secure abrogation of Kulturkampf laws.[4] The crown prince did not accept this logic. In Frederick's mind, the resolution of the conference showed that the National Liberals had completely "sold out" to conservatives and interest groups; in short, they bore no resemblance to the "good" National Liberals of the past.[5] Victoria agreed: "As far as the good National Liberals are concerned, their blindness has led to our woeful circumstances! Instead of building an oppositional bloc to Bismarck, they are only his plaything, and allow themselves to follow wherever he tells them to go."[6]

The crown prince's opposition to Bismarck's policies did not, however, mean that he wished to join forces with the Progressives, whose influence was on the rise during the early 1880s. In June 1880, Eugen Richter, leader of the Progressive Party, predicted a liberal victory comparable to the one that swept Gladstone and his Liberal Party into office in England.[7] Richter's prediction was not exaggerated: in the elections of 1881, the Progressives won an impressive victory at the expense of the National Liberals and Free Conservatives.

These events pleased the crown princess, who tried to persuade her husband to share her enthusiasm for Gladstone. When the liberals came to power in England, she wrote her husband: "She [Queen Victoria, who hated Gladstone] is probably anxious and beside herself about the elections. *My* feelings are quite the opposite! The assumption that the Liberals [in Britain] are less well-disposed towards Germany than the Tories is quite false—I believe just the opposite is true! The Liberals represent the best of what we have to offer."[8] After she met with the British prime minister in 1884, she wrote Frederick:

Last night Mr. Gladstone was at dinner, and I had the privilege of being seated next to him! How I admire this wonderful and honorable man! I don't completely agree with his foreign policy—he may err at times, but his knowledge and sensibilities are remarkable [and] evoke astonishment. . . . He talked a lot about you . . . he admires you very much, and he *sincerely* loves Germany. . . . He admires your Papa as a man and a soldier, but is apparently not sympathetic to his political views. These men [German conservatives] are such poor judges of character and call him an enemy of Germany—which God knows is not the least bit true. This elderly man fights fearlessly for what he believes to be the best interests of his country.[9]

Victoria was also pleased with the Progressives' gains in the elections of 1881. As she told her mother, "I am very glad that German elections have returned so many Liberals, and I hope it will show Prince Bismarck that Germans are not at all delighted with his government though I do not think he cares one bit."[10]

Significantly, Frederick did not share his wife's enthusiasm for either the Gladstonian liberals or the Progressives. Although he told his wife that his views on Gladstone's victory in 1880 were "similar" to those she had expressed,[11] he nonetheless sought assurances from Stockmar that the election results were not a sign of increasing radicalization in the British political system. Stockmar relayed Frederick's concern to Roggenbach and reported: "Roggenbach . . . does not believe that the change of government in England means that the country has been won over to radicalism. He attributes the Liberals' victory not to growing radicalism, but to support from the depressed agricultural population, which believed that the Liberals would ease their difficulties."[12]

After the elections of 1881, Bismarck launched a campaign to break the growing political strength of the Progressive Party. According to historian Paul Kennedy, "This campaign was motivated not only to preserve his own power in the next reign, but it also emanated from his firm belief that continued victory of the Progressives at the polls would gradually bring about a republic."[13] Pro-Bismarck newspapers informed the German people that the Progressive liberals coming to power during the coming reign of Frederick would pursue a disastrous foreign policy. "Manchester men" such as Bamberger and Richter would negotiate an anti-Russian alliance, thus precipitating the possibility of war with Russia. To keep the peace, electors were told to vote conservative in order to keep the chancellor in power.[14]

Bismarck also warned the emperor and the crown prince about the dangers of Gladstonian liberalism. He used reports on the British liberal government's difficulties with issues such as Irish reform to confirm the shortcomings of liberal practices. These reports, which effectively reinforced the emperor's prejudices against liberalism, were sent to his son in the hope that he, too, would recognize the fallibility of liberal government.[15] Given Fredrick's negative reaction to the victory of the Gladstonian liberals in 1880, there is good reason to believe that such reports on the dangers of Gladstonism had the desired effect on the crown prince.

Frederick's suspicions of the left liberals remained even after they joined forces to construct a political base for a liberal regime under the leadership of the future emperor. In 1884, the Progressive Party, weakened by losses in the elections of 1882, joined forces with the Secession Party, comprising former National Liberals who had rejected Bismarck's course in 1879. Together, they formed the Deutsche Freisinnige Partei (German Free-Thinking Party), which had 107 seats in the Reichstag. Ludwig Bamberger's notes on the foundation of the party indicate that its primary goals were the "preservation of threatened constitutional parliamentary order, and the preservation of the right to free speech and free elections." The party was committed to increasing the power of the Reichstag in fiscal matters and regulation of church laws. Bamberger stressed that the party intended to resume the process of liberal reform that had been halted by Bismarck.[16]

Victoria welcomed the creation of the Freisinn Party. As far as she was concerned, Freisinn was ideally suited to dismantle Bismarck's conservative domestic policy.[17] The crown prince, however, did not agree. Since Frederick's constitutional liberalism precluded acceptance of a stronger parliament, there is good reason to believe that he did not support the party's goals. Nor did he appear to have the energy or commitment to effect a compromise between the Freisinn program and his own ideas for a liberal Germany. Observers noted that the crown prince was depressed and had no interest in his coming reign. In 1880, Stosch told Freytag that Frederick was "low and out of spirits." He added: "the heir to the throne is already an old man. Strength not exercised dies away; he keeps aloof from activity and influence."[18] Frederick's apathy was also readily noticed by Professor Heinrich Geffcken, who was a professor of jurisprudence and a close friend of the royal couple. He wrote Roggenbach: "The crown prince seems to be more pessimistic and bitter than ever; he refused to discuss this situation with regard to his coming reign . . . . he complains about his wasted life, and I believe that the reason he feels this way is because he does not work."[19]

Given Frederick's feelings about the goals of Freisinn, it is reasonable to assume that Victoria encouraged him to send a telegram to Bamberger congratulating him on the creation of the Freisinn Party. Thereafter, the party became more commonly known as the "Crown Prince Party," and Frederick's telegram gave party members reason to believe that he supported their goals.[20] This impression aroused the fears of National Liberal leader Johannes Miquel, who told Stosch that it was necessary for Frederick to refrain "from giving free rein to his leftist policies." Stosch hastened to assure Miquel that this was simply not true: "The inner nature of the Prince is in clearest opposition to the left," he wrote.[21]

While Bismarck may have known that Frederick did not have leftist tendencies, the formation of the Freisinn Party nonetheless troubled him. With enough support, the party could help German liberalism recover from the events of 1878–1879. In Bismarck's mind, liberal recovery entailed the dismantling of his conservative policies and the formation of a dreaded "Gladstone ministry."[22]

During the election campaign of 1884, Bismarck was determined to reduce the ranks of the Freisinn Party by finding divisions on issues in its ranks. In this he was successful. Freisinn was divided on Bismarck's social welfare legislation and split after Bismarck accused left-liberals who opposed renewal of the antisocialist law as being soft on socialism.[23] According to Gordon Craig, "All in all, the renewal of the Socialist Law did little to support the idea that a new and militant liberalism was in the making."[24]

Freisinn was also unable to take a united stand when Bismarck announced his intention to acquire German colonies in Africa. Bismarck's abandonment of his decade-long opposition to German colonial acquisitions surprised friends and foes alike and has fuelled much historical debate.[25] At bottom, however, there is a good deal of evidence to support the conclusion that Bismarck pursued a colonial campaign in order to compromise the strength of the Freisinn Party, which split when Germany's drive for colonies was accompanied by worsening relations between Germany and Britain.[26] Some party members jumped on Bismarck's colonial bandwagon, whereas others refrained from doing so because of their pro-British sensibilities, not to mention those of the crown prince and his wife.

The crown prince, like the Freisinn Party, had mixed feelings about colonies: he supported Germany's acquisition of overseas colonies, but was saddened when Anglo-German relations suffered as a result.[27] Unlike her husband, Victoria vehemently opposed the drive for colonies and viewed Bismarck's support for colonies as a means to gain support for other conservative policies. As she confided to her friend Lady Ponsonby:

The Germans are always reproaching the English for having prejudices against Germany, and forget that *they* have many more and much more deep-seated ones about other countries, especially England! They *imagine* that England is jealous of Germany's attempting to have colonies. I am almost certain that the whole agitation about colonial enterprise would not have been cooked up if it were not a useful *handle for the elections.*[28]

She also told her mother:

I do not wonder that our British Colonies are enraged by this ridiculous hoisting of the German flag in all sorts of places. I think it is too senseless and nothing but a piece of vanity and brag, as I do not see what Germany wants with those places, nor what earthly good they are to her. . . . When Bismarck begins to play at Germany being a Weltreich, I think it is time for us to let him know where we are, though in perfect friendship.[29]

The election results of 1884 once again showed that Bismarck's plan to reduce the left-wing liberal opposition worked. The Freisinn bloc dropped from 107 to 67 seats, the National Liberals won 50 seats, the conservatives gained 24 seats. Yet Bismarck was hardly completely satisfied with the election results, since gains made by the Social Democrats pointed to the chancellor's failure to lure workers away from the party with his social welfare legislation.The party received 24 seats and was now big enough to have the right of representation on all major Reichstag committees.[30]

Frederick's reaction to the election results showed his disillusionment with Bismarck's system, which had only succeeded in increasing the power of the Social Democrats, while unduly strengthening the powers of the government at the same time. Such a combination, he believed, would put him in a very difficult position when he came to the throne.[31]

The rift between the crown prince and the chancellor did not go unnoticed by the liberal press. In November 1881, an article in the Progressive *Volkszeitung* stated that relations between the crown prince and the chancellor were at an all-time low because of the chancellor's attempt to remove the crown prince and his liberal cohorts from Berlin by installing the former as Statthalter of Alsace-Lorraine. Although the contents of the article were quite true, Bismarck asked for Frederick's permission to follow up the article with a retraction.[32] Frederick's reply to Bismarck's request was terse; he said that he was ready to cooperate with the chancellor "in the same friendly spirit" that had characterized their discussions on Prince William's proposed marriage to Princess Victoria of Schleswig-Holstein.[33] This comment was very sarcastic, since Frederick had gone to great pains to overcome the chancellor's objections to the match. The tone of the letter thus supports the conclusion that relations between the heir to the throne and the chancellor were cold indeed.

In 1884, the liberal journal *Reichsfreund* gave its readers every reason to believe that Frederick opposed Bismarck and was committed to the liberal cause:

The Crown Prince, for his communications to the Press, evidently selects newspapers which are not organs of the Chancellor or dependent on him. The more eagerly the

Chancellor's friends strive to commit . . . the Crown Prince to the Chancellor's present policy . . . the more frequently does the Crown Prince utter pronouncements which make it clear to the German people that one may have a different conception of the tasks of the future from that held by the Conservatives and the Chancellor, and that above all the German heir to the throne refuses to be associated in any way with the Chancellor's present policy as a whole, or to accept moral responsibility for it in the eyes of the nation.[34]

The poor relations between the royal couple and the chancellor gave Bismarck's adherents good reason to believe that if "Bismarck went on flouting the vanity and self-respect of the crown prince, it was very possible that Frederick would dismiss him out of sheer personal hatred—no matter how great the chancellor's personal prestige or how strong his political position in the Reichstag and the country."[35] This situation prompted a number of Bismarck's adherents, whose positions were more or less dependent upon Bismarck's continued tenure in office, to try to secure a rapprochement between the royal couple and the chancellor. The most prominent member of this group was Friedrich von Holstein, the senior counsellor in the Political Division of the Foreign Office. His efforts to strengthen Bismarck's position for the next reign formed a prominent theme in his diaries and correspondence.[36] Holstein obtained information on the status of relations between the royal couple and the chancellor through his contact at court, Count Götz von Seckendorff, who was the chamberlain to the crown princess and "enjoyed her confidence to a remarkable degree."[37] In 1883, Seckendorff's hand was strengthened when his protégé Count Gustav von Sommerfeld, became private secretary to the crown princess.

Thanks to his contacts at court, Holstein discovered that some of Frederick's hostility toward Bismarck was based on trivial matters. For example, the crown prince voiced his dissatisfaction when it appeared to him that Bismarck was receiving favors and honors at his expense. Holstein noted in his diary: "To this very day they [members of the crown prince's court] resent the fact that Prince Bismarck got his own private railway carriage some time ago. This railway carriage has often been mentioned to me as one reason for the Crown Prince's ill-will."[38] On another occasion, Holstein recorded that Frederick was enraged when Bismarck appeared to be usurping honors generally reserved for the crown prince:

The Crown Prince is half demented with the honours now being showered on the Chancellor for his birthday. . . . But what enrages him most is that the Sultan is sending a Pasha here to congratulate the Chancellor, and bestow on him and on the Crown Prince the highest Turkish decoration. That the Chancellor should thus be placed on the same level as the heir to the throne goes far beyond His Imperial Highness' idea of a joke. He strides up and down like a madman. "And I suppose they'll expect me to call on Prince Bismarck in full court dress to congratulate him. What's he done anyway? I was the man who first had the idea of a Reich!"[39]

Frederick's anger over such matters appears to have betrayed his deep resentment for Bismarck's power and influence, which, by the crown prince's lights, had virtually destroyed hopes for a liberal Germany. Holstein tried to prevent such outbursts by urging the chancellor to redress matters that had aroused the ill-will of the heir to the throne.[40]

Holstein and his allies believed that relations between the royal couple and the chancellor could also be improved by the removal of anti-Bismarck members of the royal couple's entourage, who encouraged their hatred of Bismarck in order to secure powerful positions for themselves in the next reign. The so-called Crown Prince Circle included Stosch,[41] General von Mischke, the crown prince's aide-de-camp, and Karl von Normann, who succeeded Ernst von Stockmar as private secretary and adviser to the crown princess after the health of the former began to fail in the early 1880s. The primary target of Holstein's campaign was Karl von Normann, whom conservatives at court called "the worst of the bad advisers of the crown prince." In 1884, Holstein expressed his agreement with this statement when he wrote, "There are many indications that Normann and his followers are trying by every possible means to bring about a split between His Imperial Highness and Bismarck."[42]

Holstein's suspicions were correct. Letters from Normann to the crown princess show that Normann had been working to maintain the breach between the royal couple and the chancellor long before 1884.[43] Normann gave Victoria the hope that Germany's future would be bright—as long as Bismarck was not at the helm. After Bismarck abandoned his alliance with the National Liberals and embarked on his conservative course in late 1879, Normann wrote the crown princess: "I trust that reason will return, and, unless I am grievously mistaken, [I believe that] the reactionary movement will have a good effect—the more we see how deficient we are in so many areas, the faster we will learn how to be reasonable again."[44] He also fuelled Victoria's hopes that the "damage" done by Bismarck was reversible:

I derive comfort from thinking about the future. It may sound fantastic, but I am convinced that the statesmen who will succeed Bismarck will be faced with a difficult but satisfying task. . . . With one blow a cleansing process can be initiated in state and private life—and this need not be a violent process. . . . Success in such a task would depend on the ability to place the right man in every post . . . there is no dearth of talented men, and he who looks carefully will see that this is true. . . . Such a future is only possible without the Emperor.[45]

Normann also flattered the crown princess' political judgment:

It is impossible for me to describe the true joy that you have bestowed upon me . . . how can I possibly describe the wealth of thoughts that you have inspired in me! I must strive to be modest, but perhaps I may be permitted to harbor the hope that you have given me regarding the future. What a blessing it is for this country that such a noble person, to whom is entrusted the wealth and happiness of the people—possesses rare qualities such as an ability to respect deeply the common people, and the ability to understand all things that inspire intelligent people.[46]

Evidently, Victoria's pleasure with such unctuous flattery worked as Normann hoped it might: in 1882 he became court chamberlain to the crown prince. It is also reasonable to assume that she secured this appointment in the hope that Normann's optimism with regard to the coming reign would rub off on the crown prince.

Normann did more than flatter Victoria; he was accused of leaking "incautious statements" about the ill will between the crown prince and Bismarck to the press.[47] The purpose behind such statements may well have been his desire to give German liberals hope that the crown prince was committed to their cause.[48]

Normann's influence began to wane, thanks to the success of Seckendorff and Sommerfeld's campaign to discredit Normann in the eyes of the crown princess. Seckendorff and Sommerfeld accused Normann of advising Frederick on certain matters without first consulting her. Seckendorff told Victoria that "Normann, who was confident in the support of the liberal parties in Germany, was trying to influence the Crown Prince without or even against the Crown Princess, and that he was representing himself as the spokesman of the German liberal element as opposed to the British liberalism of the Crown Princess."[49]

Their pressure appears to have worked. By September 1883, Victoria was singing Sommerfeld's praises at Normann's expense and made it clear to her husband that Normann's presence was no longer desirable at court. She told her husband that Normann's talents would be best served in a political post so that he could educate himself to assume a political position during Frederick's coming reign.[50]

Frederick agreed with his wife: "Given Normann's talents and his dedication to work, it would be preferable if he could expand his horizons so that he could give me [political] support in the future—but how can this be done and who should take over his present duties?"[51]

Seckendorff and Holstein were only too happy to answer this question. As soon as Holstein learned that Normann's days at court were numbered, he contacted his friend, the Prussian minister at Weimar, Count Hugo Radolinski, and invited him to become court chamberlain to the crown prince. Radolinski was a suitable choice because he was reputed to have no connection to antigovernment parties and because he was known to be "honestly devoted to the Prussian monarchy and the German cause."[52] Holstein felt that Radolinski would also be acceptable to the crown princess, for he was a widower of an Englishwoman who was well-acquainted with the British royal family. Bismarck also welcomed the appointment of one of Holstein's allies as chamberlain to the crown prince since such a change was bound to improve relations between himself and the royal couple. The chancellor was therefore happy to approve Frederick's request to appoint Normann to head the Prussian legation in Oldenburg.

It appears that Seckendorff and Sommerfeld's efforts to discredit the other two members of the so-called crown prince circle—Stosch and Mischke—were also successful. In 1885, Victoria told her husband:

It is a pity that Mischke, Normann and Stosch—who are all excellent people on an individual basis—push, intimidate and exploit each other—and give the impression that they wish to construct a clique that would dominate us. Each of them is attached to us in his own way, and each will be able to render us great services, but to have them all in one place is simply not good. We are indebted to each of them [and] what we have as yet to do is to determine what kind of positions they will have where they can do the most good.[53]

The crown prince's allies considered Normann's dismissal part of a plot to dispose of all anti-Bismarck advisers of the crown prince.[54] Frederick, however, told Stosch that Normann accepted his new post in Oldenburg so that he could become more familiar with state procedures, "until the moment comes when I am able to utilize his unusual capacity for work." Frederick added that Normann wanted the post and that it was "in his and my interest to separate him from court life."[55]

Although Frederick denied that Bismarck was trying to surround him with his own people, the departure of Frederick's anti Bismarck advisors, along with the crown prince's lack of support for the Freisinn Party must have given party members the impression that he was not interested in their cause. It was rumored in liberal circles that the royal couple was attempting to mend fences with Bismarck. In August 1884, Freisinn deputy Karl Schrader wrote his colleague Franz von Stauffenberg: "You want to know something about the political views of the Crown Prince. I am afraid that I can tell you less about them than I used to, for I have seen neither him nor the Crown Princess in a long time. They have become careful in their contacts with liberal people; it seems that word has been passed around to avoid everything that might annoy Bismarck."[56]

Schrader's fears were not unfounded.[57] Frederick was, indeed, willing to come to some sort of agreement with the chancellor for two reasons: first, Bismarck's talents as foreign minister were regarded as indispensable by all political parties, including his most bitter enemies on the left, and second, the crown prince failed to see how he, as emperor, could pursue any other course than the one mapped out by the chancellor. As he explained to his wife in 1884, Bismarck had had ample time to dazzle an entire generation of Germans with his successes and had brought them over to his point of view. This being the case, he did not anticipate that his mere accession to the throne would immediately eradicate the beliefs and practices of the Bismarckian era, and he also believed that the "healing" process could not be accomplished in one reign. The liberal transformation, if it could take place at all, would be a very lengthy and difficult process.[58]

Despite his opposition to the pro-Bismarck line taken by the National Liberals, the crown prince told the chancellor in 1884 that he intended to include leaders of that party in his government when he came to the throne. In April 1884, Holstein reported:

The Prince was frank and cordial. . . . After the Kaiser's death, which might come any day, the Crown Prince would be very glad to have Bismarck as Chancellor; he would then appoint Bennigsen and Miquel to direct Prussian affairs. Prince Bismarck replied that he had no objection to HIH's making an attempt to govern with the National Liberals; the attempt might succeed. But if HIH wanted to go one step further towards the Left, to Forckenbeck and friends, he would soon be rushing headlong down the slope to republicanism.[59]

Given Frederick's feelings about left-wing liberalism, it is reasonable to assume that he did not argue the latter point with Bismarck. If it came to a choice between ruling with the Freisinn Party or the National Liberals, Frederick's liberal constitutionalism dictated that the latter was definitely the lesser of two evils.

Frederick's ability to agree with the chancellor on several issues did not assuage his suspicions about the course the latter intended to pursue in the coming reign. His suspicions were confirmed when he learned of Bismarck's tentative plans to engineer a coup against the constitution.[60] These plans stemmed from the chancellor's growing disillusionment with the parliamentary process, which had failed to give him the kind of majority he wanted. The conservative parliamentary majority of 1879 turned against him during the decade that followed.[61] In an attempt to redress this situation, he created extraparliamentary government organs composed of pro-Bismarckian interest groups that would serve as the basis for a national assembly to replace the Reichstag.[62] One of these government organs was the Prussian State Council. Proposed by Bismarck in 1884, the council was to advise the emperor on national affairs.

Frederick was not completely aware of the chancellor's revisionist intentions when the latter offered the crown prince the presidency of the council.[63] The crown prince accepted the post because Bismarck was to serve as vice president, meaning that for once Frederick would have at least nominal authority over the chancellor. Still, the conservative composition of the council irked him. As he told Stosch, "In view of the composition of the members of the state council . . . I will be in a splendid minority." He added: "after twenty years of silence, I find an occasion to give my opinions openly in a way that gives me little pleasure."[64]

After the crown prince accepted the presidency, however, Forckenbeck told him that Bismarck wished to use the conservative council to counterbalance the power of a liberal parliament and ministry when Frederick came to the throne.[65] Frederick's biographer Martin Philippson suggests that Frederick's performance as president was purposely mediocre after Forckenbeck enlightened him about the true purpose behind the council.[66] In the end, the council did not fulfill the purpose that Bismarck intended it to serve, because the emperor regarded it as a superfluous institution, claiming that its primary functions were already performed by the Landtag. Even Bismarck was forced to agree that the council only complicated the machinery of government.[67] The council met several times in 1884 but did not meet again until 1890.

Although the Prussian council of state did not live up to Bismarck's expectations, the crown prince's concern about the chancellor's revisionist intentions made him committed to preventing the chancellor from doing as he pleased during the coming reign. When the emperor fell seriously ill in 1885, Frederick went to Stosch's estate in Oestrich and drafted proclamations to be issued to his people and the chancellor when he became emperor. It is important to note that Victoria was not present when the proclamations were drafted at Stosch's estate in Oestrich. Frederick's advisers on this project were a mixed group: Roggenbach and Geffcken wished to see Bismarck's influence limited during the coming reign, whereas Stosch and Friedberg wished to see maintenance of the status quo.[68]

The original draft of the proclamations reflects Frederick's preoccupation with both of these concerns. His first priority was to limit the influence of the chancellor. The draft makes not one but several references to restoring the prestige of the monarchy at Bismarck's expense during the coming reign: "I will be the chancellor's superior, and he will henceforth serve as my minister," he wrote.[69] In essence, he wanted Bismarck to live up to his Reichstag speech, which stated that the kings of Prussia had always determined policy. Frederick intended to apprise the chancellor of his feelings on this matter prior to releasing the final versions of the proclamations. If the chancellor refused to abide by them, Frederick made it clear that he would rule without Bismarck.[70]

The original also attests to Frederick's dissatisfaction with the empire's bureaucracy, universal suffrage, and the ongoing conflict between Catholic and Protestant interests. But he added that any effort to effect positive changes could be pursued slowly and only within the context of the constitutional status quo.[71] The final draft refined this latter point. The future emperor asked the chancellor to observe and respect "the constitutional and legal ordinances of the Empire and Prussia" and avoid "those shocks which repeated changes in the institutions and laws of the State entail."[72] He added:

The furtherance of the duties which fall to the Imperial Government must leave those stable principles undisturbed upon which hitherto the Prussian State has securely rested. In the Empire the constitutional rights of all the Federal Governments are to be as conscientiously observed as those of the Imperial Diet. . . . I am resolved to govern in the Empire and in Prussia with a conscientious observation of the provisions of their respective constitutions.[73]

These statements made it clear that Frederick had every intention of keeping the chancellor's policies within constitutional bounds.[74]

It is not known how Bismarck responded to the exact contents of the proclamations, but it is reasonable to assume that the chancellor knew enough about Frederick's liberal views to conclude that the latter would not retain a chancellor who wished to radically alter the constitution. This, in turn, may explain why the chancellor gave up his ambitious plans to change the constitution to his liking well before Frederick came to the throne.[75]

Although the chancellor could tolerate Frederick's liberal constitutionalism, he was concerned about reports indicating the crown prince's apparent unwillingness to resist his wife's determination to bring Freisinn to power. Victoria's letters to her husband show that she rejected his view that the liberalization of Germany would be difficult, if not impossible, during the coming reign.[76] She believed that the damage done by Bismarck could be rectified if the chancellor relinquished control over domestic policy to the Freisinn Party:

Abelino [Bismarck] is and remains the man for exceptional circumstances; power, energy, clear-headedness [and] genial courage are his virtues—all of which have accomplished a great deal during foreign [policy] crises! . . . This [domestic policy] requires other virtues, which are possessed by the Progressive Left—they have the insight and the drive to improve and dignify the [domestic] situation; they are committed to bringing out the best in human nature—these are the best people to work with! [77]

Freisinn would foster the development of what the crown princess saw as ideal for Germany: "a strong government that can protect the country from danger abroad . . . a good and strong army—an efficient but small navy." The new Germany, she said, would not foster "absolutism, imperialism or the development of a workers' state."[78] Victoria added that she was bowed but not broken by Freisinn losses in the elections of 1884, and she was convinced that members of the Freisinn Party felt the same way. "Their time will come," she said, and she looked forward to the time when Germany could rid itself of "clericalists, socialists and ultraconservatives" who were "enemies of freedom" and "disciples of violence."[79]

This exchange shows that Victoria did not consider the very real possibility that Bismarck would refuse to serve with ministers who wished drastically to revise his domestic policy. Frederick, on the other hand, was wary of his wife's plans but did not contradict them. Frederick's unwillingness to challenge his wife's views did not go unnoticed by Holstein. In October 1884, he wrote:

Everyone is agreed that the Crown Prince's character grows weaker year by year. And it seems certain that his wife's influence is increasing every year. The only point on which opinions vary is whether the Chancellor will restrain her influence when she is Kaiserin. Formerly, I should have felt convinced he would. Now I hope for the best, but without any certainty, for the Chancellor is growing old.[80]

Holstein was also alarmed about the way Victoria appeared to dominate her husband:

In the opinion of all the initiated, insofar as they are honest, it is absolutely inconceivable that the Crown Prince should ever, no matter what the circumstances, assert his own will in opposition to his wife's. "You only have to look what she's made of him," said S[ommerfeld] recently. "But for her he'd be the average man, very arrogant, good tempered, of mediocre gifts, and with a good deal of common sense. But now he's not a man at all, he has no ideas of his own, unless she allows him. He's a mere cipher. 'Ask my wife,' or 'Have you discussed the matter with the Crown Princess?'—there's no more to be said."[81]

Sommerfeld's views were confirmed by Radolinski, who told Holstein, "When the Crown Prince comes to power, the Crown Princess will be Kaiser."[82]

Reports of Frederick's vulnerability to his wife's influence were also confirmed by the crown prince's friends. In 1886, Frederick and Stosch discussed the composition of the government during the coming reign. Stosch observed "that a change in program would not be necessary as long as he retained Bismarck." This was agreeable to the crown prince, who also looked favorably upon Stosch's suggestion to remove the reactionary ministers of finance and the interior when he came to the throne. But Stosch told Normann in July that there was good reason to believe that Frederick would not abide by his suggestions if they were not to Victoria's liking: "The crown prince has not an atom of action . . . or reliability either."[83]

Stosch was right: his advice did not appeal to the crown princess, who made it abundantly clear to her husband that she did not approve of him: "It's a pity that his [Stosch's] irascibility and sharpness and his awkward way of interfering make him sometimes a bit dangerous." The crown princess asked her husband to refrain from relying on Stosch's advice and put himself in contact with anti-Bismarck liberals such as Roggenbach and Walther Loë. "That would make me *very* happy," she said.[84]

Stosch tried to warn the crown prince of the dangers of associating with left liberals. He told the crown prince that "a further move to the left in the Reichstag would deprive him of support of the German princes." He added that even "the National Liberals were wary of the crown prince precisely because of his wife's close contacts with the Left Liberals."[85] Stosch advised the crown prince and his wife to meet with National Liberal leaders Miquel and Bennigsen, in hopes that they could find a basis for mutual cooperation. The crown princess, however, was not interested. In April 1887, Stosch wrote that the crown prince "wanted to meet with Bennigsen, but that he dared not for fear of his wife."[86]

In March 1885, Holstein learned that Victoria was entertaining thoughts of dismissing the chancellor. Seckendorff reported that the crown princess had been in touch with Dr. Heinrich Geffcken, who was a vehement opponent of Bismarck. According to Seckendorff, Geffcken was filling Victoria's head with ideas as to how Bismarck could be tactfully eased out of power after the succession. Seckendorff asked the crown princess to refrain from associating with Geffcken, but she refused. Victoria also made no secret of her desire to make significant changes that Bismarck would hardly condone in the coming reign. In April 1885, Holstein wrote:

The Crown Princess stated again recently that in the coming transformation of society there would be no more room for "powerful" monarchs. Power was superfluous; it was enough for the sovereign to secure personal influence. In England, for example, where the Queen possessed no real power, she did nevertheless wield unusual influence, and was also generally loved and respected. The Princess went on to speak very bitterly about universal suffrage and in particular about tariffs; free trade, she said, was the only right policy.[87]

Statements such as these made it clear that the road to rapprochement between the royal couple and Bismarck lay in Holstein's ability to convince Victoria, not Frederick, that it was necessary to cooperate with the chancellor during the coming reign. In May 1885, Sommerfeld and Seckendorff made every effort to convince the crown princess that it was necessary to mend fences with Bismarck if he were to stay on during the coming reign. They reminded her of her "unpopularity and suspicion because of the un-German sentiments attributed to her," and they begged her to abandon the notion of dismissing Bismarck after the succession.[88] If Bismarck was dismissed, they warned, Prince William, who opposed his parents at every turn, could rally to the retired chancellor and form an opposition bloc that would be stronger than the liberal succession government. To this the crown princess replied that she intended to retain Bismarck, but her advisers retorted that she was mistaken in her belief that the chancellor would serve with left liberals such as Forckenbeck and Richter.

Sommerfeld and Seckendorff's arguments made an impression on the crown princess, who was well aware that their warnings about her son were not exaggerated.[89] In late June, she indicated her willingness to assure Bismarck that she wished him to stay on after the succession. She expressed these ideas in a memorandum sent to minister of justice Friedberg, a friend of the royal couple, who was to mediate between the crown princess and the chancellor. Although she did not intend to abandon her liberal beliefs, she wished to assure Bismarck that "she would not place any obstacles in his path, any more than she had done during the regency."[90]

Victoria's memorandum, however, shows that she nevertheless intended to embark on a more liberal course. The memorandum began with the observation that the imminent succession would mark the end of a glorious era in German history dominated by the emperor and Bismarck. "They have created a unique and wondrous structure [the German empire], but the structure has its weaknesses," she said.[91] The quality of German leadership, she wrote, would change when her husband came to the throne:

Instead of an elderly soldier [William] who was educated at a time when ideas and challenges were far different from those of today . . . comes a mature but energetic man, no less a soldier. He has not been unaffected by all the upheavals, events and ideological battles that have taken place since 1848. Since then he has seen much of the world, he is deeply interested in the development of modern ideas, and he is just as ambitious as his father where his fatherland is concerned.[92]

What her husband intended to do, she said, was to retain and build upon all those things that had made Prussia great. His reign would emphasize military power, industriousness, and order, but to this would be added cultural development, prosperity, and universal education of all people so that they could achieve more individual liberty and political maturity.

These noble aims, however, could not be achieved unless the central government gave up some of its authority: "The central government cannot do everything," she said, "and the division of labour is the principle that rules the world today." The new government would therefore initiate the transition to a new political order in which the administrative powers held by the central government would be gradually shifted into the hands of the people. This process, she said, would be supervised by Bismarck: "The strong hand of a Prince Bismarck will no doubt be capable of building these bridges that will safely enable us to cross into a new era that will crown his lifetime achievements."[93]

Victoria noted that her husband would be only too happy to cooperate with Bismarck; he would be considerate of the chancellor's wishes and would not overburden him. Further, she insisted that Frederick's liberalism was not an obstacle to a good working relationship with the chancellor: "The crown prince stands above the [political] parties and has not made any particular party doctrine his own; but he does have certain convictions about certain great questions which are to some degree shared by the liberal parties. [But] it will be possible for him ... to only do that which will not disrupt the natural process of [political] development."[94] She also hoped that the future would witness greater cooperation between all political parties, and that the government would adopt a milder tone toward its critics. Most of all, she hoped for an alliance of anti-socialist elements in the land, since it was the rising tide of socialism that presented the greatest threat to Germany's welfare: "State laws will not enable us to get rid of them [the socialists]; the entire society must work on this!"[95]

The crown princess closed the memorandum by insisting that she wished to be seen as an asset in Bismarck's eyes. She insisted that the rumors concerning her anti-German sentiments were simply false:

Sometimes I want to laugh, but more often I cry about all the things that are attributed to me. Among other things, it is said that I am only capable of judging things from an English ... standpoint! This does not flatter my intelligence, because one does not have to be a genius to know that the institutions of one country are not necessarily suitable for another! (Prince Bismarck's clothing would no doubt weigh heavily upon me and not fit at all). ... Although I do have faults ... I don't believe that megalomania and ambition are among them. Perhaps if Prince Bismarck would see me more often, he would see that I am not the disruptive and dangerous person that I am considered to be . . . he has never had the opportunity to see for himself that the opposite is true.[96]

Frederick did not allow this memorandum to be sent to Bismarck. He told his wife that he considered her memorandum "too artificial," which was true, given the fact that his proclamation to the chancellor and Victoria's memorandum had little in common. He also feared that it would "arouse comment."[97] There is every reason to believe that the crown prince was right: Bismarck would have soundly rejected Victoria's wish to increase the powers of the Reichstag at the expense of the central government, and he would have hardly been willing to oversee the transition to a less centralized form of government. In any case, Frederick himself was not willing to rule along the lines proposed by his wife. She wished to temper the power of the chancellor to increase the power of parliament, whereas her husband wanted to decrease Bismarck's power to increase the prestige of the crown.[98]

Since the hoped-for rapprochement between the crown princess and the chancellor did not materialize, Bismarck's allies continued to express concern about Victoria's influence over her husband. The chancellor himself was also wary of Victoria's ability to persuade her husband to agree to ideas that the chancellor considered dangerous. This was clearly the case when Victoria secured her husband's grudging consent to the marriage of their daughter Victoria to Prince Alexander of Battenberg, ruler of Bulgaria. The latter had been installed by the Russians as the puppet ruler of Bulgaria, but in 1885, he defied his Russian patrons by supporting a Bulgarian nationalist revolution and proclaiming his intention to rule an independent Bulgaria, free of Russian influence. Bismarck was vehemently opposed to the Battenberg marriage. He felt that a marriage between Alexander and the granddaughter of the German emperor would needlessly involve Germany in Balkan affairs, seriously compromise Russo-German relations, and run the risk of war between the two countries.[99]

The Battenberg marriage issue soured relations between the royal couple and the chancellor, who continued to block the marriage even after Alexander was forced by the Russians to abdicate in 1886. By Bismarck's lights, Alexander's abdication did not rule out the possibility, however slight, that he could be recalled to the Bulgarian throne. If Alexander returned to Bulgaria with his German-born wife, Germany might, indeed, be drawn into Balkan affairs. Even if Alexander never regained his throne, "the marriage of the anti-Russian prince to the emperor's granddaughter would be certain to arouse Russian suspicion."[100]

Bismarck also regarded the marriage as a potential threat to his own power during the coming reign. He got wind of Frederick's intention to appoint Alexander governor of Alsace-Lorraine[101] and probably suspected that the crown princess would have no qualms of having Alexander eventually replace Bismarck as chancellor. The chancellor therefore did everything he could to prevent the emperor from being won over to the idea of accepting the marriage. He composed a lengthy memorandum that effectively blackened Alexander's character and future ambitions. Bismarck attempted to prove that Alexander's position in Bulgaria was merely a stepping-stone toward procurement of power in Germany.[102]

Bismarck also accused the prince of stirring up the opposition parties against the government:

His first step towards this goal was a publicity campaign in the German, Austrian and British Press. . . . All the German opposition papers, Jesuit, Guelph, Radical, Polish, and Social Democratic, at once recognized in the Prince and his cause a useful weapon with which to attack the government and its foreign policy. All parties and individuals working for the overthrow of the existing order realised with unerring instinct that Prince Alexander, with his connexions [sic] with influential circles in Germany and England, could under certain conditions be used as a figurehead by the "malcontents." Since his return to Germany, Prince Alexander has the support of all those parties . . . whose [news]papers have been unanimous in their condemnation of Germany's Bulgarian policy.[103]

If Alexander became chancellor, Bismarck predicted that he "would command a majority in the Reichstag, though he would at the same time be the occasion of a split in that majority, because it is united only by its opposition to Government proposals, not by any positive aims." If Alexander did not attain the chancellorship, he would still be a threat as governor of Alsace-Lorraine. The governorship, said Bismarck, was a position that required "unswerving loyalty to the Kaiser and Reich"—a quality that Alexander, based on his relations with the tsar, did not possess: "If the Prince broke faith with the Sultan and the Tsar in order to become King of the Bulgars . . . then where is the guarantee against the possibility of his turning against the German Kaiser if he saw any prospect of becoming, possibly with French assistance, King of the Swabians or Prince or the Confederation of the Rhine?"[104] The emperor accepted all of Bismarck's arguments, as well as Bismarck's press campaign to discredit Alexander that followed.[105]

While Bismarck was able to handle the Battenberg threat during the emperor's lifetime, he feared that this would change when the crown prince came to the throne. For this reason Bismarck had to look for a way to ensure himself against being confronted with a Reichstag dominated by a pro-Battenberg opposition. Although opposition parties were defeated in the elections of 1884, Bismarck still did not have a solid bloc of support for his policies in the Reichstag.[106] Faced with an uncooperative Reichstag and a weak heir whose wife supported the anti-Bismarck opposition, Bismarck knew he had to construct a parliamentary majority for himself to remain in office.

Bismarck ultimately managed to construct an alliance against the crown princess and her pro-Battenberg sympathizers by convincing voters that international tensions demanded a new armaments bill. Bismarck anticipated that liberals would object to the long-term aspect of the bill, since this would deprive the Reichstag of the ability to control the military budget directly. When the liberal parties rejected the bill, the chancellor dissolved the Reichstag and called for new elections.[107] During the election campaign, Bismarck accused the liberal parties of endangering Germany's national security. The voters accepted this propaganda, and subsequent elections in 1887 produced a coalition of right-wing National Liberals and Conservatives, which was dubbed the Bismarck Cartel. Bismarck's victory was achieved at the expense of Freisinn, which retained only thirty-two seats after the elections of 1887.[108]

Despite the severity of their electoral defeat in 1887, many members of the Freisinn Party considered themselves to be a viable political force in Germany. Immediately after the elections, Theodor Barth's article in *Die Nation* "implied that the luck of Freisinn would turn after Frederick III came to the throne."[109] Victoria shared this view and tried to isolate her husband from anyone who felt differently.

Bismarck's parliamentary position was stronger than it had been in years, thanks to his Cartel, but the ability of the crown prince to resist his wife appeared to be weaker than ever. Stosch felt that the only way to check Victoria's domination over the crown prince was to surround the latter with "strong advisors who would persuade him to reach a speedy decision and then to face her with a *fait accompli*."[110]

But this was a suggestion, not a formulated plan, and there was nothing to prevent Victoria from upsetting Bismarck's domestic position by forcing her husband to make concessions to the left liberal opposition during the coming reign.[111] Nor did Bismarck have any assurance that Victoria would not try to push through the Battenberg marriage at the earliest possible date. Given the delicate state relations between Germany and Russia, the Battenberg marriage would have at least put a strain on the recently negotiated Russo-German Reinsurance Treaty.

In late 1887, reports on Frederick's failing health gave rise to speculation that Victoria would exploit her husband's physical weakness to get what she wanted. But as the following chapter shows, it was precisely Frederick's illness that ultimately provided the chancellor the means with which to counteract her influence during her husband's brief reign.

NOTES

1. Although many accused Bismarck of using social welfare legislation as a convenient means of garnering conservative political support, the fact remains that the legislation provided the most comprehensive protection of workers yet introduced in any country. According to H. W. Koch, "To attribute Bismarck's social legislation to mere opportunism, to a carrot-and-stick policy towards the members of the Social Democratic party . . . ignores the body of ample evidence available. This shows that Bismarck from the earliest days of his political career had recognized the social problem and considered it the state's duty to intervene

on behalf of the underprivileged." H. W. Koch, *A Constitutional History of Germany in the Nineteenth and Twentieth Centuries* (London 1984), p. 152. For a broad survey of state welfare activities, see Florian Tennstedt, *Sozialgeschichte der Sozialpolitik in Deutschland: Vom 18. Jahrhundert bis zum Ersten Weltkrieg* (Göttingen, 1981). Tennstedt argues that the controversial legislation helped the poor and that Bismarck's goal of involving workers in the state was realized, albeit long after the chancellor disappeared from the scene.

2. Liberals who opposed the legislation recommended in its stead an extension of employers' liability, more mutual aid associations, and more and larger private insurance companies. Otto Pflanze, *Bismarck and the Development of Germany. Volume 3: The Period of Fortification 1880–1898* (Princeton, NJ, 1990), p. 160.

3. Diary entry, 4 November 1884. Geheimes Staatsarchiv Preussischer Kulturbesitz, Merseburg (hereafter GStAPK Merseburg) Nachlass Friedrich III, Rep. 52, FI Nr. 7x (Diaries). However, Frederick's biographer Margarete von Poschinger writes that Frederick supported Bismarck's social welfare program: "The memorable message of 17 November 1881, in which the Emperor once more urged upon the Reichstag the active promotion of the prosperity of the labouring classes as a remedy for socialistic evils, and which was intended to show that the Emperor supported the Chancellor's policy with the whole weight of his authority, was the result of deliberations with the Crown Prince as well as the Emperor." Margarete von Poschinger, *Life of the Emperor Frederick*, (New York., 1971) p. 422.

4. Pflanze, *Bismarck,* Vol. 3, p. 161.

5. Diary entry, 30 October 1884. GStAPK Merseburg Nachlass Friedrich III, Rep. 52, FI Nr. 7x.

6. Hessische Hausstiftung, Schloss Fasanerie, Fulda (hereafter HH): Crown Princess Victoria to Crown Prince Frederick William, Botzen, 13 November 1884.

7. James J. Sheehan, *German Liberalism in the Nineteenth Century* (Chicago, 1978), p. 131. Richter's political vision is the focus of Ina Susanne Lorenz's *Eugen Richter: Der entschiedene Liberalismus in wilhelminischer Zeit 1871 bis 1906* (Leipzig, 1981).

8. HH: Crown Princess Victoria to Crown Prince Frederick William, Rome, 5 April 1880.

9. HH: Crown Princess Victoria to Crown Prince Frederick William, Balmoral, 9 September 1884.

10. Frederic Ponsonby, *Letters of the Empress Frederick* (London, 1929), p. 191.

11. HH: Crown Prince Frederick William to Crown Princess Victoria, Berlin, 7 April 1880.

12. HH: Stockmar to Crown Prince Frederick William, 26 April 1880.

13. Paul Kennedy, *The Rise of the Anglo-German Antagonism: 1860–1914* (London, 1987), p. 163.

14. Ibid., p. 165

15. Ibid., p. 164. Bismarck's war against Gladstonism was extended to foreign

policy as well. Reports concerning the "instability" of Britain were sent to Vienna and St. Petersburg to keep Germany's allies wary of Britain. The Austrians in particular were repeatedly subject to Bismarck's expression of his conviction that Gladstone's policies were "unacceptably antimonarchical, revolutionary, unpeaceful." Ibid., p. 165. Bismarck also tried to convince the crown prince that British governing practices made an Anglo–German alliance impossible: "The prospect of swiftly changing governments allowed British ministers to repudiate the obligations of their predecessors." Ibid.

16. Bamberger's notes: "Gründung der deutschen Freisinnigen Partei, März 1884." Deutsches Bundesarchiv, Abteilung Potsdam (hereafter DBAP) 90 Ba 3, Nachlass Bamberger Nr. 232 #2.

17. HH: Crown Princess Victoria to Crown Prince Frederick William, 7 November 1884.

18. Stosch to Freytag, 26 December 1880. F.B.M. Hollyday, *Bismarck's Rival. A Political Biography of General and Admiral Albrecht von Stosch* (Durham, NC, 1963), p. 133. This concern was shared by British ambassador Odo Russell, who wrote British foreign secretary Granville, "When the dear old Emperor dies—and I regret to say that he has lately shown the first symptoms of ailing health—then Bismarck's irresponsible power ought to come to an end—that is, if the Crown Prince has the moral strength to compel his Chancellor to submit to the constitution of the Empire, and accept the accidents of a parliamentary system based on universal suffrage, which, at present, Bismarck absolutely refuses to do." Russell to Granville, 19 November 1881, Paul Knaplund, ed., *Letters from the British Embassy, 1871–1874 1880–1885* (Washington, D. C., 1944), p. 231.

19. Geffcken to Roggenbach, 23 March 1883, DBAP, Nachlass Bamberger, 90Ba3, #227.

20. In response to this incident, Friedrich von Holstein (privy counsellor in the foreign office and a friend of Bismarck) commented in his diary: "The Crown Princess has said, it is stated in the Press that the Crown Prince was consulted before the German Radical Party [Freisinn] was formed, and that he gave his approval to the step. It is a lie which could only have been invented with the object of alienating the Kaiser and Chancellor from the Crown Prince." Norman Rich and M. H. Fisher, eds., *The Holstein Papers.* 4 Vols (hereafter HP) (Cambridge, 1957), Vol. 2, p. 155.

21. Hollyday, *Stosch*, pp. 218–219.

22. Gordon Craig, *Germany: 1866–1945* (New York, 1978), p. 165.

23. The accusation split the party vote on the bill, for many liberals feared being labelled as working hand in glove with the Social Democrats and voted for renewal, whereas their colleagues were unwilling to abandon their party's insistence on equality before the law regardless of person or party. Craig, *Germany*, p. 167.

24. Ibid.

25. According to historian Hans-Ulrich Wehler, Bismarck's drive for colonies was motivated by specific economic factors: after the economic crisis of 1882, the

chancellor believed that colonies would ensure safe and secure economic growth and preserve the existing social hierarchy and political structure. H. U. Wehler, "Bismarck und der Imperialismus, 1862–1890" in Wehler, ed., *Krisenherde des Kaiserreichs 1871–1918* (Göttingen, 1970), p. 120. Otto Pflanze supports this view: "Anxiety about the state of Germany's economy, concern about social stability, and the search for secure and growing markets, and the dynamics of European and world politics were the principal conditions that led to Bismarck's change on the policy of colonies." He adds, however, that Bismarck embarked on the colonial program only after he was reasonably certain that such a policy would not incur "serious harm to Germany's foreign relations in Europe." Pflanze, *Bismarck,* Volume 3, pp. 122–123. Woodruff Smith sees colonialism more as "a result of social and political changes that had occurred over the course of the whole nineteenth century." Woodruff Smith, *The German Colonial Empire* (Chapel Hill, NC, 1978), p. 3.

26. Bismarck initially felt that England would support Germany's drive for colonies. According to Norman Rich, "Bismarck had every reason to suppose that the British government would be willing to make concessions to Germany in the colonial field in exchange for Germany's benevolent neutrality during the British occupation of Egypt, especially since the British still needed German support for their occupation policies." But the Gladstone government, to Bismarck's surprise, refused to give Germany the colonial concessions that it desired. Norman Rich, *Friedrich von Holstein, 2* Vols. (Cambridge, 1965), Vol. 1, p. 146. Bismarck was undeterred by British opposition to German colonial acquisitions. Instead, he tried to turn British opposition to his advantage by embarking upon a policy of cooperation with France on colonial issues. He was all the more willing to have such a policy result in a diplomatic defeat for the liberal government of Gladstone, which he despised and would have been happy to bring down. Ibid., p. 147

27. Kennedy, *Anglo-German Antagonism*, pp. 129–130. Unlike Bismarck, the crown prince supported the idea of colonial acquisitions for Germany long before 1884. In 1873, Russell wrote Granville, "Neither he (Berhnard von Bülow, Prussian Secretary of State for Foreign Affairs, 1873–79) nor Bismarck wish for Colonies— the Crown Prince does." Paul Knaplund, *Letters from the British Embassy* pp. 118–119.

28. Crown Princess Victoria to Lady Ponsonby, 17 October 1884. Ponsonby, *Empress Frederick* (London, 1929), p. 195.

29. Egon Caesar Corti, *The English Empress. A Study in the Relations Between Queen Victoria and her Eldest Daughter, Empress Frederick of Germany* (London, 1957), p. 223. Holstein suspected that Bismarck's colonial policy was meant to compromise the reputation of the crown princess among the liberal parties, since colonial enthusiasts in the National Liberal Party considered her opposition to colonial policy to be unpatriotic. As he confided to his diary in August 1884: "The colonial question, now in its early stages, may bedevil our relations with England for a considerable period, even though an actual conflict is out of the

question. The problem is likely to pass over into the new reign. But should a conflict arise, no other question is so liable to put the future Kaiserin, with her Anglophile tendencies, in a false position vis à vis the German nation. For it is precisely the liberals and democrats who want colonies." HP, Vol 2, p. 155.

30. Craig, *Germany*, p. 168. For a survey of the history of the Social Democratic Party, see W. L. Guttsman, *The German Social Democratic Party 1875–1933: From Ghetto to Government* (Boston, 1981).

31. Diary entry, 30 October 1884. GStAPK Merseburg Nachlass Friedrich III, Rep. 52, FI Nr. 7x.

32. Bismarck to Crown Prince Frederick William, 30 October 1881. Auswärtiges Amt, Bonn, (hereafter AA) Nachlass Richthofen, 1/2 #22.

33. Crown Prince Frederick William to Bismarck (draft), 7 November 1881, AA, Nachlass Richthofen, 1/3 #22, Ad. The letter appears to have been drafted by Karl von Normann and reads: "Während in der Elsass-Lothringen Staathalterfrage keinerlei Differenz zwischen uns stattgefunden hat, habe ich die volle Bereitwilligkeit, mit welcher Sie meinen die Vermählung meines Sohnes zutreffenden Wünschen von Anfang an entgegengekommen sind, immer nur dankbar anerkennen können."

34. HP, Vol 2, p. 51 fn. This statement is very much at odds with Stockmar's concern about the crown prince's attitude toward liberalism: "I respectfully submit a newspaper article which outlines the deepest current concerns of all enlightened patriots: that is, the prevailing tendency of Your Royal Highness to totally identify himself with the present government system which diminishes hope that any change will be possible in the future. I, however, believe that it is possible for Your Royal Highness to reassert your independence." HH: Stockmar to Crown Prince Frederick William, 22 December 1881.

35. Rich, *Holstein*, p. 133.

36. Holstein's minor position belied his extraordinary influence on German affairs. He entered the Prussian diplomatic service in 1860 under the aegis of Bismarck. In succeeding years, Bismarck furthered his career in numerous posts abroad, and it was Bismarck who brought him to Berlin in the 1860s. HP, Vol. 2, pp. 132ff.

37. Rich, *Holstein*, p. 133.

38. Ibid., pp. 178–179.

39. Ibid., p. 179.

40. Ibid., p. 140. Holstein was quick to point out that the crown prince was not the only one to exaggerate the importance of trivial matters. According to Holstein, Bismarck had overreacted when he insisted that no members of his cabinet attend the funeral of left liberal leader Eduard Lasker in January 1884: "If only the Chancellor were not so violent about trifles," said Holstein. "It is all the same to him whether his opponent is alive or dead—'no peace to the wicked' is his maxim." Given Bismarck's feelings on the subject of Lasker's memorial service, Holstein made sure that the royal couple did not attend, for Holstein feared that "this would

cause a breach with the Chancellor that would not be healed for a long time." The royal couple heeded this advice; the crown princess did, however, send a letter to Ludwig Bamberger complimenting him on his memorial address at Lasker's funeral. HP, Vol. 2, p. 72, and Rich, *Holstein*, p. 140.

41. As we have seen, Stosch was a conservative in his political views, and he spent much time and effort trying to bring the crown prince closer to the chancellor. But in the process, Stosch incurred Bismarck's jealousy and hatred: Bismarck envied Stosch since he was on good terms with both the crown prince and the emperor. Since Stosch was associated with the liberal movement because he was Frederick's friend, Bismarck unjustly labelled Stosch a Gladstonian radical. See Hollyday, *Stosch*, p. 135.

42. HP, Vol. 2, p. 46.

43. In September 1879, Normann wrote: "Nothing can be more hateful to the truly sophisticated circles of our people than an othodox conservative regime. . . . Even with all the power at his disposal, Bismarck is not strong enough to restrain the evil spirits that he has liberated—and what evil spirits they are!" HH: Karl von Normann to Crown Princess Victoria, Neues Palais, 26 September 1879. Like Victoria, he was sharply critical of those liberals who chose not to break their allegiance to Bismarck after the events of 1878–1879: "Dr. Delbrück visited me recently—he . . . thinks that everything that is going on is splendid. Whatever Bismarck does is above reproach—even to err with the 'great man' is a victory." Ibid., 3 November 1879. Normann also told Victoria that Bismarck's conservative economic policy was the primary obstacle to an Anglo-German alliance: "It is quite clear," he wrote, "that England will not be receptive to the thought of allying with us as long as our policy in international trade is based on the useless retrograde theory." HH: Karl von Normann to Crown Princess Victoria, Neues Palais, 26 September 1879.

44. Ibid., 4 November 1879.

45. Ibid., 23 November 1880.

46. Ibid., 20 August 1881.

47. Marschall to Turban, Berlin, 22 June 1884. Walter Fuchs, *Grossherzog Friedrich I von Baden und die Reichspolitik 1871–1907* 4 Vols. (Stuttgart, 1968–1980), Vol. 2, p. 251.

48. Normann's talent for intrigue was evident in late 1883 when he publicized the ill-will between the crown prince and the chancellor when the latter abruptly requested the former to see the pope in Rome. Frederick asked his wife to discover the purpose of his visit . She replied: "I am not let in on secrets, and I do not know where the idea originated from, nor what the purpose [of the visit] is." HH: Crown Princess Victoria to Crown Prince Frederick William, Neues Palais, 11 December 1883. Frederick learned the purpose of the visit only after his return to Berlin, and he complained to Paul Hatzfeldt, the state secretary in the Foreign Ministry, that he had felt like "Bismarck's courier, who was forced to chase the globe without instructions or without opportunity to consult on what he was supposed to do." HP, Vol. 2 p. 44 fn. After his return, Bismarck explained that the visit was intended

to show German Catholics that reconciliation with the Vatican was not out of the question. Bismarck later said that he had deliberately kept Frederick in the dark about the Rome mission for fear that Normann would leak details of the mission to the press. Bismarck's suspicions about Normann were correct, since the latter's name was linked to the publication of Frederick's interview with the pope in the *Nationalzeitung*. The article downplayed the importance of the meeting, probably in order to appease liberals who wished to see the crown prince as someone who opposed the abrogation of Kulturkampf legislation. HP, Vol.2 p. 44 fn.

49. Rich, *Holstein*, p. 138.

50. She did not confront her husband with Seckendorff's accusations but told him that she was upset by the rivalry between Sommerfeld and Normann: "It could happen that you could lose Sommerfeld, and this would be unfortunate for you; he is a gentleman—reliable, tactful and discreet and he could do so much for you, and only you can protect him from unpleasantries." HH: Crown Princess Victoria to Crown Prince Frederick William, Neues Palais, 13 September 1883. She intimated that Normann was responsible for the rift between himself and Sommerfeld; the latter, she said, had attempted repeatedly to establish a cordial relationship with Normann, but to no avail. The crown princess also accused Normann of neglecting his duties at court because of his preoccupation with politics and concluded that his talents would be best served in a political post so that he could educate himself to assume a political position during Frederick's coming reign. When Normann became chamberlain to the crown prince in 1882, Victoria told her husband that he was not to be considered a permanent fixture at court: "Eulenburg [Normann's predecessor as chamberlain] understood that Normann's position is only to be a temporary one, and that Normann will *later* serve you in some sort of *political* capacity. . . . When you become Kaiser, we will name another Court Chamberlain, and Normann will become a Minister without portfolio or a cabinet chief of some sort." Ibid., 17 September 1882. Victoria was also wary of Normann's presence at court because she intensely disliked his wife. As she told her husband, "You know that Normann and Stockmar are my most intimate friends . . . and that I treasure them as they so deserve, but I cannot forget that Normann has a *tactless* and *ambitious* wife, who intimidates and pushes her husband, and despite all of Normann's intelligence and spirit, he does *not always* have the power to resist her. She and she alone pushed him to demand the Schloss Hauptmann title—this has created much bad blood." Ibid., 17 September 1882.

51. HH: Crown Prince Frederick William to Crown Princess Victoria, Merseburg, 16 September 1883.

52. Rich, *Holstein* p. 138.

53. HH: Crown Princess Victoria to Crown Prince Frederick William, Baveno, 20 August 1885. She added that Normann would have to serve for several years in diplomatic posts before he could assume the position as the director of a German embassy abroad. She also wished to put Stosch to work but feared that Bismarck would never accept this, and she was utterly opposed to making Mischke a gen-

eral adjutant after the succession because he was unsuited to the post.

54. Freisinn newspapers contended that Bismarck had refused to sanction Frederick's appointment as president of the council of state unless he got rid of Normann. The implication here was that Frederick was duty-bound to accept the presidency and had to sacrifice Normann in order to please his father. This view has found an echo in Frederick and Victoria's biographies. Count Egon Caesar Corti wrote: "When Frederick William reached home he found agitation was being worked up against Karl von Normann . . . the Chancellor . . . suspected that Normann was working hand in glove with the Crown Princess, the Empress Augusta and General von Stosch, and finally succeeded in separating this faithful man from the Crown Prince by sending him as Minister to Oldenburg." Corti, *English Empress*, p. 221. However, Baden's minister to Prussia, Marschall, denied the existence of a Bismarckian plot to oust Normann. He wrote: "The progressive papers have asserted that this change in personnel came about as a result of the crown prince's assumption of the presidency of the council of state [Staatsrat]. . . . This is completely untrue. The fact of the matter is that . . . the crown prince called upon the Chancellor and requested to have Normann transferred to the diplomatic service and that he would be replaced by Radolinski, to which the Chancellor readily agreed." Marschall to Turban, Berlin, 22 Juni 1884. Fuchs, *Friedrich I von Baden,* Vol. 2, p. 251.

55. Hollyday, *Stosch* p. 218.

56. Andreas Dorpalen, "Frederick III and the Liberal Movement," *American Historical Review*, Vol. 54, No. 1 (October 1948), p. 24.

57. The crown prince was grateful to Bismarck for having granted Normann the Oldenburg legation and told Stosch that this was evidence of "his [Bismarck's] completely changed attitude towards me." Hollyday, *Stosch*, p. 218.

58. HH: Crown Prince Frederick William to Crown Princess Victoria, Bornstedt, 9 November 1884.

59. HP, Vol. 2, pp. 112–113.

60. Michael Stürmer holds that Bismarck kept alive the threat of a coup against the constitution during the 1870s and 1880s. See Michael Stürmer, *Das ruhelose Reich. Deutschland 1866–1918* (Berlin, 1985), p. 116 and M. Stürmer, "Staatsreichgedanken im Bismarckreich," *Historische Zeitschrift*, Vol 209 (1969). Johannes Ziekursch believes that Bismarck contemplated a coup to protect his position against Frederick's coming reign. Johannes Ziekursch, *Politische Geschichte des Neuen Deutschen Kaiserreichs* 3 Vols. (Frankfurt am Main., 1925–1930), Vol. 2, pp. 394–394

61. Conservatives were dissatisfied with his policies, and the Center Party was displeased with the lack of confessional peace at home. In March 1883, Geffcken wrote Roggenbach: "Bismarck's prestige has declined deeply in the eyes of all the political parties." Geffcken to Roggenbach, 23 March 1883, DBAP, Nachlass Bamberger, 90Ba3, #227. See also Ernst Rudolf Huber, *Deutsche Verfassungsgeschichte seit 1789.* 4 Vols. (Stuttgart, 1957–1969), Vol. 4, pp. 146–

150, and 202–227.

62. "In public and private discussions he charted the legal course for such an action by reinterpreting the constitution as a sovereign union not of the German people but of the federal states." Pflanze, *Bismarck*, Vol. 3, p. 98.

63. The council, originally created in 1817, was abandoned in 1848 due to liberal revolutionaries' demands for a more representative organ of government. Holstein explained the Bismarck's rationale for reviving the council: "The Chancellor mentioned that he thought it might be a good thing if the Council of State gradually evolved into an Imperial Council, to strengthen the Bundesrat, and counterbalance the Chancellor and the Reichstag. The genuine underlying aim is to create a further check to prevent both the Prussian and German Parliaments from falling into the abyss. The Chancellor said in this connexion [sic] that the Princes were the Conservative element, i.e. the force that held the Reich together, and the Parliaments were the disintegrating element." HP, Vol. 2, p. 105.

64. Hollyday, *Stosch*, p. 219.

65. Martin Philippson, *Das Leben Friedrichs III* (Wiesbaden, 1900), p. 341.

66. This assertion is partially confirmed by Holstein, who wrote, "The Crown Prince's attitude to the Council of State has gone through various phases. First, opposition to it as a liberal, then interest in the work, but now complete rejection of it again." HP, Vol. 2, p. 167.

67. Pflanze, *Bismarck*, Vol. 3, p. 108.

68. Hollyday, *Stosch*, p. 231.

69. "Meine Grundsätze müssen eine dauerende Regierungspolitik tragen. . . und in entsprechender Weise den Partei Anhang des Kanzlers mindern, so dass ich der Herr des Reichskanzlers bin, der fortan wohl mein Minister aber nicht mehr als ein falscher sei." Diary entry, 1885. GStAPK Merseburg Nachlass Friedrich III, Rep. 52, FI Nr. 7x (Diaries).

70. "Es ist zu berücksichtigen, dass Fälle eintreten können in der ohne B[ismarck]. und wenn's sein muss, gegen den Ex-Kanzler und seine Partei regiert werden muss. Daher ist die Regierung so zu komponieren dass die ausschlaggebenden Kreise in Preussen Vertrauen zu derselben haben." Ibid. Frederick also considered limiting Bismarck's power by making all ministers subject to re-appointment when the crown prince came to the throne. As re-appointments were being evaluated, Frederick would have the wherewithal to set limitations on Bismarck's power vis-à-vis the throne. This plan was rejected, probably because the justification for it was constitutionally dubious [!]. Huber, *Verfassungsgeschichte*, pp. 166–167.

71. "Also status quo zum Anfang, nun so mehr als Zeit zur Beobachtung und Kenntnis der Regierungs-Maschine, freie Hand zur allmählicher Änderung, und wenn erst erforderlich, Successsiver [sic] Personenwechsel . . . Fehler, die ich vorfinde: Appetit-Reiz nach Geld gew-sen und Stellenbesitz—echt französische Verderbniss und im Widerspruch zum Alt Preuss[ischen] Beamthum. . . Confessionelle Gegensäzte . . . haben durch Fehler der Regierung unversöhnliche

Gegner erzeugt und zum polit[ischem] Machtstutz verholfen, welcher ihnen entrissen werden muss. . . Allgemeines Stimmrecht! und schlechte Presse . . . . National Occonom[ische] und sociale [sic] Fragen." Ibid.

72. The English translations of Frederick's proclamations appear in Rennell Rodd, *Frederick: Crown Prince and Emperor* (London, 1888), pp. 189–197.

73. Ibid., pp. 192–194.

74. Hollyday, *Stosch*, p. 231. With difficulty, Frederick's advisers managed to convince him to abandon his insistence on styling himself Frederick IV, in the line of the Holy Roman Emperors. Ibid., pp. 229 ff.

75. See Pflanze, *Bismarck,* Vol. 3, pp. 98 and 108.

76. HH: Crown Princess Victoria to Crown Prince Frederick William, Botzen, 8 November 1884.

77. Ibid., 7 November 1884.

78. Ibid.

79. Ibid. Victoria's passionate support for Freisinn can be explained by a letter she wrote to her mother in March 1890: "What a pity it is that the *Times* makes such superficial and prejudiced remarks about our elections! The Freisinnige are not republicans and democrats at all—they are as like the English Whigs as they can be—they want constitutional government—as little state interference as possible—and free trade, no Socialism, no repressive laws, no persecution of Jews and Catholics. Of course they do grumble about the army budget, sometimes they oppose the taxes on wheat, bread and coffee. They are especially detested by Prince Bismarck and consequentially calumniated in every possible way." Ponsonby, *Letters*, p. 409.

80. HP, Vol 2, p. 164.

81. Ibid., pp. 194–195.

82. Ibid., p. 194.

83. Ibid., pp. 232–233.

84. HH: Crown Princess Victoria to Crown Prince Frederick William, Windsor, 10 May 1886. The chancellor hated Baron Walther von Löe, whom he accused of being in league with the Empress Augusta.

85. Hollyday, *Stosch*, p. 225. He wrote: "nothing could be more dangerous for his position than reports from [Freisinn deputy] Karl Schrader."

86. Quoted in Ibid., p. 226.

87. Ibid., p. 190.

88. Rich, *Holstein*, p. 144.

89. Victoria knew too well that William would turn against his parents by siding with Bismarck. In late 1884, she wrote her husband, "He [William] is somewhat narrow-minded and hard-hearted—only time can help him do away with these evils! He only associates with hard-core officers, Junkers, and Berlin society. . . . We would only bring agony upon ourselves if we even attempted to convert William!" HH: Crown Princess Victoria to Crown Prince Frederick William, Botzen, 13 November 1884.

90. Rich, *Holstein*, p. 212.

91. HH: Crown Princess Victoria to Friedberg, 1 July 1885.

92. Ibid.

93. Ibid.

94. Ibid.

95. Ibid. Victoria's ideas on the social question were echoed by the National Liberal Reichstag representative Karl Braun, who held that a free society giving free reign to economic energies could alleviate poverty and bring class interests into harmony. See Winifried Selig, *Von Nassau zum Deutschen Reich: Die ideologische und politische Entwicklung von Karl Braun* (Wiesbaden, 1981).

96. Ibid

97. HP, Vol. 2, p. 212.

98. When the memorandum was rejected as a vehicle for rapprochement, Holstein suggested a formal meeting between Victoria and the chancellor. Victoria was willing to cooperate, but the chancellor was not. Bismarck told Holstein that a meeting would accomplish nothing: "We have no quarrel to be settled. The only thing I reproach the lady with is that she's remained an Englishwoman and exerts pro-English influence on her husband." Bismarck added that the crown prince had already given him assurances that he would be able to direct foreign policy after the succession and that he would be relieved of many of his other responsibilities that he found taxing, given his advanced age. The chancellor was relieved about this, but he was suspicious when Frederick shied away from discussing the composition of the post-succession cabinet. According to Holstein: "From this the chancellor concluded that the Crown Prince was contemplating a cabinet of a very leftist tinge. He . . . said 'I refuse to serve with Ministers I despise.' He suspected that the sole aim of Victoria's cooperation was to trap him into demonstrations which would make it appear as though he were clinging to his position." Ibid., p. 212. Victoria's memorandum shows that Bismarck's suspicions were probably correct.

99. Victoria's clash with Bismarck over the Battenberg marriage began to brew at a time when Holstein was forced to play down his efforts to effect a rapprochement between the two parties. In the fall of 1885, Holstein learned that his activities had aroused the jealousy of Bismarck's son, Herbert von Bismarck. As much as Holstein wanted the rapprochement to be effected, he knew that Herbert's jealousy, if left unchecked, could severely jeopardize his political future. Although Holstein told Herbert that undertaking the mission to improve relations between the chancellor and the royal couple was far from an enviable task, Herbert was determined to assume the role of mediator. Holstein knew, however, that Herbert's prospects for success were dismal: "Herbert will try . . . to bring the Chancellor and the Crown Prince together by acting as confidant to both," he noted in his diary. "He will not succeed, because the Crown Prince and Princess positively detest him." HP, Vol 2, p. 224.

100. Rich, *Holstein*, p. 204.

101. Any disappointment Victoria may have felt about Alexander's abdication was overshadowed by her firm belief that the Battenberg marriage could soon take place. She was anxious to reward Alexander for his bravery when he returned to Germany and pressed her husband to have Bismarck restore Alexander's lands and fortune to him. HH: Crown Princess Victoria to Crown Prince Frederick William, Campiglio, 26 August 1886. She also suggested that the prince be rewarded with the command of a Hessian division because "this has always been his dream." Frederick was willing to be even more generous than his wife: he suggested that Alexander could be appointed governor of Alsace-Lorraine during his coming reign. The crown princess wrote: "Your idea to someday appoint Sandro governor of Alsace-Lorraine [Reichsland] is excellent." Ibid., 26 August 1886.

102. Bismarck to William I, Varzin, 30 September 1886. HP Vol. 2, pp. 389. Bismarck reminded the emperor that Alexander's wish to attain power in Germany had been one of the reasons the chancellor had been anxious to keep the prince from losing his position in Bulgaria: "Already some years ago Your Majesty foresaw the possibility that in case Prince Alexander left Bulgaria, he would return to Germany to endeavour to create a position for himself here; and in consequence our diplomatic activities have been directed towards unobtrusively counteracting all efforts in Bulgaria aimed at his overthrow."

103. Ibid., p. 392.

104. Ibid.

105. Ibid., p. 393.

106. The Catholic Center Party continued to oppose him on a number of issues, and the Social Democrats were a troublesome element, and the renewal of the antisocialist law in 1886 had passed with difficulty. Bismarck considered confronting the Social Democratic threat by changing the electoral law, and he even hoped that the socialists would go to extremes and arrange a coup d'etat so that he could foster enough outrage to do away with them once and for all. Craig, *Germany*, p. 168.

107. The crown prince did not appear to oppose the military bill. As he told his wife, "Bismarck is in Varzin, but intends to make a political speech concerning the military budget. . . . Opposition is expected from the National Liberals and the Opposition, although this is not yet certain. Such a drastic increase in armaments will not fail to make its impression, but hopefully this will not have serious consequences." HH: Crown Prince Frederick William to Crown Princess Victoria, Letzlingen, 12 November 1886.

108. Rich, *Holstein*, p. 226.

109. Andreas Dorpalen, "Frederick III", p. 26.

110. Hollyday, *Stosch*, p. 227.

111. Victoria's biographer Egon Caesar Corti claims that the crown prince, who had been questioning Bismarck's methods of combatting socialism, wrote a memorandum on the subject in March 1887. Corti, *English Empress*, p. 237. But Frederick's papers show that the memorandum was merely an outline and was copied from a

draft of his wife's ideas on the subject. The outline concluded that the workers' needs could be better addressed by philanthropic interests as opposed to state socialism, a conclusion that echoed the views of prominent left liberals on the subject. HH: Drafts by Frederick and Victoria on the socialist problem, March 1887.

Chapter 7

The Illness, Reign, and Legend of Frederick III

Since the crown prince had always been prone to throat maladies,[1] he and his wife were not particularly concerned when he developed hoarseness as result of a cold in late 1886. This time, however, the hoarseness did not abate. In March 1887, Dr. Gerhardt, a throat specialist from the University of Berlin, examined the crown prince and discovered a small growth on the left vocal cord.[2] Dr. Gerhardt suspected that the growth was cancerous and asked Dr. Ernst von Bergmann, a prominent surgeon and the director of the medical school in Berlin, to confirm his diagnosis. Bergmann concurred with Gerhardt and advised an immediate operation on the larynx to prevent the spread of the disease and to save Frederick's life. After consulting with the crown prince and his wife, the doctors scheduled the surgery for 21 May.

Bismarck, however, believed that the doctors were acting too hastily and that the royal couple was not adequately informed about the risks involved in the surgical procedure.[3] Risks there were: if the doctors chose to perform a laryngectomy, the chances of surviving such surgery were slim, and postoperative patients had a life expectancy of only a few months to a little over one year.[4] Bismarck also requested that Frederick's case be reviewed by other experts. Other prominent throat specialists confirmed Bergmann's diagnosis and recommended surgery, but Bismarck was still not satisfied. He now insisted that the best non-German expert be called in for consultation, and the German doctors selected Dr. Morell Mackenzie, a noted British larnygologist.

To the surprise of the German doctors, Mackenzie believed that the growth was not cancer but a "wart or a papilloma" and insisted that the crown prince could be cured if he came to England for treatment. To substantiate his diagnosis, Mackenzie ordered Dr. Rudolf Virchow, known as the world's greatest authority on cells, to examine particles of Frederick's larynx microscopically. Virchow was able to find nothing to confirm a diagnosis of cancer.[5] With a tremendous sense of relief, the royal couple departed for England, with the doubting Bergmann and Gerhardt in tow.[6]

In July and August, Mackenzie told British reporters that the "disease was definitely not cancer and that very encouraging progress towards a cure was being made."[7] By the fall of 1887, however, Mackenzie's treatments had not cured the crown prince. Mackenzie insisted that there was still hope for a cure if the crown prince prolonged his stay in England. This course of action was rejected by the German doctors, who insisted that the crown prince would be better off under the care of his doctors in Berlin. They added that Frederick's presence was necessary in Berlin, because the health of his father was failing. The doctors finally reached a compromise: they agreed to allow the crown prince to recuperate in Toblach in the Tyrolian Alps, where the patient would benefit from the mountain air and still remain close to Germany in the event that the emperor's health took a turn for the worse.

Examination of Frederick's throat in November revealed changes in the growth that, even in Mackenzie's opinion, "looked very much like cancer."[8] The doctors now concluded that the crown prince faced two options, both equally grim: he could undergo surgery, though the doctors warned that even successful removal of the larynx would not guarantee against recurrence of the growth; or he could allow the disease to run its fatal course, and a tracheotomy could be performed to assist breathing. The crown prince opted for the latter course in writing, for he had been unable to speak for several months. He took the dreadful news bravely, and his stature in the face of death drew praise from Stosch, who wrote Normann:

I have thought back over the many difficult and dangerous days in which I saw the Prince and remembered how I always marvelled at his total calm and cold-bloodedness in such situations. . . . He must be prevented from looking death in the face and from that it follows that every operation, even the smallest, can endanger his life. May the Prince have a speedy end and keep the reputation of a courageous and fine man. He was always a handsome and lovable person, and he will remain one to the end.[9]

In early November, the royal entourage left for San Remo on the Italian Riviera, in the hope that the warm climate would improve Frederick's health.

The crown prince was not allowed to suffer in peace, for the treatment of his illness generated a deplorable domestic and international controversy.[10] Mackenzie continued to issue overly optimistic reports on Frederick's condition even as the health of his patient deteriorated, and the fact that he was championed by the royal couple angered the German doctors, who held that the postponement of surgery had been a fatal mistake and that Victoria's insistence on accepting the diagnosis of a British doctor would cost the crown prince his life.[11] This view was supported by the German conservatives, whose resentment of "British influence" was matched by their fears of Frederick's coming reign.[12] The conservatives now rallied around Frederick's son, Prince William, who sympathized with reactionary influences at court.[13] The liberals, on the other hand, supported Mackenzie and the crown prince.[14]

The agony of the royal couple was compounded when they learned that William's allies were attempting to remove the ailing Frederick from the line of succession. The most prominent members of this group were Herbert von Bismarck and General Emil von Albedyll, the chief of the emperor's military cabinet. Both were enemies of Victoria and believed that "she was issuing optimistic reports on her husband's condition to maintain the idea that he was incapable of ruling so that she could, in fact, rule herself."[15]

Bismarck shared Albedyll's fears about the crown princess; he knew that she was capable of exploiting her husband's physical weakness in order to realize goals—such as the Battenberg marriage—that could endanger Germany's security.[16] He must also have feared that Victoria could also promote the goals of the left liberals at the expense of the Cartel. Albedyll's scheme, however, was not a favorable alternative for the chancellor, since the general and his supporters wished to dismantle Bismarck's Cartel and wanted a preventive war with Russia.[17]

Faced with two unacceptable scenarios, Bismarck opted for a third course: he used the threat of a regency to restrain the crown princess when her husband came to the throne.[18] In mid-November, Bismarck presented an order for the emperor's signature that would allow Prince William to act as his grandfather's deputy in the event that the latter became "suddenly incapacitated." The order was signed without consulting the crown prince, but Bismarck gave the impression at court that the order "was a brutal act directed against the heir to the throne."[19]

The crown prince and princess were incensed by the deputization order, and Bismarck quickly came to their defense. He told the royal couple that he was in no way directly responsible for the order, nor could he have dissuaded the emperor from signing it. But he assured them that "the order had nothing to do with the succession and would automatically lapse with the accession of the crown prince, who would naturally become emperor on the death of his father."[20] This reply satisfied the crown prince and his wife, and with a sense of relief the crown princess told her mother that Bismarck looked forward to the reign of her husband and was willing to fight against any talk of Frederick's abdication in favor of his son. Victoria, however, failed to see that the chancellor's motives in blocking the regency were not altruistic; only after Frederick came to the throne did she discover that the price for the chancellor's support was submission to his will.

Meanwhile, the crown princess continued to put her faith in Mackenzie and discounted reports on the gravity of her husband's condition. Any improvement in his health she regarded as the beginning of a complete recovery. After Frederick underwent a tracheotomy in February 1888, Victoria told her mother, "Fritz is really a little better today, so I am comforted a little, and I think he is turning the corner and beginning to mend." She and Mackenzie also did what they could to convince the German public that Frederick was not on his deathbed.[21] When the crown prince was ordered back to Berlin because of the failing health of his father, the crown princess refused to allow her husband to leave, since the move from sunny

San Remo to wintry Berlin would only spoil his chances for recovery.[22]

When Bismarck telegraphed the royal couple that the emperor was seriously ill and could die at any moment, the crown princess could no longer hold out against the pressure for her husband's return to Berlin. As the royal couple and their entourage prepared to leave San Remo, the crown princess wrote her mother, "Fritz must be there to assume the responsibilities of his position, but it is grievous to think of the risks he runs and the painfulness of the whole situation!"[23] But they had delayed their departure too long. Just before noon on 9 March 1888, Frederick received a telegram at San Remo addressed to "His Imperial and Royal Majesty Emperor Frederick III." The new emperor wept at the news of his father's death, and his diary entry for that day consists of one pitiful sentence: "I do not have a Papa any more!"[24]

After he regained his composure, the new emperor wrote out his announcement of his own succession as Frederick III.[25] He then paid tribute to his wife by presenting her the highest decoration in the empire, the Order of the Black Eagle. Immediately thereafter, he turned to Mackenzie and said, "I thank you for having made me live long enough to recompense the valiant courage of my wife." The distraught new empress wrote her mother, "To think of my poor Fritz succeeding his father as a sick and stricken man is so hard!! How much good he might have done! I pray that he may be spared to be a blessing to his people and Europe."[26]

Frederick began his reign with gestures to the liberals. He bestowed the Order of the Black Eagle upon minister of justice Friedberg, who had ties to the liberal movement, and Eduard Simson, who had been president of the Frankfurt Assembly in 1848 and the first president of the Reichstag.[27] Both men were commoners and were ennobled before they could receive the Black Eagle, since the order was restricted to nobility. Liberals had high hopes about the first acts of the new emperor. Eugen Richter's newspaper, the *Freisinnige Zeitung*, printed articles expressing confidence in Frederick's ability to dismantle the Bismarck system.

The conservatives, however, were infuriated. That the first recipients of decorations from the new emperor were of Jewish origin fuelled the anger of the anti-Semitic court chaplain Alfred Stöcker, who was a close friend of Crown Prince William. General Alfred von Waldersee, the quartermaster general of the Army General Staff, regarded the Friedberg decoration "as in itself the announcement of a liberal program."[28] The ultraconservative *Kreuzzeitung* even speculated that any change in the status quo would run the risk of war.

On 12 March, Frederick's proclamations to his people and his chancellor were published in the press.[29] These documents appeared to mean all things to all people. Conservatives regarded them as "evidence that Kaiser Frederick intended no basic changes in government policy or personnel."[30] There is reason to believe that Bismarck was satisfied with his proclamation, because it showed that the crown prince had not caved in to his wife's demands for radical liberal reforms. What came as a sense of relief to the chancellor disturbed the liberals, who were disappointed that the proclamations did not include provisions for parliamentary reforms. Nonetheless, liberals hailed the "rather strong statement on religious toleration." Richter believed that the conservative tone of the proclamations did not negate the possibility of a "new era of freedom" under the new emperor.[31] The left-liberal *Frankfurter Zeitung* agreed: "The proclamation ... arouses the happy promise of a constitutional regime which will show understanding for and keep step with the demands of a cultural life and free us from the terrible nightmare of the fear of egotistical and intolerant reaction."[32]

Victoria was satisfied because the proclamations pleased Bismarck, her crucial ally at this time. As she told her mother, "I think Fritz's proclamation and also his letter to Prince Bismarck produced the right impression."[33] She also told her friend Lady Ponsonby, "Prince Bismarck has been civil and nice and feels quite at ease."[34] The supreme obstacle to achieving her goals for Germany, however, was Frederick's disease. As she told her mother:

Yes we are our own masters now, but shall we not have to leave all the work undone which we have so long and so carefully been preparing? Will there be any chance of doing the right thing, any time to carry out useful measures, needful reforms? .... All the more we shall strive to do what is wisest and safest and best! Prudence and caution are necessary now where fresh and generous regeneration of many an obsolete and used up thing would have been desirable![35]

The new empress soon discovered that she and the chancellor disagreed on the "wisest, safest and best" policy for Germany.[36] Only two weeks after Frederick's accession, the empress and Bismarck clashed when she persuaded her husband not to sign the renewal of the antisocialist law and a bill that extended the length of the Reichstag session from three to five years. Frederick told the chancellor that the extension of the Reichstag session would compromise voters' rights and that there was no point in renewing an antisocialist law that had failed to curb the progress of socialism in the country.[37] Bismarck knew that Frederick's refusal was influenced by his wife and chose to confront her on the subject.[38] The bills had been passed by large majorities, he told her, and the emperor was constitutionally obliged to sign them.[39] He added that rejection of the bills would "prejudice the future of the crown prince," which meant that Frederick's authority depended on Bismarck's support.[40] Victoria understood this and went immediately to her husband, who shortly thereafter presented the chancellor with the signed bills.

Almost immediately after Victoria tried to quash the antisocialist and Reichstag extension bills, Bismarck learned that she had resuscitated the Battenberg marriage project. In late March, he was handed a note from the emperor stating that he "wished to give Prince Alexander an army command and decorate him with the order pour le merité,"[41] adding that the prince would soon become engaged to his daughter Victoria. Bismarck was stunned by this news and wasted no time in presenting his familiar objections to the emperor. The Russians, he said, would interpret the marriage as a shift in Russo-German policy, and he would resign if the marriage took place. Frederick quickly saw the logic in Bismarck's arguments and agreed to cancel Alexander's visit to Berlin.[42] Victoria, however, refused to accept her husband's decision and ordered Radolinski to make arrangements for a celebration of her daughter's engagement.

When Bismarck learned of this, he set to work to convince the emperor, the Battenberg family, and the German public that the Battenberg marriage would trigger a chain of events that would spell calamity for German foreign policy and that he would prefer to resign rather than take responsibility for such a disaster. In a lengthy memorandum to the Battenberg family, he wrote that Germany "had succeeded in restoring a measure of trust with the tsar sufficient to offer a prospect for continued peace" but that the marriage would destroy this trust: "it would be a disaster for all of Europe if a mistake in Germany's handling of the tsar destroyed all previous diplomatic success."[43] Bismarck told the emperor that the marriage would only damage his wife's sorry reputation. German public opinion would see that a shift in Germany's policy toward Russia "could have been brought about by English influence at court, which would be blamed on the Kaiserin Victoria" and that "such hostility among the public would be difficult to handle."[44] The chancellor also told Salisbury that the marriage could harm Anglo-German relations: if the marriage went through, he said, Germany would have little choice but to "reorient her policy more toward Russia in compensation."[45] In addition, Bismarck launched a campaign in the press hinting that he would resign over the Battenberg affair.

The empress, however, was not swayed by any of Bismarck's arguments and even seemed willing to allow him to resign. In a letter marked "Private and Secret," Malet wrote Salisbury on 5 April:

He [Bismarck] said that he should retire if the design [the Battenberg marriage] were persisted in, and said that the Empress was aware of his intention to resign and had said that there were other Chancellors in Germany. He said that the Emperor was opposed to the marriage and had had a bitter scene with the Empress about it, but that he was worn out and could not resist. He said that he fears that the Empress is encouraged by the Queen [Victoria] and asked me if you had any influence to bear there. I cannot but regard the retirement of the Chancellor on such a question as a very serious matter.[46]

Rumors of the chancellor's possible resignation gave heart to left liberals, who saw the dispute over the Battenberg marriage as a smoke screen for more serious problems between the chancellor and the crown.[47] The minister of agriculture Lucius von Ballhausen noted in his diary: "The progressives are convinced that they will soon come to power; [left liberal leader] Rickert is prancing about like a proud peacock."[48] Richter shared his colleague's enthusiasm. On 8 April he wrote Bamberger: "I say with satisfaction that the approved direction will be sharply to the left [scharf links gesteuert wird]," and added that public opinion appeared no longer interested in supporting Bismarck's conciliatory policy toward Russia.[49]

Resignation rumors ended abruptly when the chancellor brought out his final and most powerful weapon against the marriage: through Radolinski, he let the empress know that her insistence on the marriage "would raise the question of her husband's fitness to rule."[50] When the empress met with the chancellor on 5 April, the empress immediately told him that the marriage could be postponed for the duration of her husband's reign.

Malet made the following conclusions about the affair:

It's now clear that there was no "Chancellor crisis" except of the Chancellor's own creation. He had only to speak quietly to the Emperor and Empress about the proposed marriage and all would have been settled. The question is, what was his object in giving the whole matter publicity and in making a European sensation by which the Imperial prestige and his own character have both suffered. I presume . . . that he considered it necessary at the onset of the new reign to prove the tremendous strength of his position in Germany— and that he did this to impress the Emperor and Empress but also and especially the present Crown Prince with whom it will be much more difficult to fight later on.[51]

Malet's comments help explain why Bismarck's demeanor toward the royal couple was so inconsistent during their reign. The chancellor was happy to stay on good terms with the royal couple as long as they abided by his wishes, but in the event that they did not, he made things very uncomfortable for them. Bismarck's exaggerated response to the Battenberg affair shows his determination to prove to Victoria and her son, who harbored his own designs of revising the chancellor's policies, that they would risk great embarrassment by going against the latter's will.

On 5 April, the empress reported to her mother: "Crisis of the Chancellor is an invention; we have never been on better terms and the understanding is perfect." The meeting between the empress and the chancellor of 5 April appears to have marked a turning point in their relations, for Victoria's activities after this meeting show that she supported the chancellor's struggle against William and his allies. Although Victoria discreetly sought advice from left-liberal leader Bamberger and asked his liberal press to come to her defense, this did not go against the grain of her agreement with Bismarck, for a publicity link between the German liberals and the court could help Bismarck in his struggle to control Prince William and his reactionary allies.[52] Her correspondence with Bamberger and others is very complimentary of Bismarck's loyalty; it was the rest of the ministers, she said, who were making life difficult for her and her husband.[53] She was, she told Bamberger, an "unjustly attacked woman. . . . I come into the line of fire and am a small part of those things that *must* be *destroyed, and must be* held up to my *sons* as a *frightening example.*" Bamberger tried to assure the empress that the "clique" that had tried to blacken her reputation had not succeeded in turning the majority of the

German people against her.[54]

Victoria added that the ministers—with the exception of Bismarck—took advantage of Frederick's physical weakness to force him to make decisions against his will. The emperor, for example, had wished to decorate left liberals Forckenbeck, Bunsen, and Schrader. Bismarck had agreed, "but the ministry," said the empress, "made a terrible row . . . and the Chancellor could not put it through; they threatened to *resign* immediately." She added that the emperor "did not have a single political friend or supporter near him, and that their own son was trying to "paralyse the emperor in every way." Bamberger advised the empress against entertaining thoughts of allowing the resignation of the hostile ministry because "the resulting confusion could not be overcome." He added that there was no use trying to institute liberal reforms, for they would only be rescinded during the coming reign of William.[55]

It was only after Frederick's death that the empress realized that the most outstanding liberal act of his reign—the ouster of Robert von Puttkamer, the reactionary minister of the interior—had been engineered by Bismarck. As minister of interior, Puttkamer was responsible for the dismissal of many liberal members of the ministry,[56] and he had also turned a blind eye to the gerrymandering of electoral districts in Prussia to favor conservative candidates. Frederick himself was eager to be rid of Puttkamer, since his practices harkened back to those of the reactionary Manteuffel era. In May 1888, the liberals felt they had a case against Puttkamer, since the election commission had come to the conclusion that the Landtag seat held by his own brother had been gerrymandered.[57] The Landtag resolution sparked a debate between liberals, who accused Puttkamer of fashioning the government system to suit his own needs and the conservatives, who supported Puttkamer.[58] In a Reichstag session on 26 May the left liberals accused the Bismarck regime of defending illegal influence on local elections and also decried government influence of the press during the Battenberg affair. Richter said:

If the hundreth part of the abuse that had been thrown at Prince Bismarck that in those weeks was hurled against the Kaiserin Victoria . . . then the prisons would be filled with hundreds of people. . . . If the elections are merely a test of how far the . . . power of the ministers . . . extends over the free will of the people, then the popular assembly is itself only a creation . . . of the government. Rather than allow such a pseudo-constitutionalism to develop . . . we should rather return to the absolutist system.[59]

Richter's newspaper, the *Freisinnige Zeitung*, reported that the speech was warmly received by the emperor himself. "The empress wrote to Bamberger that the emperor had 'nodded and smiled' when he read the speech." His wife exclaimed: "At last there is someone who defends [me]!"[60]

The speech gave the emperor and empress confidence they needed to force Puttkamer's resignation. On 26 May, Puttkamer presented the emperor a bill that extended the life of the Landtag session from three to five years. The empress, following Bamberger's advice, told her husband that he could put pressure on Puttkamer by not signing the bill, and the emperor complied. In frustration, Puttkamer pressed Friedberg to try to change the emperor's mind. Friedberg found that the emperor objected to signing the bill because such an act would constitute "a bitter disappointment for the German liberals." He then asked Friedberg to consult with his wife on the matter, and the emperor eventually signed the bill. The emperor accompanied his signature with a letter to Puttkamer stating that his signature on the bill in no way signified the emperor's acquiescence to illegal election practices. In essence, the letter was a statement of the emperor's lack of confidence in Puttkamer.[61]

Puttkamer tried to defend his administration in a lengthy report to the emperor, but this report provided the perfect pretext for his resignation. On 2 June, the empress received a letter from Bamberger that suggested that "if His Majesty replied to Herr von Puttkamer in a dissatisfied, ungracious way, he would have to go, and none of the ministers, in particular the chancellor, could complain of the kaiser's replying as he pleases to a letter he has received from a minister."[62] The letter had the desired effect: Puttkamer resigned. But the liberals' rejoicing over Puttkamer's resignation was muted. They had hoped that Puttkamer's ouster would be followed by a royal decree on freedom of elections, but no such decree was forthcoming. And as liberal August Stein put it in an article in the *Frankfurter Zeitung und Handelsblatt*, Puttkamer's resignation was not in itself a guarantee that long-ingrained habits of electioneering would not continue under his successor.[63]

These negative reactions were mostly ignored by Frederick's biographers, who extolled the ouster of Puttkamer as the last brave act of a dying man whose heart was in the right, liberal place. But Puttkamer's ouster also fitted perfectly into Bismarck's overall plan to undermine the reactionary influences around Crown Prince William.[64] Since the blame for Puttkamer's ouster was placed on the shoulders of the emperor, empress, and the left liberals, the conservatives felt duly threatened by the overwhelming left-liberal agitation for Puttkamer's dismissal. Hence, the incident also "helped to hold the Kreuzzeitung Conservatives in a cooperative position within the cartel majority."[65]

When Puttkamer resigned, Victoria told her mother: "Fritz has after much difficulty and some diplomacy got rid of Puttkamer, which I consider a great step. He will be able to carry out all sorts of other things if he can break through the wall of opposition so cleverly organised at San Remo, and in which William is so deeply involved." She also implied that the ouster was carried out in spite of Bismarck's disapproval: "To get the right things done, the wrong ones prevented, and yet not to fall out with Bismarck is a terribly difficult game to play."[66] One week after her husband's death, however, she said that it was Bismarck who had actually wished to get rid of Puttkamer and that he had placed the odium of Puttkamer's dismissal on the emperor's shoulders.[67]

Although the chancellor was able to control the empress's desire to effect liberal reforms, she tried his patience by her continued preoccupation with the Battenberg affair.[68] When Queen Victoria arrived in Germany to see her son-in-law after the Battenberg crisis in April, she found her daughter busy with plans to have the Battenberg marriage take place in secret. Bismarck knew about this but placed a number of conditions on the marriage in the hope that the empress would give up the project in frustration. The queen, however, told her daughter that she now opposed the marriage and reminded her that "her position required her to respect German interests and German wishes. Since the marriage was against those interests, it had to be given up."[69] The queen also discussed her daughter's sorry reputation with Bismarck. The audience went well, and Bismarck was particularly pleased to hear that the queen "quite understood and supported his position in the Battenberg affair." The queen, in turn, was satisfied by Bismarck's assurances that he would "stand by poor Vicky" and thwart any attempt to institute a regency in view of the emperor's failing health.[70]

The empress, however, disregarded her mother's advice about the Battenberg marriage. She told Bamberger that Bismarck no longer objected to the Battenberg marriage "but that he was under pressure from William and the Dowager Empress to state the opposite."[71] Bamberger advised the empress not to take any steps toward the marriage in the immediate future. Given the outcry against her during the recent Battenberg crisis in April, the resurrection of the marriage plan would only make things worse.[72]

In May, Victoria received a lengthy letter from Prince Alexander in which he asked to be released from any obligation to Princess Victoria, since the marriage seemed to be quite hopeless. The empress refused to believe what Alexander was saying and asked Bamberger to tell the prince personally not to give up hope, and she told Bamberger that she would reopen the matter with Bismarck. Bamberger advised against this course of action; if the Battenberg affair was reopened during her husband's reign, this would "hand her enemies a devastating weapon."[73] Victoria accepted this logic and now began a campaign to make certain that the marriage would take place after her husband's death. She asked Friedberg to persuade the emperor to include a demand in his will that the marriage take place and believed that her son's opposition to the union had ended. On 11 June, she wrote Friedberg:

Yesterday my son sent C[ount] von Liebenau to me and he asked me to consider a "waiting period" in the matter of our daughter's marriage! A waiting period of one year! This seems rather long after four years of waiting—but I considered this to be a concession which I . . . gratefully accepted, [and] at this moment I feel somewhat calmer and more hopeful. I owe this [concession] to your conversation with the kaiser . . . for which I am grateful! Now [everything] depends on whether William will wish to heed and carry out the clearly written wish of his father! [74]

By the time that Victoria secured the inclusion of the Battenberg marriage in her husband's will, the emperor was a dying man. On 1 June, he ordered the royal court to be moved from Charlottenburg to the Schloss Friedrichskron in Potsdam, since the emperor wished to die in the palace where he was born. By 10 June, the disease that Mackenzie still maintained was not cancer had impeded his ability to swallow food, and he was forced to take nourishment through a rubber tube. Incredibly, even in the light of these developments, the liberal papers maintained that the emperor's general health was good and "that there was no special danger at present."[75]

On June 14, the emperor summoned Bismarck in order to obtain his promise that the empress would be treated well after his death. In a symbolic gesture, he took his wife's hand and placed it in the chancellor's and pressed them both together with his own. Bismarck understood what the emperor was trying to say and replied "Your Majesty can be sure that I shall never forget that Her Majesty is my queen."[76] On the following day, the emperor wrote his last words on a piece of paper—an incomplete sentence: "Victoria, me, the children . . ." and thereafter fell into unconsciousness. He died before noon on Friday, 15 June, 1888 in the presence of his wife and children.

When Victoria informed the chancellor of her husband's death, she hastened to remind him of his last promise to the emperor, "Now that he is no more you will certainly always remember his request of yesterday. He dies as a hero, his soul lives with the angels."[77] It was soon clear, however, that Bismarck had no intention of abiding by his promise, and the ill treatment that Victoria and the memory of her husband suffered at the hands of the chancellor and the new emperor compelled Victoria to play a major role in constructing the legend of Frederick III. The legend not only made Frederick the progressive liberal he never was in life but also obscured the truth about his liberal views and their impact on German history.

Victoria's trials began even before her husband was in his grave. As soon as it was known that Frederick was dying, soldiers surrounded Friedrichskron, so that no documents might be removed without knowledge of Crown Prince William, and the head of the imperial household was given orders to let no one carry on any correspondence with the outside.[78] Victoria felt as though she and her entourage were under arrest. She tried to talk to Bismarck in the hope that he would call off the guards, but the chancellor replied that he was "too busy" to see her.[79]

William's order to surround the palace with guards was meant to put a stop to the shipment of his parents' private papers to England. During Frederick's illness, Victoria feared that their private papers could be suppressed or exploited to make her husband and herself appear in the worst possible light during the coming reign of William, so she persuaded her confidants to smuggle private papers—including Frederick's diary from the Franco-Prussian war—to England.[80] When German newspapers reported that Frederick's diaries were missing, William suspected that the missing documents would reveal how different the views of his parents were from his own and that they could discredit the Hohenzollern monarchy, and he demanded the return of his father's war diary for inspection.[81]

Victoria soon discovered that Bismarck had no intention of abiding by his agreement to allow the Battenberg marriage to take place after the emperor's death. Immediately after her husband's funeral, Victoria asked Friedberg to remind William, the dowager empress Augusta, and the grand duke of Baden of Frederick's dying wish to have the marriage take place.[82] William, however, broke the engagement without consulting his mother and explained to Prince Alexander that the "rupture was because of the profound conviction held by my late deceased grandfather and father."[83] This statement was true, since Victoria put her dying husband under pressure to consent to the union before his death.

William also overrode his mother's wishes not to have an autopsy performed on her husband after Bergmann told him that "German medicine must have the opportunity to vindicate itself against Dr. Mackenzie's skullduggeries."[84] The results of the autopsy showed that Frederick had suffered from cancer, and disproved any incompetence with respect to Bergmann's tracheotomy.[85] Pleased with these results, the German doctors asked Mackenzie to write up the autopsy report, which confirmed the latter's misdiagnosis.[86] Mackenzie complied but later tried to save his reputation with his book, *The Illness of Frederick the Noble*, in which he argued that his treatments had prolonged the life of the emperor and that Frederick would not have survived the surgery recommended by Bergmann and Gerhardt.[87] As usual, Victoria accepted Makenzie's view and was infuriated when her son refused to allow publication of Mackenzie's book in Germany.

Victoria was humiliated in a number of other ways. Although she was permitted to assume the title "Empress Frederick," the name of the palace where Frederick died was changed from Friedrichskron back to the Neues Palais, disregarding his final wishes. And when William opened the first Reichstag of his reign on 25 June, he paid homage to his grandfather and promised to follow his path but said nothing about his recently deceased father.

The liberal newspapers attempted to compensate for the government's lack of consideration for Frederick's memory. The *Frankfurter Zeitung* proclaimed that Frederick's ideals would live on: "The good that he did, the greatness he strove for, this remains a living thing for his family, for the nation, and for the world." The *Vossische Zeitung* praised Frederick as "a soldier of progress . . . a Siegfried . . . whose sword banishes gloomy night," and the *Freisinnige Zeitung* wrote that Frederick's memory would serve as an example to be followed in the future.[88]

Victoria echoed these sentiments in her letters to her mother. Three days after her husband's death, she wrote:

We had a mission, we felt and knew it—we were Papa's and your children! We were faithful to what we believed and knew to be right. We loved Germany—we wished to see her strong and great, not only with the sword, but in all that was righteous, in culture, in progress and in liberty. We wished to see the people happy and free, growing and developing in all that is good. . . . We had treasured up much experience! Bitterly, hardly bought!!!—

that is now all wasted.[89]

The Queen tried to comfort her daughter and encouraged her to carry on her husband's work, but the empress replied: "I disappear with him. My task was with him, for him, for his dear people. It is buried in the grave. My voice will be silent forever. I feared not to lift it up—for the good cause—for him."[90]

A few months later, however, Victoria rallied sufficiently to take her mother's advice. She wrote Frau Stockmar of her wish to establish a "Kaiser Frederick Society" that would spread his thoughts and ideals among the German people:

Although we are forced to survive without Emperor Frederick and his genuine concern and support, we should not allow his thoughts and ideas to disappear! The comparison is perhaps presumptuous, but Christ also left the world and his doctrine did not die, his example did not cease to inspire people as long as modest men cultivated his ideas . . . [and] His ideas did not die out! . . . . A small army of people must rally around Emperor Frederick's name and programme. . . . If the government has neither the time nor the inclination for this project, we will have to take it upon ourselves. There was once, after all, a Nationalverein in Germany! It was very powerful and influential; German unity could not have been achieved without it. I think that if a movement (called the Kaiser Frederick Society) were fostered throughout Germany, it could promote all the points contained in his programe . . . it could have as its organs *Die Nation, Volkswohl,* the *Vossische Zeitung* and the *Volkszeitung*—and these would promote the spreading of the liberal reconstruction of Germany among the masses. It would be a peaceful but an effective organization.[91]

Although Victoria insisted that the Kaiser Frederick Society was not to serve as a means to oppose the conservative government, she wanted it to be staffed by members of the opposition Freisinn Party: "Members of the German Progressive party must be at the heart of the Society, but they must attract other types of people as well." Victoria wished to lead the organization herself if she were deemed "suitable for the job." Germany's problems, she concluded, could only be solved if handled in the "modern, liberal sense."[92]

Victoria's plans for the organization bearing her husband's name show that what she perceived to be her husband's ideals far more resembled her own. Her plans for the society imply that her husband's "programme" and the goals of the Freisinn Party were linked, yet, as we have seen, Frederick's "programme" stressed preservation of the constitutional status quo, and he never had any intention of cooperating closely with the Freisinn Party, whose goals he did not support.

Victoria was not the only one eager to glorify her husband's memory. In September 1888, Professor Heinrich Geffcken, the most vehement opponent of Bismarck in Frederick's entourage, anonymously published selections from Frederick's Franco-Prussian war diary in the *Deutsche Rundschau*. Although the documents published did not include Victoria's "contributions" to her husband's war diary,[93] they nonetheless attested to Frederick's association with prominent liberals such as Roggenbach and Simson and showed how energetically he had worked to make Bismarck and William I overcome their opposition to the creation of the German Reich.[94] Readers of the article came away with the impression that Bismarck exaggerated the extent of his contribution toward the creation of the German Empire.[95]

Victoria was immediately suspected of having leaked the diary to the press, but she told her mother that she had had nothing to do with it:

The Marmor Palais and Berlin are in a state of fury and excitement about the publication of Fritz's Tagebuch. . . . I cannot imagine how it got into the *Rundschau* . . . Fritz had several copies lithographed and gave them to his more intimate friends. . . . Everyone now thinks that I have done this and to play Prince Bismarck a trick to revenge myself, etc. Of course this is all a mischievous lie! . . . . I was advised to put a denial into the newspapers, that I had nothing to do with the publication—this I refused to do! I was also advised to write in the same sense to Prince Bismarck, which I also refused. But I have sent him word that I could not understand who could have published this, and that it appeared to me a want of tact and judgement to print what partook of a private and intimate character while the people named in the book are alive.[96]

William tactlessly told his mother that Frederick had had no business writing such "impudent" things in his diary, and the empress was infuriated by a critique of the diary selections that appeared in the pro-Bismarck newspaper, the *Post*. As Victoria told her mother, the *Post* article compared Frederick with "Emperor Joseph of Austria, saying that the latter had been a failure, and implying what a blessing it was for Germany that Fritz had not reigned longer as his principles must have led to failure!!!"[97]

Criticism of Frederick's diary was not enough for Bismarck. By his lights, the diary contributed to the emerging legend of Frederick III, which had the capacity to "lead to the formation of a common liberal front against him."[98] He launched an investigation into the matter and did not regard it as closed even after it was discovered that Geffcken was the culprit. Although Bismarck believed the diary selections to be genuine, he told the emperor that the diary was a forgery: William I, said Bismarck, had not allowed the chancellor "to inform Frederick of state policy during the Franco-Prussian war," since the old emperor feared that "his son would betray secrets to the Francophile English court."[99]

On 30 September, Geffcken was arrested and brought to trial on libel charges. Other liberal members of Frederick's entourage were also persecuted: although Roggenbach knew nothing about the publication of the diary selections, his home was searched by the police. Stosch believed that Roggenbach was accused of complicity in the affair simply because the chancellor wished to destroy a man who had had the potential to succeed him. Stosch, Roggenbach, and Freytag were called as witnesses at Geffcken's trial. In an attempt to protect himself from prosecution, Stosch burned what he called "all letters of importance."[100]

Bismarck continued his campaign against Frederick's legend after charges against Geffcken were dismissed. In December 1888, the *Kölnische Zeitung* "revealed" that the British ambassador to Russia, Sir Robert Morier, had "betrayed" German state secrets to the French during the war of 1870.[101] According to Stosch, these accusations "served as Bismarck's smokescreen in his attack against the Empress Frederick and her husband."[102] But this campaign backfired when Morier published his correspondence with Herbert Bismarck, which disproved the chancellor's charges and placed Herbert in a very unfavorable light.[103] By early 1889, even William had become disenchanted with the chancellor's campaign, especially when it became clear that the public reaction to the whole affair was negative.[104]

Although the persecution of Frederick's supporters failed to discredit the late emperor, Bismarck's campaign appears to have discouraged Victoria from pursuing her ambitious plans for the Kaiser Frederick Society. The Geffcken affair made it clear that any attempt to keep her husband's memory alive would be immediately and indiscriminately attacked by her son and the chancellor.[105] Although in the past Victoria had sharply criticized her husband for his policy of passive resistance, she now adopted this policy herself rather than face possible persecution by her enemies. Victoria's friend, Lady Mary Ponsonby, explained the logic behind the dowager empress's passive stance in a letter to Queen Victoria in 1889: "The Empress Frederick is a very powerful personality in Europe and as such, quietly, silently, but very surely ... this very strong individuality will gather round one centre all that is first rate in society and in the artistic and literary world; later it is probable also in the political world, but for this it is obvious that anything like *interference*, active or passive, in politics, would be fatal to Her Majesty's peace."[106]

Though Victoria was unable to agitate publicly on behalf of her husband's memory, her clandestine agitation on his behalf nurtured the growth of Frederick's legend. Significantly, as was the case with her plans for the Kaiser Frederick Society, Victoria continued to paint a picture of her husband that was most mostly fictitious. We know that Frederick needed Bismarck as foreign minister. Victoria told her mother differently: "Fritz did not need Bismarck and his diplomatic band to keep up good relations with the other powers! He possessed the friendship and the confidence of the rulers, and the sympathies of their people! This was always gall and wormwood to Bismarck, who feared a rival in prestige, and would have had to do Fritz's bidding if Fritz had been well and could have enforced his will."[107] Further, though Frederick supported the 1878 antisocialist law, Victoria told her mother: "My beloved Fritz was so much against the passing of the [anti]Socialist Law! He foresaw what the Liberal party always foresaw and which has now happened, i.e., it would only encourage the growth of Socialism and teach the Socialists to organize themselves into a body secretly. This is now done."[108]

She also used her son's ineffectiveness to make Frederick look good in contrast. For instance, in a November 1888 letter to her mother she wrote:

W[illiam] only reads the papers prepared for him, does not understand or care for all the difficult and intricate questions of the internal Government, and is utterly ignorant of social, industrial, agricultural, commercial and financial questions, etc., [and he is] only preoccupied with military things, with a smattering of foreign affairs. . . . Bismarck wishes his head to be thoroughly turned, his vanity and pride to be still greater than they are already.[109]

Her consternation was more vehement two years later: "He [William] is absolutely ignorant! He never studied politics. . . . He knows not a single political man. Of the Liberals in Germany he does not know one!!! He was always taught to avoid our friends, and now there is no one to tell him the truth. He never asks what his father would have done, but takes the advice of the oddest and most incompetent people."[110] Victoria insisted the sorry state of affairs would never have happened during her husband's reign: "Fritz and I were intensely anxious . . . that the Government and Ministers . . . should work hand in hand, assisting each other in the cause of true culture, civilization and progress."[111]

Why the deception? Victoria and her allies forged the liberal legend of Frederick III, hoping his memory would be a rallying point for the liberal movement. Although this particular goal was not realized, the legend had several important outcomes. First, the legend neutralized the negative image of Frederick that the conservative government conjured up after his death.[112] Second, it gave Frederick's biographers the erroneous impression that he was sympathetic to the left-wing liberalism of his wife and the Freisinn Party. The legend also reinforced Bismarck's negative reputation in the eyes of his critics. The fallout from Victoria's criticism of Bismarck persists to this day in historical works asserting that his system contributed to Germany's tragic course. Witness Erich Eyck's case against Bismarck, supported, in part, by a letter written by Victoria after her husband's death:

Why are we, so to speak, in opposition? Because our patriotism wanted to see the greatness of our fatherland connected with the noble sense for right, morality, for freedom and culture, for individual independence, for the improvement of the single person as man and as German, as European and as cosmopolitan. Improvement, progress, ennoblement— that was our motto. Peace, tolerance, charity—these most precious possessions of mankind, we had to see them trampled upon, laughed at. . . . *Blood and iron* alone had made Germany great and unified—all national vices were called patriotism![113]

Finally, the legend effectively obscured the Frederick's true accomplishments. The conclusion attempts to separate Frederick from his legend in order to assess the impact of his views on the course of German liberal development.

NOTES

1. When Frederick fell ill with an intestinal infection in 1872, he told his wife: "I am so accustomed to suffering from colds in the throat, hence this departure from my usual pattern is rather strange." Hessische Hausstiftung, Schloss Fasanerie, Fulda (hereafter HH): Crown Prince Frederick William to Crown Princess Victoria, Karlsruhe, 14 November 1872.

2. Sir Frederick Ponsonby, *Letters of the Empress Frederick* (London, 1929), p. 224.

3. As Bismarck noted in his memoirs: "the doctors [were] determined to make the Crown Prince unconscious, and to carry out the removal of the larynx without having informed him of their intention. I raised objections, and required that they should not proceed without the consent of the Crown Prince." Ponsonby, *Letters*, p. 331. The correspondence shows that the royal couple was kept in the dark about Frederick's illness. During his cure at Bad Ems, the crown prince told his wife that Gerhardt had nothing definite to say about the cause of his hoarseness. He added, "How can one possibly make any sense of this?" Nor did his entourage appear willing to enlighten him: "Stosch has nothing to say, and the same is true of Radolinski and the others—all they tell me is that I must follow doctor's orders!" HH: Crown Prince Frederick William to Crown Princess Victoria, Bad Ems, 13 May 1887.

4. Dr. Jain A. Lin's recent account of Frederick's illness confirms the danger that the crown prince faced: "As a general surgeon, Dr. Bergmann performed seven laryngectomies between 1882 and 1889. Post-operative survival of his patients averaged from seventeen weeks, and the longest was one and a half years. One year after Fritz's death, he operated on a laryngeal cancer patient who died shortly after surgery." Jain I. Lin, *The Death of a Kaiser: A Medical-Historical Narrative* (Dayton, OH, 1985), p. 118.

5. Lin, *Death of a Kaiser*, p. 28.

6. Frederick appeared in a parade for the Queen Victoria's Golden Jubilee parade in June, and his "magnificent appearance in a white uniform drew the loudest and longest cheers from the crowd, some of whom saw him variously as Charlemange, Siegfried, Lohengrin, or a new Barbarossa." J. Alden Nichols, *The Year of the Three Kaisers: Bismarck and the German Succession, 1887–1888* (Champaign, IL, 1987), p. 21.

7. The crown prince was so pleased with his physician that he persuaded Queen Victoria to have Mackenzie knighted in September. Shortly thereafter, the crown prince sent a letter to the Prussian Grand Masonic Lodge that included the statement: "Full of trust I look to God and hope that, recuperated, in the not too distant future I can return with my family to My Residence in the midst of My Beloved Fatherland." Nichols, *Three Kaisers*, p. 22. Mackenzie, however, was not admired at the court of the crown prince. He alienated members of Frederick's household by his terse requests for exorbitant fees. After he presented Radolinski

with a bill for £2,625 (or $13,125.00) in June, he explained: "The fees may seem high, [but] they would be the same to private individuals. . . . I have been paid on the same scale by such private persons, even when no operation has been required." Mackenzie to Radolinski, 29 July 1887, Deutsches Zentralarchiv, Abteilung II, Merseburg, (hereafter DZA Merseburg) Rep. 52, 7a (Nachlass Friedrichs III), Korrespondenz der Hofmarschälle. Radolinski complained to Hausminister Count Stolberg about Mackenzie's avarice, adding that Mackenzie had quoted the same prices to Queen Victoria's physician even before he received the call from the German doctors to go to Berlin. Radolinski to Stolberg, 16 August 1887, ibid.

8. Nichols, *Three Kaisers*, p. 22.

9. Frederic B. M. Hollyday, *Bismarck's Rival: A Political Biography of General and Admiral Albrecht von Stosch* (Durham, NC, 1960), pp. 237–238. The crown princess, however, refused to accept the fact that her husband was terminally ill. As she told her mother: "I cannot and will not give up all hope. . . . We must leave the future in God's hands and not trouble about it, but fight this illness the best we can, by remaining cheerful and hopeful." Ponsonby, *Letters*, p. 260.

10. The treatment of Frederick's illness is still discussed among physicians. Although Jain Lin's *Death of a Kaiser* provides a wealth of medical detail on Frederick's illness, it is flawed as a work of history. For example, Lin notes that the crown princess in 1888 was "in her mid-forties, a little chubby after six children, one of whom died in childhood." (p. 15) The crown princess had not six but eight children, two of whom died in childhood.

11. The rumor that Victoria and her mother had originally selected him because of their mistrust of German medicine was "confirmed" by the conservative German press. In November 1887, Sir Edward Malet, Britain's ambassador to Germany, asked Herbert von Bismarck to set the record straight: "Now as a matter of fact, of which I am sure you are aware, the Crown Princess had nothing to do with calling in Sir Morell Mackenzie, still less the Queen. The report that the Crown Princess sent for him originally is doing her great injury, and is devoid of truth." Malet requested that Herbert print a statement to this effect in the government newspapers. Herbert, however, told Malet that such a statement would only be disputed by the German doctors and that this, in turn, would only make matters worse. Bismarck agreed, and no statement was published. Ponsonby, *Letters*, pp. 229–230.

12. Popular biographer Emil Ludwig summed up the sentiments of conservatives who opposed Victoria and Mackenzie when he wrote: "Her [Victoria's] distrust of German therapeutics has come to be regarded as largely responsible for his [Frederick's] tragic and untimely end." Quoted in ibid., pp. 227–228.

13. During their stay in England, the crown princess discovered that her son William had told the emperor not to believe Mackenzie's optimistic reports on Frederick's condition. In disgust, the crown princess told her husband that their son was filling the emperor's head full of "lies" to make "mischief" and to make himself feel important. HH: Crown Princess Victoria to Crown Prince Frederick

William, Royal Yacht, 14 July 1887. The crown prince agreed: "William," he wrote his wife, "is dominated by a combination of youthful immaturity, unbridled ambition, and absolute vanity; these qualities would be piteously laughable, if it were not for the evil souls who exploited them—and my throat ailment—in order to advance their own selfish aims!" HH: Crown Prince Frederick William to Crown Princess Victoria, Buckingham Palace, 13 July 1887. Victoria maintained that the evil influences around William could be eliminated when her husband came to the throne: "this lovely game [William's intrigues] . . . will continue until you have the power . . . to put an end to this folly. This can be done in 24 hours." HH: Crown Princess Victoria to Crown Prince Frederick William, Royal Yacht, 16 July 1887.

14. The support in the liberal press for the crown prince and Mackenzie was not sufficient to quash malicious gossip about Victoria's character and her feelings about her husband. In the fall of 1887, Holstein learned from Radolinski and others that the crown princess was in love with Seckendorff, indifferent to Frederick's illness, and doing everything possible to hasten her husband's demise. Norman Rich and M. H. Fisher, eds., *The Holstein Papers* 4 Vols. (Cambridge, 1957), Vol. 2, pp. 344–351 (hereafter HP). There is ample evidence from the British ambassador and from Victoria's letters to her husband and mother to indicate that the rumors were false. See Malet to Salisbury, 21 May 1887, "Private and Personal," Public Records Office, Kew, Richmond (hereafter PRO), FO 348/8, #63 (Malet Papers); Crown Princess Victoria to Queen Victoria, 2 June 1887. Ponsonby, *Letters*, p. 238 and HH: Crown Princess Victoria to Crown Prince Frederick William, Norris Castle, 20 August 1887.

15. Nichols, *Three Kaisers*, p. 24. Holstein also shared this view. As he confided to his diary: "If the Kaiser dies overnight it seems to me unavoidable that the dying prince shall be made to renounce his claim to the throne, because under present conditions his wife could do all manner of mischief in a few months." HP Vol. 2, p. 357. As soon as Albedyll and Herbert learned of the gravity of Frederick's illness, they asked the emperor for permission to disclose the news to the German public. Accordingly, a bulletin appeared in the official *Reichsanzeiger* on 12 November stating that the crown prince's illness was of "a carcinomatous nature." The announcement was meant to arouse fears about the stability of the government in view of the emperor's advanced age and the illness of his heir, and Albedyll hoped to parlay these fears to persuade the emperor and Bismarck to have William made regent. Nichols, *Three Kaisers*, p. 28.

16. Bismarck and the conservatives were not the only ones wary of what the empress might do. Salisbury expressed grave concern that the empress would damage Anglo-German relations by constantly appealing to her countrymen for advice and counsel. Salisbury advised Malet: "It is of course to be hoped that the Empress may never confide to you any of her feelings as to the internal policy of Germany, and may never ask your advice. . . . But if perchance you should be forced to give her advice . . . your wisest course will be to discourage any leaning to English notions of policy. . . . she must not be detected trying to shape Ger-

many to an English pattern. Otherwise she will incur [the] most serious risk. If I had the misfortune. . . . to advise her now, I should frame all my advice on the principle that it is her role to be mildly Bismarckian or intensely German." Salisbury to Malet, 14 March 1888, PRO, FO 343/9 #273 (Malet Papers). Salisbury had also heard that the empress would try to "utilize the next two or three (?) months to give a permanent direction to German policy in an anti-Bismarckian sense" and added, "I am still more anxious that it should not be possible to suggest that England had meddled in the matter." Ibid. This exchange indicates that they believed the empress would not shrink from creating problems in Anglo-German relations to advance her own aims.

17. Albedyll and his allies aimed to "achieve control of the Junker Conservative party as a whole and move it out of the Cartel into an association with the Catholic Center." Bismarck also knew that any attempt to bypass the succession of Frederick would arouse the anger of the National Liberals, who formed a crucial part of his Cartel. Ibid., p. 340. In the end, Albedyll's scheme had little hope for success. It would have been difficult to proclaim William regent on the constitutional grounds that his father had become "permanently incapacitated." Although the crown prince could not speak, his other faculties had not been impaired. As Victoria told her mother, "Fritz is as well able to *think, read and write*—and transact business as he ever was." She added, "I think it would be such a satisfaction to Fritz to be able to be of use to his country, nation, army—and to Europe, if only for a limited time. If he felt too ill to discharge business—later on, *he* could then institute a Regency!" Nichols, *Three Kaisers*, p. 28.

18. Ibid.

19. Ibid., p. 33.

20. Ibid., pp. 29–30.

21. Ponsonby, *Letters*, p. 288. Mackenzie reopened his offensive against the German doctors when he insisted that Frederick's poor health after the tracheotomy could be attributed to the ineptness of Dr. Bramann, who had performed the operation. That the treatment of the crown prince was doing more harm than the illness itself was a sentiment that was accepted by the left-liberal press. Ponsonby, *Letters*, p. 287.

22. Ibid., p. 288.

23. Ibid., p. 281 15 March.

24. Geheimes Staatsarchiv Preussischer Kulturbesitz, Berlin-Dahlem, Rep. 52, (Nachlass Friedrichs III) Tagebuch Friedrichs III, Jahre 1888. Although the new emperor and his father had been estranged for some time, the emotional reaction of Frederick may be attributable to the fact that he had always admired and respected his father, despite their differences. His illness played a role in his reaction. For several months, Frederick had undergone painful treatments and endless poking and prodding of his throat by a parade of specialists. He must also have been aware of the bitter debate raging in the press on his condition. Nor could he have failed to notice that the conservatives appeared to be looking forward to his

premature death, whereas his wife and the left liberals exhibited an optimism about his condition that he probably did not share.

25. Although this idea had been rejected soundly by advisers who assisted him in drafting his proclamation as emperor in 1885, Frederick never truly abandoned his desire to put himself in the romantic line of the medieval Holy Roman Emperors as Frederick IV. As Frederick explained to Roggenbach in late 1887, "I alone created the German Empire. My father considered it a matter of secondary importance and still treats it like that. I intervened; when Bismarck spoke to me after Sedan about crossing the line of the Main River, I bound to him the idea of the German Empire. When I left Berlin last May, Bismarck came to speak to me about the death of the Emperor. He said: 'I must know what title you will assume.' I answered as above. He said no word to me in reply and therefore agrees; with that all the expert, scholarly and juristic opinions which I have gotten in the matter lose their meaning." The Crown Princess later told Roggenbach: "All my arguments do not help a bit here; he insists on it." Hollyday, *Stosch*, p. 232. Bismarck finally vetoed the idea in 1888 and explained that there was no connection whatever between the the German Empire and the Holy Roman Empire. According to Nichols, Frederick's stubborn adherence to the Frederick IV idea attests to his "truly naive and romantic conception of the monarchy." *Three Kaisers*, p. 183.

26. Ponsonby, *Letters*, p. 287 9 March.

27. Ibid., p. 182.

28. The general also complained that Frederick's order on mourning for Emperor William I was hardly an adequate tribute to the dead emperor's memory: "Most of the German princes have proclaimed public mourning; the king of Prussia leaves it to each person to do what he wants!" Ibid., p. 183.

29. Discussion of the proclamations appears in Chapter 6.

30. Ibid., p. 186.

31. Ibid.

32. Koppel S. Pinson, *Modern Germany* (New York, 1966), p. 275.

33. Ponsonby, *Letters*, pp. 291–292.

34. Ibid., p. 293.

35. Ibid.

36. Ernst Huber points out that Frederick wished to make his wife his representative in the event he became incapacitated instead of his son. Bismarck objected on the grounds that German animosity against England would only increase in the event that the "English" empress became her husband's representative. Frederick agreed and made his son his representative. Ernst Huber, *Deutsche Verfassungsgeschichte seit 1789* 4 Vols. (Stuttgart, 1957–1969), Vol. 4, p. 168. Huber adds, however, that she became a de facto representative, since Victoria was involved in every decision that her husband made.

37. Nichols, *Three Kaisers*, p. 198.

38. The empress' meddling in this affair was confirmed by Hohenlohe, who wrote, "Boetticher is complaining that the Empress is meddling in [government]

business. She is said to have told the emperor not to sign the antisocialist law, and it was only after Bismarck clarified matters that the emperor gave in. He [the emperor] has little resistance to the influence of the empress, who in turn is under the influence of the wives of liberal leaders Schrader, Helmholtz and Stockmar." Ernst Feder's remnant, found in Deutsches Bundesarchiv, Abteilung Potsdam (hereafter DBAP) Nachlass Bamberger 90Ba3, #227.

39. Nichols, *Three Kaisers*, p. 198.

40. Ibid., pp. 197–198. Victoria's opposition to the extension of the antisocialist law and the legislative period of the Reichstag had the backing of the left liberals, but their agitation for specific changes in policy was awkward. For example, the Freisinn Party tried to bolster support for the new regime by circulating the rumor that the liberal-minded minister of justice Friedberg was responsible for blocking conservatives' attempts to institute a regency. An article to this effect appeared in the *Freisinnige Zeitung*, but the rumor was denied by Friedberg himself, and an official contradiction appeared on 20 March in the *National Zeitung*. This incident is discussed in a letter from Malet to Salisbury of 20 March. PRO, FO 64-1186, #90 (German Correspondence, Prussia and Germany).

41. Nichols, *Three Kaisers*, p. 206.

42. According to Bamberger, the emperor was so moved by Bismarck's arguments against the marriage that "he raised himself up and embraced Bismarck." Ernst Feder, ed. *Bismarcks Grosses Spiel: Die Geheimen Tagebücher Ludwig Bambergers* (Frankfurt am Main, 1932), p. 343.

43. Quoted in Nichols, *Three Kaisers*, p. 208.

44. Ibid., p. 209.

45. Ibid. This pressure seems to have worked. Members of the British foreign office suggested that the queen cancel her planned visit to Germany since it could be construed as a sign that she supported the Battenberg marriage. But the queen refused; on 13 April, she wrote Salisbury, "I cannot understand Bismarck's excitement. . . . but . . . I cannot abandon my intention of seeing the dear suffering Emperor." Ponsonby, *Letters*, p. 300.

46. Malet to Salisbury, 5 April 1888, PRO, FO 343/2, #284 (Malet Papers). Holstein also put pressure on the empress to abandon the Battenberg marriage, since he had learned that Alexander was in love with someone else. The empress, however, refused to believe the "rumors." Alexander's liaison was confirmed by the British foreign office. Colonel Leopold Swaine, the military attache in Berlin, who wrote the Prince of Wales on 13 April that the Prince of Bulgaria "is now reported to have ein zärtliches Verhältnis with a member of the histrionic art." Ponsonby, *Letters*, p. 299.

47. Nichols, *Three Kaisers*, p. 217.

48. Ernst Feder's notes in DBAP 90Ba3, #227 (Nachlass Bamberger). "Fortschrittler überzeugt jetzt zur Regierung zu kommen, Rickert umherstolziert wie der Stoch im Salat."

49. Richter to Bamberger, 8 April 1888, DZA Potsdam, 90Ba3, #227 (Nachlass

Bamberger). Schrader, however, wrote Bamberger on 5 April that the chancellor had cooked up the resignation crisis just to gain attention. Schrader to Bamberger, 5 April 1888. DZA Potsdam, 90 Ba3, (Nachlass Bamberger) Nr. 188.

50. Nichols, *Three Kaisers*, p. 213. This pleased Bismarck, who offered to reward the empress for her patience; he told her that 9 million marks of Emperor William's property would be divided between herself and her four daughters. Ibid., p. 211. Delivery of the sum may well have been contingent on Victoria's willingness to let the press campaign against her continue. What Bismarck offered in exchange was to wean her eldest son from the right-wing reactionaries, whom she despised, and to bring the crown prince and his right-wing conservative friends back into a pro-government position. Ibid., p. 213.

51. Malet to Salisbury, 21 April 1888. PRO, FO 343/9, #61 (Malet Papers).

52. Nichols, *Three Kaisers*, p. 263.

53. Ibid., p. 261.

54. Victoria's tolerance for press attacks against her came to an end after developments in her husband's condition sparked another round of salvos between pro- and anti-Mackenzie factions in the German press. On 12 April, Dr. Bergmann had received an urgent call from Mackenzie, who arrived to find the emperor barely able to breathe since the cancer blocked the flow of air through a tracheotomy tube. Bergmann's treatment left the emperor able to breathe, but he suffered from bleeding from the affected area, high fever, and general weakness. Mackenzie and his adherents practically accused Bergmann of incompetence, charging that repeated insertions of the canula had been "unnecessary." The German doctors, supported by the *Kölnische Zeitung*, in turn blamed Frederick's declining health on Mackenzie's "right-angled breathing tube." Mackenzie wished to defend himself against this accusation, but the empress forbade him to do so for fear of making matters worse. She did, however, ask Friedberg to have the chancellor do something about the criticism of the emperor's treatment in the press: "No one supports the idea of freedom of the press more than I . . . but this case is different—it should be possible to defend ourselves against shameless attacks!" Ibid.

55. Ibid., p. 264.

56. An article by Kenneth Barkin and M. L. Anderson disputes the idea that Puttkamer's actions constituted a setback for the liberal cause. See "The Myth of the Puttkamer Purge and the Reality of the Kulturkampf: Some Reflections on the Historiography of Imperial Germany." *Journal of Modern History*, 54 (1982), pp. 647–686.

57. Nichols, *Three Kaisers*, p. 306.

58. Ibid., p. 307. The accused minister only made matters worse for himself by going on the defensive. He declared that "the resolution was an attempt by the House of Deputies to get control over the administration and thus infringe upon the rights of the crown."

59. Ibid., p. 308.

60. Ibid., p. 310.

61. Ibid.

62. Ibid., p. 321.

63. Ibid., p. 326. Liberals also would have been even more disappointed had they known that Frederick had supported the wish of Bismarck to appoint conservative Christian Robert von Zedlitz-Truetzschler, governor of Posen, as Puttkamer's successor, against the wishes of the empress and Bamberger, who wished to see National Liberal leader Johannes Miquel in that post.

64. Ibid., p. 312.

65. Ibid., p. 330.

66. Ponsonby, *Letters*, p. 313.

67. On 22 June 1888, Hohenlohe confided to his diary: "Empress Victoria is making it known that the Puttkamer affair was orchestrated not by her but by the chancellor. Bismarck wanted to get rid of Puttkamer, and put the odium of his dismissal on the emperor." Feder remnant—notes for Hohenlohe, Bd. III, 1888, S. 440. DBAP, 90Ba 3 #227 (Nachlass Bamberger).

68. Bismarck did not rest easy even after Victoria agreed to postpone the marriage in April. According to Bamberger, "Bismarck told Roggenbach that he was satisfied that the Empress had given up the project [sich ergeben habe], but that it was impossible to rely on a woman's word; he is uneasy, and this problem painfully agitates his nerves [regt seine Nerven schmerzlich auf]." Feder, *Bismarcks Grosses Spiel*, p. 343, 21 April 1888.

69. Nichols, *Three Kaisers*, p. 249.

70. Ibid.

71. Ibid., p. 267. He added that Bismarck's threats of a regency were a bluff: "Since the chancellor did not want a regency, there was no danger."

72. Ibid.

73. Ibid., p. 322.

74. HH: Empress Victoria to Friedberg, 11 June 1888.

75. Nichols, *Three Kaisers*, p. 335.

76. Ibid., p. 336.

77. Ibid., p. 337.

78. Ponsonby, *Letters*, p. 318.

79. Ibid.

80. Frederick took private papers with him when he went to England in 1887, and Victoria also asked Mackenzie's colleague, Dr. Mark Hovell, to smuggle three volumes of Frederick's diary from the Franco-Prussian war to England. Ponsonby, *Letters*, p. 339. Only a few days before Frederick's death, Victoria "informed her mother that she was sending yet another box of papers through the English Embassy, to be stored with the others. Sir Edward Malet thought that the box contained jewels." Nichols, *Three Kaisers,* p. 329.

81. On 19 July 1888, Victoria informed Friedberg that she and her husband had nothing to hide: "The boxes have arrived. It is *all* my property! [mein Eigenthum ist es alles!] Come and look through [them], and you can select the papers you

wish to have deposited at the Ministry of the Interior! I am prepared to immediately surrender any papers solely devoted to official matters!" HH: Empress Victoria to Friedberg, 19 July 1888. Victoria added that it was her husband who originally suggested that his papers be deposited in England: "You *know* very well that my beloved husband disliked the way in which people trample all over the possessions of the departed. In the event that he had to spend a great deal of time away [from home], he felt it would be best that our papers be kept with my mother! The papers of Emperor William and Empress Augusta [from the years] 1848–1849 were kept there [as well]."

82. HH: Empress Victoria to Friedberg, 20 June 1888.

83. Ponsonby, *Letters*, p. 321.

84. Nichols, *Three Kaisers*, p. 337.

85. Ibid.

86. Ibid., p. 331. In his autopsy report, Mackenzie obligingly wrote: "It is my opinion that the disease from which the Emperor Frederick III died was cancer" and added that the larynx had become affected at a very early date. In dealing with the question as to whether Frederick would have been saved by early surgery, Dr. Jain Lin notes: "the answer is probably yes. From the discovery of the growth to the time of death, only 15 months elapsed. The cancer was not widespread. . . . But would he have survived surgery at the hands of Dr. von Bergmann? The answer probably is no. Total or partial laryngectomy, which any competent laryngologist can perform without difficulty today, was still experimental then. In his book [*The Illness of Frederick the Noble*] Dr. Mackenzie painstakingly collected almost 200 cases of thyrotomy and partial or total laryngectomy in which the majority of patients died shortly after surgery." Lin, *Death of a Kaiser*, p. 119.

87. In his book on Frederick's illness, Mackenzie took his campaign against Bergmann one step too far. He charged that Bergmann was drunk when he treated the blockage in Frederick's throat in April 1888 and had created the wound that had become abscessed, causing a fever and the decline in Frederick's condition that had hastened his death. This charge was so scandalous that Mackenzie was censured by the British Medical Association and the Royal College of Surgeons and was forced to resign from the Royal College of Physicians. His reputation ruined, Mackenzie outlived his royal patient by only a few years. Nichols, *Three Kaisers*, p. 240. Mackenzie's version of Bergmann's treatment was supported by Victoria. Two months after Frederick's death, she wrote her mother, "The end was hastened and the strength to resist the disease was impaired by Bergmann's mismanagement of the after-treatment of the tracheotomy, and the injury he inflicted on my poor darling Fritz by so awkwardly forcing the tube back into its place when no force was required." Ponsonby, *Letters*, p. 308. Ponsonby supports this assessment: "His [Frederick's] malady had been somewhat aggravated by the maladroitness of Professor Bergmann, which proved to be one of the turning points of the case." Ibid. Werner Richter, however, casts doubt on accusations of Bergmann's incompetence: "Mackenzie maintained that Bergmann's failed opera-

tion caused an abscess in the area surrounding the trachea. It is impossible to determine whether or not this is true; the autopsy did not mention an abscess." Richter, *Kaiser Friedrich*, p. 340.

88. Nichols, *Three Kaisers*, pp. 338–339. Nichols points out that these obsequies not only expressed the left liberals' "sentimental attachment to Frederick" but also revealed their ability to cloud the reality of Frederick's brief reign in a shroud of "idealism that conveniently fogged over the political reality and prevented them from forming a practical, popular program." Ibid., p. 339.

89. Ponsonby, *Letters*, p. 320.

90. Ibid.

91. HH: Empress Frederick to Frau Stockmar, 8 August 1888.

92. Ibid.

93. The Silvesterbetrachtung and other passages that attest even more strongly to "Frederick's" liberalism do not appear in the *Deutsche Rundschau*. See Chapter 4.

94. Julius Rosenberg, ed., *Deutsche Rundschau*, Vol. 57 (October–December 1888), pp. 12–14.

95. Ponsonby, *Letters*, p. 343.

96. Ibid., p. 344.

97. Ibid., p. 345.

98. Lothar Gall, *Bismarck, the White Revolutionary* (London, 1988), p. 199: "Bismarck had obtained the young emperor's consent to this course by hinting at allegedly threatened national interests and above all by discreetly suggesting that this placing of his father on the pedestal of liberal legend did his own position no good, nor did it favour the requisite focusing of present expectation on himself."

99. Hollyday, *Stosch*, p. 245. Since the war diary was not genuine, Bismarck told the young emperor, the editor of the *Deutsche Rundschau* "could be brought to trial under the law of libel," and even in the unlikely event that the diary was proved to be genuine, "the editor could be punished under the law against disclosing state secrets." Ibid.

100. Ibid., p. 248. According to Stosch: "The Chancellor had gone to the Emperor with extracts from Roggenbach's confiscated papers and had convinced him that he harbored 'a viper in his bosom.'"

101. Ibid.

102. Ibid. In June 1889, the left liberal *Freisinnige Zeitung* labelled the dismissal of Frederick's friend, minister of justice Friedberg, as a part of Bismarck's purge against the late emperor's memory.

103. Ibid.

104. Gall, *Bismarck*, p. 200. William was also impressed by the argument that "Bismarck's scarcely veiled attacks on the late emperor were likely to do general harm to the monarchical idea."

105. During the height of the Geffcken affair she wrote her mother: "The two men on whom I ought to be able to rely are Minister Friedberg and the Haus

Minister, but they are servants of the state, of William and Bismarck, and have neither the interest nor the courage to defend me where I am wronged. I have only my sense of right, my good conscience, the affection of many sections of the public and the liberals to rely on—nothing else! For all that, I shall not allow myself to be driven away from Germany, nor shall I abandon those who are true to Fritz's beloved memory and principles." Ponsonby, *Letters*, p. 354.

106. Ibid., pp. 375–376.

107. Ibid., p. 360.

108. Ibid., p. 404.

109. Ibid., p. 359.

110. Ibid., p. 404.

111. Ibid., p. 360.

112. Shortly before Frederick's death, Victoria wrote her mother: "If Fritz goes, I do not the least care what becomes of me. . . . Fritz and I will be more than avenged one day by the course events will take when these people come to power." Ibid., p. 313.

113. Erich Eyck, *Bismarck and the German Empire* (London, 1968), p. 299.

Conclusion

This study has focused on the evolution of Frederick III's liberal views within the larger context of liberal development during his lifetime. As far as can be seen from the previous record, Frederick had little in common with the legend that was created by his wife and nurtured by her liberal supporters. As we have seen, the legend obscured several truths about his liberal views: it downplayed Frederick's opposition to British-style liberalism, his alliance with Bismarck during the latter's period of cooperation with the liberals, his rejection of the idea of ruling alongside the left-liberal Freisinn Party when he came to the throne, and, above all, his bouts of depression and his lack of enthusiasm about his coming rule that dominated the last decade of his life. In the final analysis, the legend says a lot more about Victoria's political views than those of her husband. It was Victoria, not Frederick, who wanted to dismantle Bismarck's system and convert Prussia and Germany to genuine parliamentary governments.

However, the fact that Frederick had little in common with his legend should not diminish his contribution to the course of German liberal development. As a youth, Frederick underwent a conversion from conservative prince to constitutional liberal. The conversion was genuine: he was the only ruler of Germany who never wavered in his conviction that the monarch and the people were subject to the rule of law and that the constitution was a binding agreement between the monarch and the people that had to be upheld at all costs.

Frederick felt he had good reason to reject Victoria's view that it was necessary to adopt British political institutions in Germany. To compromise the power of the monarchy by giving the people greater power, he felt, would invite the dreaded "revolution from below," since the German people were politically too immature to use wisely the gift of increased political power. As he saw it, the monarchy was responsible for responding to the needs of the people, whereas the role of parliament was to assist the monarchy in its efforts to ensure their welfare. His political ideal was achieved during the new era, a time when government and parliament appeared to share a mutual desire to pursue liberal reforms—such as free expression, free trade, and popular education—within the framework of the constitutional status quo.

To Frederick's dismay, however, the issue of army reform ended the new era. The ensuing conflict between crown and parliament put the crown prince in a difficult position since both monarchy and parliament agitated for changes that Frederick found unacceptable: he opposed the king's willingness to reject parliamentary rights guaranteed by the constitution, as well as the liberals' attempts to alter the constitutional status quo at the expense of the monarchy. Frederick suggested a foreign policy victory to break the deadlock between crown and parliament. Such a victory, he believed, would tone down liberal agitation for radical parliamentary reforms. But his advice was ignored, since his father and powerful conservatives erroneously assumed that the crown prince sympathized with the political goals of the opposition.

When Bismarck became minister-president in 1862, he appeared to embody everything that the crown prince despised: disdain for the constitutional process and the nationalist cause. Bismarck's use of Lückentheorie and his rejection of nationalists' demands during the Schleswig-Holstein crisis only served to confirm this view. Frederick's Danzig speech was motivated by Bismarck's dubious interpretation of the constitution and his wish to assure the people of his hope that the king would see his way clear to upholding constitutionalism. This hope appeared to be dashed when the king and Bismarck threatened to subvert the constitution in order to put an end to the constitutional conflict, which impelled Frederick to embark upon his policy of passive resistance against the government.

Bismarck, however, did not make good on his threat to subvert the constitution, and in 1866, Frederick joined forces with Bismarck, since the latter appeared to have come to the conclusion that it was in Prussia's best interests to uphold constitutionalism and cooperate with the liberal-national movement for the unification of Germany. Together, the crown prince and Bismarck thwarted conservatives' attempts to use Prussia's victory over Austria as a pretext to subvert the constitution and convinced the king that it was necessary to negotiate a lenient peace with Austria and make peace with the liberal majority by means of the indemnity bill. The crown prince's cooperation with the chancellor during the Franco-Prussian war was also based on a mutual desire to uphold the constitutional status quo—this time to thwart the design of Progressives, who wished to alter it in a more liberal direction, and Prussian conservatives, who wished to once again exploit military victory to initiate a policy of reaction.

It would be an exaggeration, however, to state that the crown prince became a full-fledged advocate of Bismarckian methods and practices during their period of cooperation. Frederick never trusted the chancellor and, most of all, despised his ability to manipulate the emperor. The crown prince conjured up the vision of the newly unified Germany—which would soon be under his leadership—as a new and improved successor state to the Holy Roman Empire. Frederick's statement to his wife: "Bismarck's stamp belongs on *his* creations, but my mark will be made on what I hope to achieve later. .... in time, you and I will consecrate anew that which has sprung from Bismarck's cabinet," meant that his regime would divorce itself from the idea that the chancellor would dictate to the emperor what was best for Prussia and Germany. In other words, he used the idea of the old empire to distance himself from Bismarck's vision of Germany. From this it follows that Frederick advocated the idea of personal rule of the monarch, but this desire to place himself above all ministers and subjects was tempered by his devotion to the constitution, which stipulated that no monarch was above the rule of law.

Despite his prevailing mistrust of the chancellor, Frederick supported efforts undertaken by Bismarck and the liberal majority to consolidate unification and combat particularist forces in the empire during the early 1870s. Indeed, the new empire closely resembled what Frederick wanted most for Germany: liberal policies pursued within the framework of the constitutional status quo; the "Liberal era" was, in essence, the basis of what Frederick intended to pursue during his coming reign.

However, Frederick's enthusiasm for his reign waned as the fortunes of the liberals declined during the latter half of the decade, and it vanished in 1879 as he witnessed Bismarck's destruction of ideas and institutions upon which the former intended to base his rule. The abandonment of free trade, the dismantling of the Kulturkampf, and the co-opting of nonliberal interest groups into the power structure of the empire all represented a step backward to a time when conservatism and particularism ruled the day. Worse still, these developments drove the liberal movement into two directions, both of which Frederick found unacceptable: he resented the National Liberals, who felt they had little choice but to support Bismarck's policies, as well as the liberal Left, because it advocated increasing the powers of parliament. Further, Frederick's regency gave him a disillusioning preview of things to come during his own future reign. Unable to find a political home and convinced that the passage of years would render any attempt to dismantle Bismarck's system impossible, Frederick became indifferent toward his approaching reign during the 1880s. He languished in the background, letting his wife give liberals the impression that he shared her desire to cooperate with left liberals during his coming reign.

But although he felt it would be well-nigh impossible to resurrect the liberal era during his coming reign, Frederick was nonetheless determined to prevent Bismarck from subverting the constitution and creating a Staatsstreich, a move that would have most certainly completed the chancellor's retrograde transformation of political life in Germany. Frederick's adherence to constitutional liberalism, as articulated in his proclamations, forced the chancellor to abandon his plans to tamper with the constitution during the coming reign.

It is difficult to determine whether or not Bismarck was justified in his fear that Victoria would exploit her husband's bouts of depression to achieve her radical liberal aims during his coming reign. As we have seen, Frederick successfully resisted his wife's attempts to convince him to join forces with left liberal parties such as the Progressives and Freisinn. Nonetheless, Frederick's acquiescence to the Battenberg marriage project proved that Victoria could give her husband ideas having dangerous consequences. Bismarck managed to construct an alliance in the Reichstag against the crown princess and her pro-Battenberg sympathizers, but this victory was clouded by Frederick's declining health, which raised fears that his wife would exploit her husband's weakness to achieve her aims. Bismarck once again managed to counter this threat by using the threat of a regency to restrain the crown princess when her husband came to the throne.

Though we cannot know what a healthy Frederick would have done as emperor, he almost certainly would have retained Bismarck as long as the latter agreed to abide by the principles stated in Frederick's proclamation—in which case German policy would not have changed. Had illness or death forced Bismarck from the scene, however, it is difficult to say whether Victoria and her allies would have been able to exploit Frederick's depression to adopt constitutional amendments for genuine parliamentary government. Of course, the conservatives could have wielded enough power to thwart these reforms.

In conclusion, the previous record does not convincingly support either side of the historical debate on the impact of liberalism on the course of German history. On one hand, Frederick's unwillingness to see the adoption of British-style political institutions in Germany appears to support the theory that the ideological weaknesses of the liberal movement led to its failure. Also, Frederick's conviction that the conservative tide in politics was "irreversible" after 1879 appears to support to the theory that the failure of the liberal movement was inevitable after 1879.

One the other hand, however, this study has produced evidence suggesting that the notion of the inevitable decline and fall of the liberal movement is in need of revision. The fact that Bismarck found it necessary to devote a great deal of time and energy in attempting to counteract the influence of Victoria and her left liberal allies during the 1880s indicates that he at least saw his "system" as anything but impregnable. The resurgence of left liberalism in the 1880s, which Bismarck was able to neutralize only through the construction of his Cartel in 1887, indicates that it was not the liberal movement in general that went into a state of decline after 1879, but only the *kind* of liberalism that Frederick had so wholeheartedly supported. What Frederick bemoaned in 1879 was not the apparent emasculation of the power and influence of the liberal movement, but the complete decline in the power and influence of the National Liberals of the early 1870s, who appeared to share Frederick's conviction that it was in Germany's best interests to pursue liberal reforms within the framework of the status quo.

Frederick's bouts of depression and his vulnerability to his wife's influence during the last few years of his life should not, however, cast a pall on his achievements. As we have seen, Frederick was far from idle when he believed the future of constitutionalism to be in jeopardy. He was an influential agitator on behalf of the preservation of constitutionalism when he saw it being threatened by Bismarck in the early 1860s, by the conservatives in the aftermath of the war of 1866, and by

Bismarck once again during the 1880s. While Frederick's constitutional liberalism did not give him nearly as much potential to change the course of German history in a liberal direction as many historians have claimed, it was thanks to him that the basis for the survival of liberalism as a political movement—the constitution—remained intact.

Selected Bibliography

ARCHIVAL SOURCES

Germany

Auswärtiges Amt, Bonn
Deutsches Bundesarchiv, Abteilung Potsdam
Geheimes Staatsarchiv Preussischer Kulturbesitz, Berlin-Dahlem
Geheimes Staatsarchiv Preussischer Kulturbesitz, Merseburg
Hessische Hausstiftung, Schloss Fasanerie, Fulda

Great Britain

Public Records Office, Kew, Richmond

PUBLISHED SOURCES

Ackerknecht, E. H. *Rudolf Virchow*. Stuttgart, 1957.
Allinson, A. R., trans. *The War Diary of Frederick III*. London, 1957.
Anderson, Eugene. *The Social and Political Conflict in Prussia, 1858–1864.* Lincoln, NE, August 1954.
Anderson, Margaret L. *Windthorst: A Political Biography*. Oxford, 1986.
————, and Barkin, K. "The Myth of the Puttkamer Purge and the Reality of the Kulturkampf: Some Reflections on the Historiography of Imperial Germany." *Journal of Modern History*, 53 (1982): pp. 647–686.
Anderson, Pauline. *The Background of Anti-English Feeling in Germany*. Washington, D.C., 1939.
Arblaster, Anthony. *The Rise and Decline of Western Liberalism*. Oxford, 1984.

Askew, William, and Wallace, Lillian, eds. *Power, Public Opinion and Diplomacy.* Durham, NC, 1959.

Aufermann, M.L. *Der persönliche Anteil der Kaiserin Friedrich an der deutschen Politik.* Berlin, 1932.

Bamberger, Ludwig. *Erinnerungen.* Berlin, 1899.

————. *Gesammelte Schriften.* 5 vols. Berlin, 1894–1898.

Barkeley, Richard. *The Empress Frederick.* London, 1956.

Barker, Michael. *Gladstone and Radicalism: The Reconstruction of Liberal Policy in Britain, 1885–1894.* Bristol, 1975.

Barth, Theodore. *Politische Porträts.* Berlin, 1904.

Becker, Josef. "Zum Problem der Bismarckischen Politik in der Spanischen Thronfrage." *Historische Zeitschrift.* Vol. 23 (1971).

Bennett, Daphne. *Vicky: Princess Royal of England and German Empress.* London, 1971.

Berdahl, Robert. *The Politics of the Prussian Nobility: The Development of a Conservative Ideology, 1770–1848.* Princeton, NJ, 1988.

Bergsträsser, Ludwig. *Geschichte der politischen Parteien in Deutschland.* Munich, 1960.

Bernhardi, Theodor von. *Aus dem Leben Theodor von Bernhardi.* Leipzig, 1893–1895.

Beyerhaus, Gisbert. "Die Krise des deutschen Liberalismus und das Problem der 99 Tage." *Preussische Jahrbücher,* Vol. 239 (1935).

Blackbourn, D., and Eley, G. *Class, Religion and Local Politics in Wilhelmine Germany: The Centre Party in Württemburg before 1914.* New Haven CT, 1980.

Blackbourn, D., and Eley, G. *The Peculiarities of German History: Bourgeois Society and Politics in Nineteenth Century Germany.* New York and Oxford, 1984.

Block, Hermann. *Die parlamentarische Krisis der Nationalliberalen Partei, 1878–1880.* Münster, 1930.

Böhme, Helmut. *Deutschlands Weg zur Grossmacht.* Cologne, 1973.

————, ed. *The Foundation of the German Empire: Select Documents.* London, 1971.

Bonnin, Georges, ed. *Bismarck and the Hohenzollern Candidature for the Spanish Throne: Documents in the German Diplomatic Archives.* London, 1957.

Börner, Karl Heinz. *Kaiser Wilhelm I.* Cologne, 1984.

Bruch, R., von, ed. *Weder Kommunismus noch Kapitalismus: Bürgerliche Sozialreform in Deutschland bis zu Ära Adenauer.* Munich, 1985.

Buckle, George E., ed. *The Letters of Queen Victoria. Second Series. A Selection from Her Majesty's Correspondence and Journal Between the Years 1862 and 1878.* London, 1926.

Bunsen, Marie von. *Kaiserin Augusta.* Berlin, 1940.

Bussman, Walter, ed. "Zur Geschichte des deutschen Liberalismus im 19.

Jahrhundert." *Historische Zeitschrift* 186 (1958): 527–657.

———. *Staatssekretär Graf Herbert von Bismarck: Aus seiner politischen Privatkorrespondenz.* Göttingen, 1964.

Cahn, Wilhelm, ed. *Aus Eduard Laskers Nachlass. Fünfzehn Jahre parlamentarischer Geschichte, 1866–1880.* Berlin, 1902.

Carr, William, *Origins of the Wars of German Unification.* London, 1991.

Corti, Egon Caesar Conte. *Leben und Liebe Alexanders von Battenberg,* Graz, 1949.

———. *The English Empress. A Study in the Relations Between Queen Victoria and Her Eldest Daughter, Empress Frederick of Germany.* London, 1957.

Craig, Gordon. *Germany: 1866–1945.* New York, 1978.

Crew, David. *Town in the Ruhr. A Social History of Bochum, 1860–1914.* New York, 1979.

Dahrendorf, Ralf. "Warum die Deutschen den Kronprinzen nicht mögen." In *Reisen nach innen und aussen.* Stuttgart, 1984.

Dawson, William H. *The German Empire.* London, 1919.

Delbrück, Hans. *The Government and the Will of the People. Academic Lectures.* New York, 1923.

Dix, Arthur. *Die deutschen Reichstagswahlen, 1871–1930, und dieWandlungen der Volksgliederung.* Tübingen, 1930.

Dohme, Robert. "Erinnerungen an Kaiser Friedrich." *Deutsche Revue,* Vol. 157 (1922).

Dorpalen, Andreas. "Frederick III and the German Liberal Movement." *American Historical Review,* Vol. 54, No. 1, (October 1948).

Eisfeld, G. Die Entstehung der liberalen Parteien in Deutschland, 1858–1870: *Studien zu den Organisationen und Programmen der Liberalen und Demokraten.* Hanover, 1969.

Eley, Geoff. *From Unification to Nazism, Reinterpreting the German Past.* Boston, 1986.

Elm, Ludwig. *Die bürgerlichen Parteien in Deutschland.* Leipzig, 1970.

Evans, Ellen Lovell. *The German Center Party, 1870–1933: A Study in Political Catholicism.* Carbondale, IL, 1981.

Eyck, Erich. *Bismarck and the German Empire.* London, 1968.

Eyck, Frank. *The Prince Consort. A Political Biography.* London, 1959.

Faber, K. G. "Strukturprobleme des deutschen Liberalismus im 19 Jahrhundert." *Der Staat,* 14 (1975): pp. 201–228.

———. *Deutsche Geschichte im 19. Jahrhundert: Restauration und Revolution von 1815 bis 1851.* (Handbuch der deutschen Geschichte, no. 3/I, part 2) Wiesbaden, 1979.

Farago, Ladislas. *Royal Web.* New York, 1982.

Feder, Ernst, ed. *Bismarcks Grosses Spiel: Die Geheimen Tagebücher Ludwig Bambergers.* Frankfurt am Main, 1932.

Fischer, Fritz. *Bündnis der Eliten: Zur Kontinuität der Machtstrukturen in*

Deutschland 1871–1945. Düsseldorf, 1979.

Fisher, M.H. and Rich, Norman, eds. *The Holstein Papers*. Cambridge, 1957.

Freytag, Gustav. *The Crown Prince and the German Imperial Crown*. London, 1890.

Freund, Michael. *Das Drama der 99 Tage: Krankheit und Tod Friedrichs III.* Cologne, 1966.

————. "Der Kaiser der Liberalen-Friedrich III." In Friedrich Wilhelm von Preussen, ed., *Preussens Könige*. Gütersloh, 1971.

Friese, Johannes. *Die politische Haltung der Kronprinzessin Victoria bis zum Jahre 1871*. Berlin, 1973.

Fuchs, Walter. *Grossherzog Friedrich I von Baden und die Reichspolitik, 1871–1907* 4 Vols. Stuttgart, 1968–1980.

Fulford, Roger, ed. *Dearest Child. The Private Correspondence of Queen Victoria and the Princess Royal: 1858–1861*. London, 1964.

Fulford, Roger ed., *Your Dear Letter: The Private Correspondence of the Queen Victoria and the Crown Princess,of Prussia 1865–1871* London, 1968.

————. *Dearest Mama: Private Correspondence between Queen Victoria and the German Crown Princess, 1861–1864*. London, 1968.

————. *Darling Child: The Private Correspondence of Queen Victoria and the German Crown Princess, 1871–1878*. London, 1976.

————. *Beloved Mama: The Correspondence of Queen Victoria and the German Crown Princess, 1879–1885*. London, 1981.

Fyfe, Hamilton. *The British Liberal Party*. London, 1928.

Gagel, Walter. *Die Wahlrechtsfrage in der Geschichte der Deutschen Liberalen Parteien*. Düsseldorf, 1958.

Gagliardo, John. *Reich and Nation: The Holy Roman Empire as Idea and Reality 1763–1806*. Bloomington, IN 1980.

Gall, Lothar, ed. *Liberalismus*. Cologne, 1976.

————. "Der deutsche Liberalismus zwischen Revolution und Reichsgründung." *Historische Zeitschrift,*228 (1979): pp. 98–108.

Gerloff, Wilhelm. *Die Finanz und Zollpolitik des deutschen Reiches, nebst ihren Beziehungen zu Landes und Gemeindefinanzen von der Gründung des Norddeutschen Bundes bis zur Gegenwart*. Jena, 1913.

Gillis, John. *The Prussian Bureaucracy in Crisis. 1840–1860: Origins of an Adminstrative Ethos*. Princeton, 1971.

Guttsman, W. L. *The German Social Democratic Party 1875–1933: From Ghetto to Government*. Boston, 1981.

Hamerow, Theodore. *The Social Foundations of German Unification. Ideas and Institutions*. Princeton, NJ, 1969.

Harris, James. *A Study in the Theory and Practice of Liberalism. Eduard Lasker, 1829–1884*. New York and London, 1984.

Hartwig, Otto. *Ludwig Bamberger, eine biographische Skizze*. Marburg, 1900.

Haym, Rudolf. *Das Leben Max Dunckers*. Berlin, 1891.

Hengst, Hermann. *Friedrich Wilhelm, Kronprinz des Deutschen Reiches und von Preussen, Ein Fürstenbild aus dem Neunzehnten Jahrhundert.* Berlin, 1883.

Herre, Franz. *Kaiser Friedrich III. Deutschlands liberale Hoffnung.* Munich, 1987.

Herzfeld, Hans. *Johannes von Miquel.* Detmold, 1938.

Hess, Adalbert. *Das Parlament, das Bismarck widerstrebte. Zur Politik und sozialen Zusammensetuzung des preussischen Abgeordnetenhauses der Konfliktszeit, 1862–1866.* Cologne, 1964.

Hess, Jürgen. *Bibliographie zum deutschen Liberalismus.* Göttingen, 1981.

Heyderhoff, Julius, ed. *Im Ring der Gegner Bismarcks: Denkschriften und politischer Briefwechsel Franz von Roggenbachs mit Kaiserin Augusta und Albrecht von Stosch, 1865–96.* Leipzig, 1943.

—— and Wentzke, P. eds. *Deutscher Liberalismus im Zeitalter Bismarcks.* 4 Vols. Bonn, 1925–1926.

Hohenlohe-Ingelfingen, Prinz Karl zu. "Eine Kriegserinnerung an Kaiser Friedrich." *Preussische Jahrbücher,* Vol. 64 (1889).

Holborn, Hajo. *History of Modern Germany, 1840–1945.* New York, 1969.

Hollenberg, Günter. *Englisches Interesse am Kaiserreich: Die Attraktivität Preussen-Deutschlands für konservative und liberale Kreise in Grossbritainnien, 1860–1914.* Wiesbaden, 1974.

Hollyday, Frederic B. M. *Bismarck's Rival. A Political Biography of General and Admiral Albrecht von Stosch.* Durham, NC, 1963.

Hubatsch, Walter, ed. *Schicksalswege Deutscher Vergangenheit.* Düsseldorf, 1950.

Huber, Ernst Rudolf. *Deutsche Verfassungsgeschichte seit 1789.* 4 Vols. Stuttgart, 1957–1969.

Hunt, J. C. "Peasants, Grain Tariffs and Meat Quotas: German Protectionism Reexamined." *Central European History* Vol 7, (December 1974): 311–331.

——. "The Bourgeois Middle in German Politics, 1871–1933." *Central European History* 19 (1978): 83–106.

Jarausch, Konrad and Jones, Larry, eds. *In Search of a Liberal Germany.* London, 1990.

Jones, Larry Eugene and Retallack, James, eds. *Elections, Mass Politics and Social Change in Modern Germany.* Washington, 1991.

Käbele, Hartmut. "Der Mythos von der rapiden Industrialisirung in Deutschland." *Geschichte und Gesellschaft,* 9 (1983).

Kahan, Alan. "The Victory of German Liberalism? Rudolf Haym, Liberalism, and Bismarck." *Central European History.* Vol. 22, (March 1990).

——. *Aristocratic Liberalism: The Social and Political Thought of Jacob Burkhardt, John Stuart Mill, and Alexis de Tocqueville.* New York, 1992.

Kaiser Wilhelm II. *Ereignisse und Gestalten aus den Jahren 1878–1918.* Leipzig, 1922.

——. *Aus meinem Leben, 1859–1888.* Berlin, 1927.

Kämpf, Fritz. *Gustav Freytag und das Kronprinzpaar Friedrich Wilhelm.* Leipzig,

1923.

Kennedy, Paul. *The Rise of Anglo-German Antagonism, 1860–1914.* London, 1987.

Kent, George O. *Bismarck and His Times.* Carbondale, IL, 1978.

Knaplund, Paul, ed. *Letters from the British Embassy, 1871–1874, 1880–1885.* Washington, DC, 1944.

Koch, H. W. *A Constitutional History of Germany in the Nineteenth and Twentieth Centuries.* London, 1984.

Koch, Rainer. *Demokratie und Staat bei Julius Fröbel, 1805–1893: Liberales Denken zwischen Naturrecht und Sozialdarwinismus.* Wiesbaden, 1978.

Kohn, Walter S. G. *Governments and Politics of German-Speaking Countries.* Chicago, 1990.

Kohut, Thomas. *William II and the Germans: A Study in Leadership.* New York, 1991.

Königin Augusta von Preussen. *Bekentnisse an eine Freundin.* Dresden, 1935.

Krieger, Leonard. *The German Idea of Freedom: History of a Political Tradition.* Chicago, 1957.

Kutsch, Ruth. *Queen Victoria und die deutsche Einigung.* Berlin, 1938.

Lamer, Reinhard. *Der englische Parlamentarismus in der deutschen Theorie im Zeitalter Bismarcks, 1857–1890.* Lübeck, 1963.

Langer, William L. *European Alliances and Alignments.* London, 1950.

Langewiesche, Dieter. *Liberalismus in Deutschland.* Frankfurt am Main, 1988.

————, ed. *Liberalismus im Neunzehnten Jahrhundert: Deutschland im europäischen Vergleich.* Göttingen, 1988.

Lee, Arthur G., ed. *The Empress Frederick Writes to Sophie.* London, 1955.

Lee, W. R. and Rosenhaft, Eve, eds. *The State and Social Change in Germany, 1880–1890.* New York, 1990.

Lidke, Vernon. *The Outlawed Party: Social Democracy in Germany, 1878–1890.* Princeton, NJ, 1986.

Lin, Dr. Jain I. *The Death of a Kaiser: A Medical-Historical Narrative.* Dayton, OH, 1985.

Lloyd, Trevor. *The General Election of 1880.* Oxford, 1968.

Lorenz, Ina Susanne. *Eugen Richter: Der entscheidene Liberalismus, 1871–1906.* Leipzig, 1981.

Lutz, Heinrich. *Zwischen Habsburg und Preussen. Deutschland, 1815–1866.* Berlin, 1985.

Marks, Erich. *Kaiser Wilhelm I.* Leipzig, 1897.

Martel, Gordon, ed. *Modern Germany Reconsidered, 1870–1945.* New York, 1992.

Martin, Theodore. *The Life of HRH the Prince Consort.* 3rd ed. London, 1880.

Massie, Robert K. *Dreadnought. Britain, Germany and the Coming of the Great War.* New York, 1991.

McClelland, Charles E. *The German Historian and England: A Study in Nineteenth Century Views.* Cambridge, 1971.

Meisner, Heinrich Otto, ed. *Kaiser Friedrich III, Kriegstagebuch 1870–1871*. Berlin und Leipzig, 1926.

———, ed. *Kaiser Friedrich III. Tagebücher von 1848 bis 1866*. Leipzig, 1929.

Kaiser Friedrich III, Kriegstagebuch 1870–1871. Berlin und Leipzig, 1926.

———. *Der preussische Kronprinz im Verfassungskampf 1863*. Berlin, 1931.

Mommsen, Wilhelm, ed. *Deutsche Parteiprogramme*. Munich, 1960.

Müller-Bohn, Hermann. *Kaiser Friedrich der Gütige*. Berlin, 1900.

Nichols, J. Alden. *The Year of the Three Kaisers: Bismarck and the German Succession, 1887–1888*. Champaign, IL, 1987.

Niederhommert, Charlotte. *Königin Viktoria und der deutsche Kronprinz Friedrich Wilhellm*. Emsdetten, 1934.

Nipperdey, Thomas. *Deutsche Geschichte, 1800–1866: Bürgerwelt und starker Staat*. Munich, 1984.

Obenhaus, Herbert. *Anfänge des Parlmentarismus in Preussen bis 1848. (Handbuch der Geschichte des Deutschen Parlamentarismus*. Düsseldorf, 1984.

O'Boyle, Lenore. "Liberal Political Leadership in Germany, 1867–1884." *Journal of Modern History*, Vol. 28, (December 1956): 522–540.

———. "The German Nationalverein." *Journal of Central European Affairs*, 16 (1957): 338–352.

Olden, Rudolf. *The History of Liberty in Germany*. London, 1946.

Oncken, Hermann. *Rudolf von Bennigsen: Ein Deutscher Liberaler Politiker*. Stuttgart, 1910.

———, ed. *Grossherzog Friedrich von Baden und die deutsche Politik von 1854–1871*. Stuttgart, 1927.

Pflanze, Otto, ed. *The Unification of Germany*. New York, 1968.

———. *Bismarck and the Development of Germany*, 3 Vols. Princeton, NJ, 1990.

Philippson, Martin, *Das Leben Friedrichs III*. Wiesbaden, 1900.

———. *Max von Forckenbeck, Ein Lebensbild*. Dresden, 1968.

Pinson, Koppel S. *Modern Germany: Its History and Civilization*, 2nd ed. New York, 1966.

Pöls, Werner, *Sozialistenfrage und Revolutionsfürcht in ihrem Zusammenhang mit den angeblichen Staatsreichplänen Bismarcks*. Düsseldorf, 1960.

Ponsonby, Sir Frederick, ed., *Letters of the Empress Frederick*. London, 1929.

Poschinger, Hermann von. "Franz Roggenbach und Kaiser Friedrich." *Deutsche Revue* 35 (1910).

Poschinger, Margarete von, *Life of the Emperor Frederick*. New York, 1971.

Puttkamer, Albert von. *Staatsminister von Puttkamer: Ein Stück Preussischer Vergangenheit*. Leipzig, 1928.

Ramm, Agatha. *Sir Robert Morier: Envoy and Ambassador in the Age of Imperialism, 1876–1893*. Oxford, 1973.

Retallack, James. *Notables of the Right: The Conservative Party and Political Mobilization in Germany, 1876–1918*. London, 1988.

Rich, Norman. *Friedrich von Holstein*. Cambridge, 1965.

————— and Fisher, M. H., eds. *The Holstein Papers*. 4 Vols. Cambridge, 1957.

Richter, Eugen. *Im alten Reichstag. Erinnerungen*. 2 Vols. Berlin, 1894–1896.

Richter, Werner. *Friedrich III: Leben und Tragik des Zweiten Hohenzollern Kaisers*. 2nd ed. Munich, 1981.

Ritter, Gerhard. *Social Welfare in Germany and Britain*. New York, 1986.

—————, ed., *Die deutschen Parteien vor 1918*. Cologne, 1973.

Rodd, Rennell. *Frederick, Crown Prince and Emperor*. London, 1888.

Rohe, Karl, ed., *Englischer Liberalismus im 19, und frühren 20. Jahrhundert*. Bochum, 1987.

Röhl, J.C.G. "The Disintigration of the Kartell and the Politics of Bismarck's Fall from Power, 1887–90." *Historical Journal*, Vol. 9, No. 1, (1966): 60–89.

—————. *Wilhelm II: Die Jugend des Kaisers, 1858–1888*. Munich, 1994.

Rosenberg, Arthur. *The Birth of the German Republic*. New York, 1931.

Rosenberg, Hans, ed. *Die Nationalpolitische Publizistik Deutschlands vom Entritt der Neuen Ära in Preussen bis zum Ausbruch des Deutschen Krieges*. Munich, 1935.

—————. *Grosse Depression und Bismarckszeit*. Berlin, 1967.

Rosenberg, Julius ed. *Deutsche Rundschau*, Bd. LVII (October–December 1888).

Salomon, Felix. *Die deutschen Parteiprogramme*. Leipzig, 1907.

Schieder, W. ed. *Liberalismus in der Gesellschaft des deutschen Vormärz*. Göttingen, 1983.

Schrader-Breymann, Henriette. *Ihr Leben aus Briefen und Tagebüchern*. 2 Vols. Berlin, 1927.

Schulze, Johannnes, ed. *Max Duncker. Politischer Briefwechsel aus seinem Nachlass*. Osnabrück, 1967.

Schuster, Georg, ed. *Briefe, Reden und Erlasse des Kaisers und Königs Friedrich III*. Berlin, 1907.

Seeber, G. *Zwischen Bebel und Bismarck: Zur Geschichte des Linksliberalismus in Deutschland, 1871–1893*. East Berlin, 1965.

Selig, Winifried. *Von Nassau zum Deutschen Reich: Die ideologische und politische Entwicklung von Karl Braun*. Wiesbaden, 1981.

Sell, F. C. *Die Tragödie des deutschen Liberalismus*. Stuttgart, 1953.

Sheehan, James J. *German Liberalism in the Nineteenth Century*. Chicago, 1978.

Silvermann, Dan P. *Reluctant Union: Alsace-Lorraine and Imperial Germany, 1871–1918*. State College, PA, 1972.

Smith, Woodruff. *The German Colonial Empire*. Chapel Hill, NC, 1978.

Snell, John. *The Democratic Movement in Germany, 1789–1914*. Chapel Hill, NC 1976.

Stadelmann, Rudolf. *Social and Political History of the German 1848 Revolution*. Columbus, OH, 1975.

Steefel, L. D. *The Schleswig-Holstein Question*. Cambridge, 1941.

Stern, Fritz. *Gold and Iron. Bismarck, Bleichröder and the Building of the German Empire*. New York, 1977.

————, ed. *The Failure of Illiberalism: Essays on the Political Culture of Modern Germany.* New York, 1972.

Stoltenberg, Gerhard. *Der Deutsche Reichstag, 1871–1873.* Düsseldorf, 1955.

Stosch, Ulrich von. *Denkwürdigkeiten des Generals und Admirals Albrecht von Stosch.* Stuttgart, 1904.

Stürmer, Michael. "Staatsreichgedanken im Bismarckreich" *Historische Zeitschrift,* 209 (1969).

————. *Regierung und Reichstag im Bismarcksstaat, 1871–1880.* Düsseldorf, 1974.

————. *Das Ruhelose Reich. Deutschland, 1866–1918.* Berlin, 1985.

Suehlo, W. *Georg Herbert, Graf zu Münster.* Hildesheim, 1968.

Taffs, Winifried. *Lord Odo Russell, A Biography.* London, 1954.

Taylor, A.J.P. *Germany's First Bid for Colonies 1884–1885.* London, 1968.

Tennstedt, Florian. *Sozialgeschichte der Sozialpolitik in Deutschland: Von 18. Jahrhundert bis zum Ersten Weltkrieg.* Göttingen, 1981.

Tent, J. F. "Eugen Richter and the Decline of German Progressivism." *The Maryland Historian* (Fall, 1979).

Thorwart, Friedrich, ed. *Hermann Schultze-Delitschs Schriften und Reden.* Berlin, 1909.

Tisdall, Evelyn P. *She Made the World Chaos: The Story of the Empress Frederick.* London, 1944.

Valentin, Veit. *Bismarcks Reichsgründung im Urteil Englischen Diplomaten.* Berlin, 1937.

————. *1848: Chapters of German History.* London, 1940.

————. *The German People. Their History and Civilization from the Holy Roman Empire to the Third Reich.* New York, 1962.

Valjavec, F. *Die Entstehung der politischen Strömungen in Deutschland.* Düsseldorf, 1978.

Veblen, Thorstein, *Imperial Germany and the Indisutrial Revolution.* 2nd ed. New Brunswick, NJ, 1990.

Wehler, Hans-Ulrich, ed. *Krisenherde des Kaiserreichs, 1871–1918.* Göttingen, 1970.

————, ed. *Das Deutsche Kaiserreich.* Göttingen, 1973.

————, ed. *Sozialgeschichte Heute.* Göttingen, 1975.

Wemyss, Rosslyn. *Memoirs and Letters of Sir Robert Morier.* London, 1911.

Whittle, Tyler. *Kaiser Wilhelm II.* Munich, 1979.

Wilhelm, Rolf. *Das Verhältnis der süddeutschen Staaten zum Norddeutschen Bund 1867–1870.* Husum, 1978.

Windelband, Wolfgang. *Berlin-Madrid-Rom. Bismarck und die Reise des deutschen Kronprinzen 1883 auf Grund unveröffentlichen Akten.* Essen, 1939.

Winkler, Heinrich August. *Preussischer Liberalismus und deutscher Nationalstaat. Studien zur Geschichte der Deutschen Fortschrittspartei, 1861–1866.* Tübingen, 1964.

Witt, Peter. *Finanzpolitik des Kaiserreiches, 1903–1913.* Lübeck, 1970.

Wolbe, Eugen. *Kaiser Friedrich: Die Tragödie des Übergangenen.* Hellerau, 1931.

Wolf, H. J. *Die Krankheit Friedrichs III und ihre Wirkung auf die englische und deutsche Öffentlichkeit.* Berlin, 1938.

Ziekursch, Johannes. *Politische Geschichte des Neuen Deutschen Kaiserreiches.* Frankfurt, am Main, 1925–1930.

Ziemissen, Ludwig. *Friedrich, deutscher Kaiser und König von Preussen, ein Lebensbild.* Berlin, 1888.

Zucker, Stanley. "Ludwig Bamberger and the Politics of the Cold Shoulder: German Liberalism's Response to Working Class Legislation in the 1880's." *European Studies Review,* 2 No. 3 (1972): 201–226.

———. *Ludwig Bamberger, Liberal Politician.* Pittsburgh, 1975.

———. *Kathinka Zitz-Halein and Female Civic Activism in Mid-Nineteenth Century Germany.* Carbondale, IL 1991.

Index

Albedyll, Emil von, 169, 185 n.15, 186
    n.17
Albert, Prince of Saxe-Coburg,
    [Consort of Queen Victoria of
    England], advises Crown Prince
    Frederick William and William I,
    11-15, 16, 30; influence on Crown
    Prince Frederick William, 10;
    influence on Princess Victoria, 6-
    7, 9-10, 12-13, 15-17
Alvensleben, Gustav von, 49 n.53
Arndt, Ernst Moritz, 5
Auerswald, Leopold von, 5
Augusta, Princess of Prussia and
    German Empress, 1-2, 6, 19 n.12,
    20 n.32, 20 n.34, 176, 178
Augusta Victoria, Princess of
    Schleswig-Holstein, 141
Augustenberg, Frederick von, 55-56,
    59-61, 71 n.2, 72 n.5

Ballhausen, Lucius von, 172
Bamberger, Ludwig, 92, 139, 172-173,
    175-176, 188 n.40, 190 n.63, 190
    n.68
Barth, Theodor, 154
Battenberg, Alexander (Prince of
    Bulgaria), 152-154, 165 n.101, 165
    n.102, 169, 171-174, 176-178, 183

n.6, 188 n. 46, 189 n.54, 191 n.87
Baumgarten, Heinrich von, 68-69
Beaconsfield, Lord (Benjamin
    Disraeli), 124
Benedetti, Count Vincent, 84, 91-92
Bennigsen, Rudolf von, 47 n.16, 69,
    71, 125, 131 n. 37, 149
Bergmann, Ernst von, 167, 178, 183
    n.6, 189 n.54, 191 n.87
Bernhardi, Theodor von, 37, 47 n.16,
    69
Bernstorff, Count Albrecht, 27
Bismarck, Herbert von, 164 n.99, 181,
    185 n.15
Bismarck, Otto von, and Frederick's
    reign, 169-174; attempts to
    discredit Frederick's legend, 180-
    181; clashes with Frederick on
    foreign policy, 57-68, 70, 125;
    clashes with Frederick on
    domestic policy, 36-40, 67, 114-
    115, 117-118, 137-138, 146;
    concern with Frederick's succes-
    sion, 139-142, 148-150, 152-154,
    169; cooperation with Frederick,
    79, 81-84, 89-92, 95, 97-98, 110-
    113, 121-124; manipulates
    Frederick's regency, 116-118;
    offers Frederick governorship of

Alsace-Lorraine, 117-118, 132
n.59, 141; opinion of Crown
Princess Victoria, 9, 42, 53 n.112,
164 n.98; opposition to
Battenberg marriage, 152-154,
171-172, 176, 178; promotes
Hohenzollern candidacy for
Spanish throne, 89-91, 102 n.52;
vetoes Frederick's surgery, 167,
183 n.3
Blackbourn, David, xi
Bockum-Dolffs, Heinrich, 64
Bucher, Lothar, 103 n.59
Bunsen, Georg, 125, 174

Camphausen, Otto, 115
Carol, Prince of Rumania,116-117
Center Party, 111, 116-118, 120, 125,
133 n.65, 137, 165 n.106, 186 n.17
Christian X (King of Denmark), 55,
59-61, 71 n.2
Clarendon, Lord George, 90
Coburg intrigue, 66-67, 69
Congress of Berlin (1878), 121, 123
Conservative Party, 116
Constitutional Party,
(Wochenblattspartei) 5, 11, 26, 51
n.94, 69
Corti, Count Egon Caesar, 44, 161
n.54
Craig, Gordon, 140
Crown Prince Party. *See* Freisinnnige
Partei
Curtius, Ernst, 3, 5

Dahlmann, Frederick, 1, 5
Delbrück, Hans, 90, 125-126, 159 n.43
Dorpalen, Andreas, xii
Duncker, Max von, 40-41, 47 n. 21, 48
n.42, 62, 65, 71, 75 n.62

Eley, Geoff, xi
Eyck, Erich, xii, 182

Falk, Adalbert, 111, 125, 131 n.45
Forckenbeck, Max von, 119, 120,
125, 150, 146, 174
Franckenstein, Baron von, 120
Frederick I, Grand Duke of Baden,
37-38, 41, 98, 178
Frederick Charles, Prince of Prussia,
4, 34
Frederick William (Crown Prince of
Prussia and German Emperor),
and war of 1864, 58, 62-66; and
Prussian State council, 146, 162
n.63; as a historical problem, 1, 3;
bouts of depression, 17, 119-121,
125-127, 137, 139-140, 148-149;
childhood, 1-3; conflict with
William I, 28, 30-31, 38-40, 43-45,
73 n.16, 117; courtship and
marriage, 8-9; Danzig speech, 38-
41, 57; fixation with Holy Roman
Empire, 96-97, 106 n.89, 106 n.90,
187 n.25; illness, 167-169;
jealousy of Bismarck, 142-143;
legacy, 198-199; opposes
appointment of Bismarck, 34;
opposes William I's wish to
abdicate, 33-34; passive resistance, 31, 44, 37-38, 87-88, 98-99;
personality, 3, 6,17, 29, 41, 99 n.2,
168; political views during New
Era, 10, 16-17, 23 n.97; proclamation as emperor, 147-148, 170-171;
promotes intervention in Hesse-
Kassel conflict, 27, 31-32, 46 n.13;
relationship with Queen Victoria
and Prince Albert, 8, 10, 22 n.64;
support for constitutionalism, 16-
18, 30-32, 34, 38-39, 42-45, 65, 71,
82-83, 95-98,110-111, 146; war
diary of 1870-1871, 93-95; war of
1866, 63, 65-69, 71; works for
Anglo-German alliance, 121-122,
124-125

Frederick William IV, 4, 11, 14
Free Conservative Party, 116, 135
    n.102, 135 n.104
Freisinnige Partei (Crown Prince
    Party), 139-141, 148, 154, 179, 188
    n.40, 195
Freytag, Gustav, 37, 92, 95, 180
Friedberg, Heinrich von, 43, 118, 150,
    170, 176, 178, 188 n.40, 190 n.81,
    192 n.102
Fröbel, Julius, 2, 18 n.5

Gastein Convention (1864), 64
Geffcken, Heinrich, 139,147, 149, 179,
    161 n.61, 180-181, 192 n.105
Gerhardt, Karl Dr., 167, 178, 183 n.3
Gerlach, Leopold von, 5, 8, 100 n.20
Gladstone, William Ewart, xi, 138-139,
    156 n.15, 157 n.26
Godet, Frederic, 3
Goethe, J. W., 1
Granville, George, 110
Gramont, Antoine de, 91

Hagen motion, 26-27
Hatzfeldt, Paul, 159 n.48
Haym, Rudolf, 45, 69, 110
Hesse-Kassel conflict, 27, 32, 36
Heyderhoff, Julius, xii
Heydt, August von, 29
Hohenzollern Candidacy for the
    Spanish throne, 89-91
Holborn, Hajo, xii
Holstein, Friedrich von, 142-143, 145,
    148, 149-150, 156 n.20, 157 n.29,
    158 n.36, 164 n.99, 185 n.14, 188
    n.46
Hovell, Mark, 190 n.80

Karl Anton (Prince of Hohenzollern-
    Sigmaringen), 104 n.62
Königgrätz, Battle of, 79, 81, 84
Kreuzzeitung Party, 31, 175

Kulturkampf, 111,118, 127, 137

Langewiesche, Dieter, 119
Lasalle, Ferdinand, 65, 75 n.58, 119
Lasker, Eduard, 92, 125, 158 n.40
Leopold, Prince of Hohenzollern-
    Sigmaringen, 89-90, 103 n.60, 104
    n.62
Lindau, Robert, 125
Loë, Walther, 149
Loftus, Augustus, 66
Ludwig, King of Bavaria, 88, 95, 99
Luxembourg crisis (1867), 84-86

Mackenzie, Morell, 167-168, 170, 178,
    183 n.7, 184 n.11, 184 n.12, 186
    n.21, 191 n.54, 191 n.86, 191 n.87
Malet, Sir Edward, 172-173, 184 n.11,
    185 n.16, 190 n.80
Manteuffel, Edwin von, 29, 75 n.63,
    100 n.20
Manteuffel, Otto von, 5, 12, 174
Marschall von Bieberstein, Adolf,
    161 n.54
Mathy, Karl, 41
Mensdorff-Pouilly, Count Alexander,
    66-67
Miquel, Johannes, 140, 149, 190 n.63
Mischke, Albert, 125, 143, 145
Moltke, Helmuth von, 85, 92, 99
Mommsen, Theodor, 62
Morier, Sir Robert, 43, 181
Münster, Count, 124, 134 n.90

Napoleon III, Emperor of France, 15,
    69, 81, 77 n.84, 91-93
National Liberal Party, 84, 92, 110,
    114, 116, 118-119, 125, 135 n.104,
    137-138, 141, 165 n.107, 186 n.17
Nationalverein, 13, 17, 55
New Era, 12, 14-15,18, 26
Normann, Karl von, 125, 143-145, 149,
    159 n.43, 160 n. 50, 161 n.54, 168

North German Confederation, 81-82

Pinson, Koppel S., xii
Ponsonby, Lady Mary, 140, 171, 181
Progressive Party, 12, 80, 84, 97, 110, 116, 126, 138-139
Puttkamer, Robert von, 125, 174-175

Radolinski, Count Hugo von, 143, 149, 172-173, 183 n.3, 185 n.14
Rechberg, Count Johann von, 63
Reformverein, 55
Richter, Eugen, 138-139, 150, 170, 172, 174
Rickert, Heinrich, 172
Rochau, August, 13
Roggenbach, Hans von, 41, 69, 138-139, 147-149, 180, 187 n.25, 190 n.68
Roon, Albrecht von, 29, 33, 35, 90, 92
Rosenberg, Arthur, xii
Russell, Odo (Lord Ampthill), 110-111, 127 n.4, 128 n.12, 120 n.13, 156 n.18, 157 n.27

Saburov, Count, 123
Salisbury, Robert, 124, 172, 185 n.16
Schleswig-Holstein, 27-28, 45, 57-64, 71 n.1, 71 n.2, 196
Schrader, Karl, 125, 145, 174, 188 n.49
Schultze-Delitzsch, Hermann, 51 n.94, 64-65, 75 n.59
Seckendorff, Count Götz von, 142-144, 149-150, 160 n.50
Sedan, Battle of, 92, 95
Sheehan, James, xii, xiii
Sigismund, Prince of Prussia, 79, 100 n.2
Simson, Eduard, 35, 98, 170, 180
Social Democratic Party, 115, 137, 141, 156 n.23, 165 n.106
Sommerfeld, Count Gustav von, 142-

144, 149-150, 160 n.50
Stauffenberg, Franz von, 120, 125-126, 145
Stein, August, 175
Stöcker, Alfred von, 170
Stockmar, Ernst von, 35, 59, 68, 70-71, 138, 158 n.34
Stockmar, Frau, 179
Stolberg, Count, 122-124, 183 n.7
Stosch, Albrecht von, 87, 112, 114, 130 n.28, 132 n.57, 139-140, 143, 145, 147, 149, 154, 159 n.41, 161 n.54, 168, 180-181, 183 n.3
Stürmer, Michael, 161 n.60
Sybel, Heinrich von, 35, 69, 110

Three Emperors' League, 123
Treaties of London (1852), 56-58, 60
Treitschke, Heinrich von, 110

Valentin, Veit, xii
Versen, Major von, 90, 103 n.59
Victoria, Queen of England, xii, 2-3, 6, 20 n.34, 20, n.35, 41, 57, 66, 70, 77 n.72, 90, 103 n.55, 138, 176, 179, 181, 183 n.6, 184 n.11, 183 n.7
Victoria (Crown Princess of Prussia and German Empress), anti-Russian sentiments, 121; children, 21 n.62; courtship with Frederick, 7-8; dissatisfaction with new German Empire, 97-99; edits Frederick's war diary of 1870-1871; 93-94; encourages William I's abdication, 33-34; influence on Frederick, 10, 30-31, 35, 38-39, 59, 62-63, 86-88, 121, 125-126, 152-154; insists on unification after war of 1866, 80-83; manipulates legend of Frederick III, 179, 181-182, 195, 197-198; marriage, 9, 17; opposes Frederick's association with

Bismarck, 86-87; opposition to Bismarck's foreign policy, 58-59, 62-66, 80, 94; personality, 7, 17, 21 n.43; plans for Frederick's reign, 148-152; promotes Battenberg marriage, 152-154, 172-173, 176-178; publicizes Frederick's liberalism, 42, 52 n.100; supports left-wing liberalism, 16-17, 34, 65, 138-140, 144, 148-150, 154, 163 n.79, 179

Victoria, Princess of Prussia, 152, 171, 176

Vincke-Oldendorff, Georg, 35, 41, 45, 57

Virchow, Rudolf, 36, 157

Waldeck, Benedikt, 42

Waldersee, Alfred von, 170

Wehler, Hans-Ulrich, xiii

William I, King of Prussia and German Emperor, abdication attempt, 33; and Battenberg affair, 152-153; and constitutional conflict, 33, 46 n.4; assassination attempts, 115, 117; death, 170; marriage, 1, 3; opposition to Dual Alliance, 121-123; political views, 5, 10; reaction to Frederick's Danzig speech, 39-40, 84, 91-92, 95

William, Prince of Prussia, 10, 17, 112-113, 134 n.94, 150, 163 n.89, 168-169, 173, 175, 177, 178, 181-182, 184 n.13, 186 n.17

Windthorst, Ludwig, 118-119, 133 n.54, 133 n.70

Winter, Leopold von, 39

Wochenblattpartei. *See* Constitutional Party

Wrangel, Ernst von, 58

Ziekursch, Johannes, xii

Zollparlament, 88

Zollverein, 6, 21 n.38, 59

About the Author

PATRICIA KOLLANDER is Assistant Professor of History at Florida Atlantic University and has written articles on 19th-century German history.